LEAVING GUANTANAMO

This multilayered work follows a group of Guantanamo detainees from a single Middle Eastern country, Kuwait, portraying their lives before their capture, their experience at Guantanamo, their ultimate release, and the lives they have been challenged in remaking after returning home. It is an intimate look at real men held for years without charge and without hope.

Eric L. Lewis has represented Guantanamo detainees for more than twenty years, and he conducted the hearings that gained the release of the last two Kuwaiti "forever prisoners." As part of a committed team, he spent time with these men and their families, fighting to gain access to courts and navigating the politics and diplomacy of the Global War on Terror. In addition to telling the story of his time with the Guantanamo detainees, Lewis also analyzes how Guantanamo has changed American law and culture and how its legacy continues today.

ERIC L. LEWIS is a human rights lawyer, Chair of the law firm Lewis Baach Kaufmann Middlemiss, and President of Reprieve US. Mr. Lewis, along with Reprieve, has represented over seventy Guantanamo detainees and oversees the Life After Guantanamo project for returned detainees. He holds degrees from Princeton, Yale, and Cambridge.

LEAVING GUANTANAMO

How One Country Brought Its Men Home
from the Forever Prison

ERIC L. LEWIS

Shaftesbury Road, Cambridge CB2 8EA, United Kingdom

One Liberty Plaza, 20th Floor, New York, NY 10006, USA

477 Williamstown Road, Port Melbourne, VIC 3207, Australia

314–321, 3rd Floor, Plot 3, Splendor Forum, Jasola District Centre, New Delhi – 110025, India

103 Penang Road, #05–06/07, Visioncrest Commercial, Singapore 238467

Cambridge University Press is part of Cambridge University Press & Assessment, a department of the University of Cambridge.

We share the University's mission to contribute to society through the pursuit of education, learning and research at the highest international levels of excellence.

www.cambridge.org
Information on this title: www.cambridge.org/9781009681377

DOI: 10.1017/9781009681407

© Eric L. Lewis 2026

This publication is in copyright. Subject to statutory exception and to the provisions of relevant collective licensing agreements, no reproduction of any part may take place without the written permission of Cambridge University Press & Assessment.

When citing this work, please include a reference to the DOI 10.1017/9781009681407

First published 2026

A catalogue record for this publication is available from the British Library

A Cataloging-in-Publication data record for this book is available from the Library of Congress

ISBN 978-1-009-68138-4 Hardback
ISBN 978-1-009-68137-7 Paperback

Cambridge University Press & Assessment has no responsibility for the persistence or accuracy of URLs for external or third-party internet websites referred to in this publication and does not guarantee that any content on such websites is, or will remain, accurate or appropriate.

For EU product safety concerns, contact us at Calle de José Abascal, 56, 1°, 28003 Madrid, Spain, or email eugpsr@cambridge.org

For Emily, our children, and grandchildren

CONTENTS

List of Figures   *page* x
Acknowledgments   xi

Introduction   1

1   The Long Journey beyond the Rule of Law   6
    Arrival at Guantanamo   6
    Presumed Guilty   9

2   Why Should Kuwait Be Different?   15
    The Kuwaiti Experience: Affluence and Trauma   16
    The Quiet Emirate in a Difficult Neighborhood   17
    An Indelible Identity Forged in War and Suffering   22
    The Iraqi Invasion and Dismantling of the Kuwaiti Nation   25
    "This Shall Not Stand": The First President Bush and the Liberation   27
    The Aftermath of 9/11 and the Challenge for Kuwait   28

3   Strategizing in a New World: Navigating the New Paradigm   30
    The Rights of Foreigners Outside the United States   39
    Post-Rasul/Al Odah Defiance   43
    What Process Was Due: The Post-Rasul/Al Odah Stonewalling   44
    Congress Seeks to Cut Out the Courts   46

4   The Rules of the Road: The Lower Courts Define a Narrow Path   51
    Standard and Burden of Proof   52
    Evidentiary Presumptions   58
    Admission of Hearsay   59
    Evidence Tainted by Coercion or Torture   60

5   Twelve Men   71
    Omar Rajab Amin   77

Khalid Abdullah Mishal Al Mutairi   84
Fouad Al Rabiah   87
Abdulaziz Al Shammeri   92
Abdullah Kamal Al Kandari   95
Adel Zamel Abd Al Mahsen Al Zamel   98
Nasser Najiri Al Amutairi   102
Abdullah Saleh Al Ajmi   104
Mohammed Al Daihani   111
Saad Al Azmi   114
Fawzi Al Odah and Fayiz Al Kandari: Forever Prisoners?   118
Fawzi Al Odah   119
Fayiz Al Kandari   123

6 The Final Four: Habeas Hearings for the Last Four Kuwaiti Detainees   132
Khalid Al Mutairi   132
Fouad Al Rabiah   137
Fawzi Al Odah   143
Fayiz Al Kandari   149

7 The US Government Re-engages   154

8 The First Periodic Review Board   166
Another Habeas Challenge   169
Meeting in Guantanamo   174
Meeting the Al Odahs   181
Mama's Boy   182
Abu Fawzi   184
Brother and Sisterhood   188
Rehabilitation and Security   189
Countdown to the Periodic Review Board Hearing   196

9 And Then There Was One   203

10 Lessons Learned   221
Guantanamo Remains an Iconic Part of American Life   222
American Exceptionalism: A City on the Hill without Rules   225
The Least Dangerous Branch: Law and Its Limits   228
Ignorance and Islamophobia   230
Truth Is the First Casualty of War   232
Bureaucracy Responds to Power and Its Own Prerogatives   233
Navigating a New Paradigm for Foreigners   234

Don't Be in a Hurry and Never Give Up   234
Know the Rules: Keep Calm and Carry On   235
Try to Keep Talking   236
What Does Your Counterparty Need? What Can You Do?   237
Know the Rules of Decision and the Mindset of the Decision-Makers   238
Be Prepared in Tone and Substance   239

Notes   241
Index   257

FIGURES

5.1 US Embassy Protest by Kuwait Family Committee Led by Khalid Al Odah.   *page* 120
8.1 Radio GTMO.   176
8.2 Joint Task Force Guantanamo.   177
8.3 Kuwait prison: doll. Photo by author, May 2014.   190

ACKNOWLEDGMENTS

I am grateful to so many people who were instrumental in this book becoming a reality. First, the three members of the Core Team, Abdul Rahman Al Haroun (ARH), William Brown, and Marcia Newell, not only fought for fourteen years for the release of the detainees but also generously shared their time and experience, recounting the long history of the process before I became actively involved in the release of the final two detainees.

ARH had the initial idea for telling these stories, both because they were important in themselves and because of the useful lessons that they might provide, not just for Kuwaiti statecraft but for effective engagement with superpowers in a complex world. He inspired this book and supported it in every way at every juncture. This book would never have been written without him, and it is as much his as mine. I am grateful for his friendship, judgment, and kindness.

He, William, and Marcia worked side by side with me in thinking through the objectives of the book and in outlining its structure; they read each chapter as it was completed and provided essential editing suggestions, clarifications, and factual background. They also made certain that I had access to all of the relevant actors, both in putting together our successful efforts to get Fawzi Al Odah and Fayiz Al Kandari released and in filling numerous factual gaps with Kuwaiti officials and the detainees themselves. They also worked with me to recast the book as a series of human stories within a framework of law and politics, rather than as a legal treatise. This is a book for general audiences.

Khalid Al Odah, the head of the Family Committee, and his family were not only generous hosts, but Khalid also facilitated my visits with his and Fayiz's families and with the detainees in Kuwait after their release. I am also grateful to the five men who recounted with patience and even good humor the stories of their awful and seemingly endless incarceration.

Abdullah Alharoun, Abdul Rahman's son, and a terrific lawyer and scholar in his own right, provided great assistance and editorial direction, especially with respect to Chapter 2, which focuses on the politics and society of Kuwait.

My dearest friend of nearly fifty years, David Remnick, who also happens to have some editorial experience as the editor of the New Yorker for more than a quarter century, read an early draft and guided me toward focusing on telling the stories of these twelve men, which I think made for a much more interesting and better book. My stepdaughter, Carina Guiterman, Vice President and Executive Editor for fiction at Simon & Schuster, provided helpful guidance in negotiating the publication process, as did my friend and fellow human rights lawyer, Clive Stafford Smith.

I am also grateful to Tobias Ginsberg, Chloe Quinn, and Gemma Smith at Cambridge University Press for believing in a first-time author whose manuscript was something a bit different for an academic publisher, and for Hemapriya Eswanth, the Team Leader in preparing the manuscript for publication. My assistant of more than thirty years, Nancy Ciffolilli, typed and revised innumerable drafts.

And finally, to Emily for her love and patience throughout the process.

While I had a great deal of assistance, any errors are my own.

Introduction

This is a book about twelve men who spent their best years locked up at Guantanamo Bay. None has ever been convicted of anything or ever will be. What they share is that they are all from the same small country of Kuwait. They are all Muslims.

All were beloved family members in a close-knit society where there is great family cohesion. They left mothers and fathers, wives and children, brothers and sisters behind. Some had children who were born after they had been captured, children they did not meet until those children were four or five years old. Some had parents who died while they were away. What they also share is that they were all tortured under the authority of and by personnel of the US military and intelligence apparatus.

This is also a book about families, the families of these twelve men who lost their sons, husbands, and brothers and never knew when or if they would ever get them back. They grieved, but they also organized. They formed the "Family Committee," headed by an American-trained military pilot, Khalid Al Odah, the father of one of these men, Fawzi Al Odah. The Family Committee began their long and uncertain journey to gain the release of their sons without funding, without a plan, and without support from their government. The Family Committee had the wisdom, however, to reach out to two lawyers based in the Gulf, one Kuwaiti and one American, and a Washington-based colleague, to work with them on a daily basis for more than fourteen years to secure the release of their children.

These three brave and capable people – Abdul Rahman Al Haroun, William Brown, and Marcia Newell – formed the "Core Team," which persuaded the Kuwaiti government, unlike others, to lend its sovereign influence and resources to bringing its boys home. They initiated and coordinated extensive legal efforts in the United States that were necessary to gain the release of these twelve detainees. They did so not because they thought courts were likely to order them released, but because they knew that using the courts was indispensable in keeping their ordeals visible to the public and to a legal system that at least paid lip service to the rule of law. They never received any payment for their long and patient efforts.

Abdul Rahman Al Haroun (known to all as ARH) was and remains one of the leading commercial and energy lawyers in the region. But more than that, he had warm and trusting relationships throughout Kuwaiti society. Khalid Al Odah was a distant cousin, and his son Fawzi was one of the last two Kuwaitis held at Guantanamo, when it seemed he might be one of the "forever prisoners," never charged but indefinitely detained without due process and possibly for life. For ARH, this was not only a legal matter, but one that implicated his country, his government, his profession and his family. He funded the initial American legal efforts from his own pocket.

ARH also wanted the stories of the long ordeal of the Kuwaiti detainees – legal, diplomatic, and personal – told, and he asked me to write this book. He helped me with access to both the men and Kuwaiti officials; he provided support while I completed the manuscript without ever asking for anything other than that these stories be preserved; he inspired this project, while never suggesting in any way what I should write.

I was fortunate enough to have been engaged by the Core Team to handle the hearings and negotiations to get the last two men, Fawzi Al Odah and Fayiz Al Kandari, back to Kuwait. I was able to write about Fawzi and Fayiz and their families from personal experience. But that was the last lap of a marathon run by the Family Committee and the Core Team, which shared with me their history over more than a decade of effort before I came on the scene – the victories, the defeats, and the sorrows of those years.

The Core Team and I were also able to spend invaluable time with five of the twelve men after their release. We talked at length about their lives before they were detained, their time at Guantanamo, and their efforts to regain what they had lost when they returned home years later to a very different place. This allowed the stories of those five to be told with greater richness and detail than those of some other detainees whose backgrounds came largely from US dossiers and hearings, many of which were filled with wildly improbable accounts pieced together from unreliable jailhouse informers or confessions coerced by torture. We also tried to understand the legacy of a Kuwaiti who lost his sanity and became a suicide bomber. This act surprised none of his fellow Kuwaiti detainees who witnessed his decline and could not understand why he was released while they remained.

The stories of the Guantanamo detainees are complicated and sometimes ambiguous. One of the reasons I was engaged was that I had done

Guantanamo work for detainees from many countries over many years, and not all of my clients were necessarily innocent. The complete truth is often elusive, but the rule of law relies on evidence, not perfect insight. Sometimes, inconsistencies mask lies about fundamental issues; sometimes, they are just inconsistencies or confusion about details years after the fact.

I do not labor under the delusion that every one of my clients at Guantanamo told me the complete truth; no lawyer does. One of my clients, from the United Kingdom, was released early because Tony Blair was owed a favor by George Bush. He was a Jamaican-British convert to Islam who had been tortured by both the Taliban and the Americans. He spent more than a decade after his release living quietly as a web designer in Manchester with a wife and five kids. He was radicalized by mass killings of civilians in Syria, joined ISIS, and became a suicide bomber. It is hard to know why.

Sometimes, you feel that you can see into your clients' hearts and minds; sometimes, they remain opaque. I have tried as objectively as possible, with sometimes limited information, to weigh the evidence, but I was also an advocate for some of these men; I spent time with their families. What is important is a process that seeks to get at the truth and that does not simply accept the government's story at face value or that sweeps up hundreds of men and tortures them to try to find out what happened. Truth finding was not the process employed at Guantanamo.

The stories of the detainees from Kuwait are in many ways less ambiguous, less uncertain than those of other detainees. The Core Team had high confidence from their investigations that the Kuwaitis were innocent of terrorist acts. By and large, these men were middle or upper-middle class, most were highly educated, and many had successful careers. Those factors might not preclude terrorist sympathies, but they did not fit the expected profile. They lived with their families and had no history of radicalism in Kuwait, which is a pious but not extremist place. Many had well-established and documented histories of doing charitable work in poor Muslim countries long before September 11th. They had generally journeyed to Afghanistan or Pakistan before the US bombing of Afghanistan in October 2001. Once the US bombing began, they along with hundreds of others tried to flee the country, but they were handed over to US troops, frequently for bounties, and ultimately ended up at Guantanamo Bay.

Are there things about this group of detainees that are still not known? Did someone fire a weapon or support the Taliban against the Northern Alliance in the Afghan Civil War? It is likely in some cases. But it is also clear that none of these Kuwaitis had anything to do with the planning or execution of 9/11. Indeed, one of the great tragedies of Guantanamo, as we will see, was that the senior officers running the facility knew within the first few months that they had no high-level terrorists there and that most of the men (they were all men) should not have been there at all. Yet they were not released, and the abuse continued to feed a political narrative that the United States was capturing and interrogating "the worst of the worst."

Detainees were released over the years in what appears to have been a haphazard or transactional manner, including over time ten of the twelve Kuwaitis. But Fayiz Al Kandari and Fawzi Al Odah, the last two, looked like they might remain forever. Indefinite detention without trial was a new development in American life, a precedent that remains in place as of this writing in autumn 2025. Their families and the Core Team that had worked for so long to release the other ten men were concerned that, at the end, their mission to bring all the boys home would fail and that Khalid Al Odah, who organized the Family Committee, would never see his son again.

This book is about these men and their families trapped in a Kafkaesque world where Muslim men were rounded up, overwhelmingly by Pakistani and Afghan bounty hunters, handed over to the United States, presumed to be terrorists, and treated as such, even after it became clear that the United States had not captured anyone of significant interest. They were caught up in a unique moment when a country had lost its bearings after September 11. It is a story that still has not ended for fifteen men still at Guantanamo at this writing, for men who spent years and, in many cases, decades at Guantanamo (the Biden administration finally released a sizable group just before leaving office). For those who remain, their fates are uncertain. For the eleven Kuwaitis who have survived, they are trying to rebuild their interrupted lives. The Kuwaitis were the lucky ones; they had a government that, after initial hostility and delay, pressed for their release and had the resources and diplomatic skill to secure it. Many men came from countries that were poor, unstable, or disengaged, and some of those men are still paying with their freedom for the deficiencies of their governments.

Nearly 800 men went through Guantanamo, only a handful of whom had any material role in terrorist acts, and the significant majority of whom were wholly innocent. To be clear, there are nine men who are so-called High Value Detainees, including Khalid Sheikh Mohammed, who appear to have been involved with 9/11. But those men were held for years in "black prisons" outside the United States and were not brought to Guantanamo until 2006, more than four years after all the rest had been sent. Two of those men were convicted by military tribunals, one at trial and one through a plea, and are serving sentences. Of the remaining seven, six tried to plead guilty before the military tribunals in exchange for the dropping of the death penalty, but after two years of negotiation, the Biden administration reneged on the agreement, and the validity of the pleas is in the civilian courts. So, the current record after twenty-three years is 780 men tortured and abused, thousands of years served under harsh conditions, 765 released, two convictions, seven awaiting trial, and six men without charge, of whom three have been cleared for release (but no country will take them) and three have not. Statistics are hard to come by, but it is a good estimate that more than $13 billion has been spent in maintaining Guantanamo, and hundreds of millions per year are likely to continue to be spent for years if not decades into the future.

The legacy of Guantanamo goes beyond these statistics and the human costs behind them. Post-9/11 fear, political imperatives, and a legal system that proved largely incapable of preserving the rule of law in a critical time came together to create a perfect storm of cruelty and injustice for these many men. In many ways, they and we live in a world shaped by Guantanamo and that still projects its shadows. It is no coincidence that, at the time of this writing, Guantanamo is being used again to cycle through migrants labeled without evidence as criminals or terrorists. The "worst of the worst" narrative, in secrecy and without due process, continues today with migrants because fear is a powerful weapon against the rule of law.

This book provides an analysis of the unique legal history of Guantanamo, while also providing a detailed factual narrative regarding these men's lives, and a first-person description of my experience as an advocate. It also reflects on the legal, political, and cultural legacy of Guantanamo, having had the opportunity to consider nearly a quarter century of the Guantanamo experience and the "Global War on Terror," which is not yet over.

1

The Long Journey beyond the Rule of Law

The Kuwaiti government jet lifted off and thrust quickly through the humid morning sky. It was Friday, January 8, 2016, at Guantanamo Bay, a US naval base at the edge of Cuba. The United States has occupied that base for more than a century, according to the terms of a lease with Cuba, signed just after it was granted its nominal independence from Spain and came under the American sphere of influence. The lease can only be cancelled by mutual agreement, and the United States has never agreed. The annual lease payment is the value of $200 in gold set in 1934. It has been recalculated periodically, and the current lease amount is $4,085 per annum for forty-five square miles of territory.[1] Since Castro took over in 1959, Cuba has never cashed the annual check, except once by mistake, while the United States has used the facility for everything from disaster relief to its most notorious iteration, as a high-security detention facility.

The Kuwaiti government plane would arrive the next morning in Kuwait City. On that flight was Fayiz Al Kandari, the last of the dozen Kuwaiti citizens who had been imprisoned at Guantanamo. Fayiz, as well as the other Kuwaitis and hundreds of others, had arrived at Guantanamo by military cargo jet. They were trussed up in wrist and ankle shackles looped through waist chains, functionally without hearing because of military-grade noise-canceling earphones; they were unable to see because of eye shields that left them in total darkness. They were put in diapers. The huge military jets had limited insulation, and the men lay on the cargo bed floors shivering on their journeys from Afghanistan and Pakistan that took more than twenty-four hours.

Arrival at Guantanamo

These men had been coming since January 2002, although no new prisoner had been brought there in nearly a decade when Fayiz's jet lifted away from the airstrip that winter morning in 2016. The vast majority of the men detained there had already left the same way they had arrived – blindfolded, deafened, and shackled – to be sent back to their home countries or to third countries willing to accept them. Kuwait, unlike most other countries, actively wanted and had fought for years to bring its citizens back and welcomed them on government jets that could make the long journey home nonstop, escorted by senior Kuwaiti government officials and medical personnel, and reunited in nationwide celebrations with their families. The Kuwaiti government had been persuaded to dedicate substantial resources to bringing its boys home, and once that commitment was made, it was total.

Initially, however, the families of these Kuwaiti detainees had been entirely alone in their quest to repatriate their sons. Indeed, the families and other Kuwaitis had contributed their own resources to support them in the legal battle ahead, but they were initially directed by Kuwaiti authorities to stop these efforts; the relevant authorities even refused to grant the license required to collect charitable funds from the public. It took nearly two years, but eventually the Kuwaiti government came to be convinced by the Core Team and the Family Committee that these men were not terrorists at all, and the then-Emir of Kuwait directed that the government throw its full support behind repatriating its nationals, the only government publicly to have done so.

On this January morning, eleven of the twelve Kuwaitis had already gone home. Fayiz Al Kandari, the last of the detainees, would return to his country, but not to his home. He would have a year of rehabilitation in the rehabilitation facility that the Kuwaitis had constructed within the hospital wing of the Kuwait Central Prison. The facility was not luxurious, but it offered the medical, psychological, spiritual, and rehabilitative resources that would enable him to rejoin a society that had changed dramatically after his fourteen years away. The US government had insisted that he spend this year in rehab. This condition was carefully negotiated between the US and the Kuwaiti governments, with the Core Team and me as their US lawyer, playing the role of intermediary over a period of years to learn what Kuwait could legally do, what the United States would require, and how the circles of that Venn diagram could be made to overlap.

Fayiz had endured years of isolation, cruelty, abuse, uncertainty, and fear, first in Afghanistan and Pakistan, then marooned on a corner of a far-off, divided island. Although he would be at the rehabilitation center, he would finally be able to see his mother and father, his siblings, and his extended family. His father was ill and would pass away a few months after his return. His mother had been treated for cancer; his original departure to do charity work had been prompted by the widespread cultural belief that good deeds would aid the recovery of a loved one. His mother appreciated this gesture, but she had never wanted him to leave Kuwait. Fayiz had spent fourteen years hoping against hope that he would see his parents again.

The long odyssey of Fayiz Al Kandari, Fawzi Al Odah, and the other ten Kuwaiti detainees is the subject of this book. It is a journey that began on the Afghan–Pakistan border, moved to prisons in Afghanistan, Pakistan, and elsewhere, where so many of these men were brutally tortured, followed by the trip in darkness, silence, and cold to Guantanamo Bay, where they remained, never charged, never tried, or convicted of any crime.[2]

The initial arrivals at Guantanamo in early 2002, which included six of the twelve Kuwaitis, were sent to Camp X-Ray, a makeshift, outdoor prison, where the prisoners slept in open-air cages with cement floors and tin roofs behind razor wire walls. They were given thin mats, no blankets, and buckets for bodily functions. Camp X-Ray had been built on an emergency basis to house refugees from Haiti during the migrant crisis of 1991.[3] Abandoned for more than a decade, the officers in charge were given three weeks to ready the facility to hold 300 men.[4] The detainees described them as "sheep cages" or "dog cells."[5] Animals ran through the camp. Detainees were bitten by snakes and the ever-present hordes of mosquitos. They were kept company by "banana rats," the local term for Cuban hutias, large rodents shaped like bananas that can grow up to two feet in length and weigh up to nineteen pounds.[6] The base is also populated by the Cuban rock iguana, one of the world's largest, which can grow up to five feet and weigh up to twenty pounds. They are protected, and soldiers can be disciplined for harming them, even as the soldiers were insulated from the consequences of the physical harm they inflicted on detainees.[7]

The weather in Guantanamo is generally hot and humid year-round. Every day, thousands of crabs crawled out of the sea and scuttled through Camp X-Ray and elsewhere on the island, hunting for food.[8] Unlike the crabs, the prisoners never saw the sea; their view was always blocked by layers of razor wire and canvas-covered fencing. Bright floodlights remained on all night.[9] Urination and defecation took place in the open, visible to other prisoners, guards, and the numerous military, executive branch, and congressional delegations that came through the camp.[10] The prisoners had two fifteen-minute breaks outside their cells each day; each detainee was taken alone in shackles to a small pen to exercise.[11] The first detainees remained at Camp X-Ray from the time of the first arrivals in January 2002 through the end of April of that year, when Camp 3, which became known as Camp Delta, opened.

The Camp X-Ray prisoners were transferred to Camp 3, which isolated them all in solitary confinement but was at least indoors. Detainees were held in single cells eight feet long, six feet eight inches wide, and eight feet high. The buildings were surrounded by six concentric rings of razor wire. Cell walls were partially constructed of metal mesh material that let in filtered light and air, with a steel roof.[12] Each cell had its own flush toilet and sink. Detainees were not housed adjacent to one another, so they could not speak to fellow detainees. Giant "white noise" machines – oversized fans – ran all day long, making it impossible for detainees to communicate with each other even by shouting. Solitary and sensory deprivation were essential to the planned design for Camp 3. The lizards and banana rats may have been gone, but the isolation was far more debilitating.[13]

Detainees were allowed a Quran in their cell, a light blanket, and basic toiletries, but virtually nothing else. Given the repeated abuse of the Quran by guards, many prisoners asked for their Qurans to be taken away; many of the detainees were "hafeezes," who had memorized the Quran; they did not need the Holy Book to pray, and they were outraged and deeply troubled by its desecration. Others had their Qurans taken away as punishment for one of the innumerable offenses enforced by military guards.[14]

Each prisoner was taken out alone for an hour or two per day unless Camp Delta was subject to one of the frequent lockdowns. Recreation was in a small courtyard ringed by razor wire. Guards in these early days were instructed not to talk to detainees. The men could sit or pace in the humid, airless yard; recreation periods were often at night. Many preferred to remain in their cells, where it was cool; they could sleep, and they did not need to submit to invasive searches, including body cavity searches, or shackling, only to be moved to a sweltering cement rectangle.[15]

Presumed Guilty

The long odyssey of the Kuwaiti and other detainees was precipitated by the reaction of the United States to September 11, 2001. The Bush administration launched an assault on Afghanistan beginning around four weeks later, on October 7. Osama bin Laden had maintained his headquarters in Afghanistan after his Saudi citizenship had been revoked; he had spent four to five years in Sudan before returning in 1996. No one knew where he was, and it would be another decade before he was located and killed, not in Afghanistan but in Abbottabad, Pakistan.[16]

After September 11, the United States and its proxies grabbed anyone they could find on the Afghan–Pakistan frontier, generally men of Arab descent. The vast majority of these men were not captured on an active battlefield but handed over by Afghans or Pakistanis for $5,000 or more in bounties, which was equivalent to two years' average earnings in that impoverished border area.[17] The US government dropped thousands of leaflets advertising the bounty program. One flyer read: "Get wealth and power beyond your dreams. You can receive millions of dollars helping the anti-Taliban forces catch Al Qaida and Taliban murderers. This is enough to take care of your family, your village, your tribe for the rest of your life."

Secretary of Defense Donald Rumsfeld said that leaflets fell over Afghanistan "like snowflakes in December in Chicago."[18] Not surprisingly, Afghans and Pakistanis eagerly rounded up foreigners, and the United States eagerly accepted them without any real scrutiny.

The United States desperately needed to find terrorists in those panicked post-9/11 days. It had to show it was fighting back. It needed to demonstrate that it was making tangible progress in the "Global War on Terror." It did not know whom it had captured, and it seemed not to care. The idea seemed to be to torture everybody and see what intelligence could be collected. There was much torture in those days, but very little actionable intelligence. Within the first few weeks, the senior general in charge of the Joint Task Force admitted that "the major portion of his prisoners were not particularly dangerous or hardened terrorists," and a senior Marine intelligence officer, Tim Nichols, concluded that the largest group "had nothing of substance to offer and should not have been there at all."[19] A senior Army intelligence officer formed the view by the spring of 2002 that "we're not getting anything because there might not be anything to get." Colonel Lawrence Wilkerson, chief of staff to then Secretary of State Colin Powell, filed a remarkable declaration in court stating that he attended the daily high-level briefings, and concluded

> [A]s early as August 2002, and probably earlier to other State Department personnel who were focused on these issues, that many of the prisoners detained at Guantánamo had been taken into custody without regard to whether they were truly enemy combatants, or in fact whether many of them were enemies at all. I soon realized from my conversations with military colleagues as well as foreign service officers in the field that many of the detainees were, in fact, victims of incompetent battlefield vetting. There was no meaningful way to determine whether they were terrorists, Taliban, or simply innocent civilians picked up on a very confused battlefield or in the territory of another state such as Pakistan.[20]

A confidential report prepared by the Central Intelligence Agency (CIA) as early as October 2002 concluded that most of the detainees did not belong there. Major General Jay Hood, a former Guantanamo commander, conceded, "Sometimes we just didn't get the right folks," and despite knowledge that the bulk of the detainees had no involvement in terrorism or intelligence to offer, Hood said that they were not released because "nobody wants to be the one who signs the papers."[21] The deputy commander, Brigadier General Marin Lucenti, stated that these men "weren't fighting," but "running."[22]

Despite the open secret early on that the detention dragnet had yielded virtually nothing of value, bureaucratic fear and inertia and profound indifference to the lives of these men, whose culture, religion, and language were alien to their captors, meant that they remained detained and abused. Secretary of State Rumsfeld wanted actionable intelligence, and the interrogations continued as the Pentagon ratcheted up the abusive tactics against men who had nothing to say.

The United States could not and would not accept what quickly became obvious: that it had brought to Guantanamo hundreds of men, many of whom were following a long-standing tradition in the Gulf of going to perform charitable work in poor Muslim lands. Afghanistan was a war-torn country with massive drought, population dislocation, and a lack of access to food, water, and health care. It was the subject of global aid programs on a massive scale.[23] Many of these men would go for a few weeks each year, generally on annual vacation, and many had been doing so long before anyone had heard of Osama Bin Laden or Al Qaida.[24] Islamic charities had established programs working in conjunction with American and international NGOs.[25] Others were traders or students. The United States would not believe that most of these men simply happened to be in Afghanistan or Pakistan after the United States began bombing in October 2001. Hundreds of these men, wanting no part in a war against a superpower, fled and tried to find safe haven in Pakistan and return home.

To be sure, some of the men who were captured were low-level foot soldiers in the fighting. Some had been part of the group of "Afghan Arabs," who migrated to Afghanistan from the Gulf in the late 1970s and early 1980s to fight the Soviets – with vast American support. Many of them stayed on; a small number formed the core of Al Qaida, but most of those who stayed were not involved with violent activity. No one centrally involved in planning 9/11 was brought to Guantanamo in the early days.[26]

Torture in Afghanistan, in the dark prisons, and at Guantanamo was endemic and approved at the highest levels, including by the Secretary of Defense, top generals, a future head of the Central Intelligence Agency, who supervised a dark prison in Thailand, and many others.[27] The high-value detainees were elsewhere for four years while hundreds of traders, teachers, preachers, project builders, or low-level soldiers were picked up on the Afghan–Pakistan border. The abuse was not only shameful; it was senseless and deeply counterproductive to US interests and moral authority. It still is.

None of the men who began arriving in early 2002 had anything to do with 9/11, but it did not matter. Rumsfeld had declared the men at Guantanamo the "worst of the worst," and the guards there were indoctrinated with this view and generally treated detainees accordingly. Some of the guards had served at sites that were hit on 9/11, and they were sent to Guantanamo to confront the men they were being told were responsible for the death of their comrades.

Rumsfeld and the defense and intelligence agencies at the highest level knew surprisingly early on they were not holding the architects or implementers of 9/11, but that was not the message that the president, the vice president, or the people of the United States wanted to hear, or that Rumsfeld was inclined to communicate.[28] The truth took second place to the construction of the post-9/11 narrative. The president could not say, "Well, we have bought and paid billions of dollars for an assortment of Uighur merchants, teachers of Arabic, prayer leaders, mosque builders, well diggers and the occasional barely trained soldier who had been shown how to fire a Kalashnikov for an afternoon." Perhaps, there was a driver or a messenger or a cook for Al Qaida. But no one who mattered had been sent to Guantanamo during the first four years, and the Bush administration knew it. The United States had come up empty, but the administration refused to admit it.

Guantanamo was chosen to be a "legal black hole," a place controlled *by* the United States but not *in* the United States, where these men were to be interrogated and held without process. President Bush promptly declared that the Geneva Conventions did not apply at Guantanamo Bay, a first chink in the wall of the rule of law.[29] This had never happened before. While violations of the Conventions had certainly occurred, no American leader had openly stated that the United States had no obligation to follow them. In giving legal approval to the authorization to ignore the Geneva Conventions on January 25, 2002, just as the detainees were arriving at Guantanamo, White House Counsel Alberto Gonzales said that "the war against terrorism is a new kind of war" and "this new paradigm renders obsolete Geneva's strict limitations on questioning of enemy prisoners and renders quaint some of its provisions."[30] Common

Article Three prohibits "cruel treatment and torture [and] outrages to dignity." Common Article Three was intended by its terms to prohibit torture in all cases. Now, a half century later, this moral consensus borne of the traumas of the twentieth century was viewed as somehow outmoded sentimentalism. The purported "new paradigm" of the Global War on Terror would be much like a very old paradigm; as Vice President Cheney stated, aided by the twisted logic of compliant lawyers, Al Qaida required the United States to "take off the gloves."[31]

For some months, the families of many of these men did not know whether they were alive or dead. Finally, the Kuwaiti government was notified in the first part of 2002 that there were twelve Kuwaitis being detained at Guantanamo, and, under pressure and insistence by the newly established Family Committee and the Core Team, the Kuwaiti government notified their families.

For the families of the Kuwait detainees, this was a personal tragedy, a living nightmare. Their lives were shattered. They understood their sons or husbands had gone to do a few weeks of charitable work, an annual summer ritual throughout the region. Many of the families pleaded with their sons to come back after September 11. These young men had no idea that Afghanistan was about to be attacked, and they hoped to stay for some additional weeks and finish up what they were doing.

For the Kuwaiti government, this was an international political and legal crisis and a foreign policy dilemma. The United States was a critical ally, which had liberated the country from the invasion and depredation of Saddam Hussein's Iraq just a decade before. As discussed in Chapter 2, Kuwait was a small country in a dangerous neighborhood that literally owed its very existence to the United States. It lacked the power or the inclination to engage in public conflict with the world's superpower.

Was Kuwait producing terrorists? If Kuwait was encouraging terrorism among its young people or failing to stop it, then the breadth and width of the problem throughout the world was probably far greater than had been previously imagined. And if Kuwait had a terrorism problem, then its own domestic security was threatened as well as its relations with the United States and its Western allies. Were Kuwait's sons strangers to their own families and to the moderate brand of Islam and conservative politics of their parents?

America had the most sophisticated global intelligence operation and the most powerful military in the world. Presumably, it was detaining people for a reason. But what if these detentions were arbitrary and unjustified? And even if that were the case, what could a small nation do to make sure that its men were treated fairly and with due process, especially when Gulf states were looked at with suspicion after 9/11 and Islamophobia was sweeping the United States? Perhaps, the rights and interests of one's own nationals had to yield to Kuwait's foreign policy priorities.

The Guantanamo Bay situation presented a compelling argument to any foreign government to adopt an appeasement strategy, given that the attacks of 9/11, the Afghan War, and the capture of purported terrorists were matters of international attention and deep political tension. To a Joint Session of Congress on September 20, 2001, President Bush announced, "Every nation, in every region, now has a decision to make. Either you are with us, or you are with the terrorists."

For Kuwait, this was not a good moment to pick a fight with an angry, panicked superpower. The easiest course was to let the United States do as it chose in dealing with these detainees. Every other country appeared to be taking that view. Why should Kuwait take the risk of being different, of being "with the terrorists"?

2

Why Should Kuwait Be Different?

Men from nearly fifty countries were brought to Guantanamo. Many came from failed states, desperately poor and riven by war, violence, and chaos. Afghans were the largest group (29 percent), followed by Saudi Arabians (17 percent), Yemenis (15 percent), Pakistanis (9 percent), and Algerians (3 percent). The breakdown was not surprising. Afghanistan had been in chaos for decades; after a series of pro-Soviet governments were threatened by Islamist groups, the Soviet Union invaded and spent a decade being bled by the Islamist mujahideen, who were actively supported by the United States, Saudi Arabia, and others. The war drew in numerous fighters, including the so-called Afghan Arabs, estimated at up to 35,000 fighters. Many remained after the departure of the Soviets when the Taliban took over and fought a vicious civil war against various warlords.[1] Pakistan's Inter-Services Intelligence recruited many of the fighters, which accounts for the large Pakistani contingent. Yemen, both then and now, was a failed and unstable state, and many young men left for the opportunity to fight and earn money in Afghanistan. Many Saudis had been encouraged by radical preachers to support fellow Muslims in crisis.

The men at Guantanamo were, in sum, a diverse group, in their piety, the sophistication of their faith, their familiarity with and acceptance of global culture, their education, their age, and their economic status. Twenty-one of the men captured were under eighteen, including three who were thirteen or fourteen and another three who were likely to have been under sixteen.[2] Under international law, anyone under eighteen is defined as a juvenile and must receive special protections.[3] Seventeen men were between fifty and sixty; eight were between sixty and seventy; and two were over seventy, with one aged eighty-nine.[4]

The Kuwaiti detainees constituted a quite different demographic. Although the average age of the group was similar to the general population, a bit over twenty-nine, there were no very young or very old detainees. The youngest was around twenty-two and the oldest forty-two. They were more highly educated, affluent, and worldly than the general population of detainees, reflecting Kuwait's very different political and economic history. A number spoke good English and could communicate with their captors. They were an important communications bridge, as there were few Arabic speakers among the military guards.

Kuwait presented the question after 9/11 of how the United States would treat men who were largely middle class, relatively cosmopolitan, pious but not extremist or violent in orientation, and who came from a country that was a longtime ally with close connections and gratitude toward the United States. The answers were not good.

The Kuwaiti Experience: Affluence and Trauma

After being liberated from Iraq by the United States and Coalition troops in the First Gulf War in 1991, Kuwait had rebuilt itself from the wanton destruction inflicted by Saddam Hussein's troops and, by 2001, was again one of the wealthiest countries in the world. Its population was small and generously provided with social welfare benefits and high living standards. Upon getting married, Kuwaiti males could obtain a social welfare loan of 6,000 Kuwaiti Dinars (KD) (around $19,000), of which one-third was forgiven and the rest could be repaid over time without interest. Kuwaiti nationals were also granted a plot of land for a house and an interest-free loan of 70,000 KD (around $227,000) to build it.

Unlike the governments of some in the region, Kuwait is a constitutional principality, with a hereditary Emir, an elected Parliament, a relatively free press, and a very vocal public sphere. It is widely viewed as one of the most open and stable countries in the region. In the GCC region, Kuwait is the only country designated as "Partly Free"[5] by Freedom House. If that seems like damning with faint praise, the fact is that all other GCC countries and Kuwait's neighbors are considered "Not Free."[6] The government makes certain that the religious establishment stays under government supervision. The Kuwaiti Parliament has been viewed as a generally ineffective "talking shop," preoccupied with its prerogatives at the expense of modernization and riddled with corruption, but, nevertheless, it is an elected deliberative body – the only one in the region – where a wide range of viewpoints are expressed. It has been periodically suspended, including by the newest Emir, who suspended the Parliament for four years to relatively little public outcry in May of 2024. It remains to be seen whether this is a temporary measure to try to compel Parliamentary reform and responsibility or a longer-term power play.[7]

Kuwaitis have long been accustomed to interaction with foreigners, including non-Muslim expatriates from South Asia, the United States, and Europe. English is widely spoken. It is prosperous, hard-working, and family-oriented. Its government has managed its vast hydrocarbon resources carefully, and for good or ill, the government remains the primary source of employment in the country. This has inhibited economic dynamism in recent decades but has provided economic security. Nearly eighty percent of employment is in the public sector, although many work the mandatory seven hours per day, beginning at 7 or 8 a.m., and then leave in the early afternoon to pursue their own private business ventures. There is no personal income tax, but employees contribute 7 percent of their income to the Public Institution for Social Security, the government pension fund, and the government contributes an additional 11 percent. The social safety net is generous.

The Quiet Emirate in a Difficult Neighborhood

Kuwait sits uneasily between Iraq to the north and western borders and Saudi Arabia to the south and west; the Gulf is to the east. The southern and western parts of the Gulf are populated principally by Arabs, who generally call it the Arabian Gulf. Iran sits nearby across the warm waters of this same Gulf, where it is called the Persian Gulf. At their closest point, the borders of Iran and Kuwait sit fourteen miles apart. Iraq and Iran are majority Shia; Saudi Arabia is majority Sunni. Kuwait is approximately two-thirds Sunni and one-third Shia. A significant majority of its population – nearly 70 percent – are not Kuwaiti citizens at all, but expatriate workers at both the highest and lowest levels of employment. The Sunni/Shia divide has been far less of a flashpoint in Kuwait than elsewhere in the region.

Islam is constitutionally defined as the state religion and a major (but by no means the only) source of legislation, as well as for charity to the poor. The Constitution guarantees freedom of belief, and there are licensed churches of various denominations in the country.[8] The Muslim Brotherhood has had a presence in Kuwait since the 1950s, and is active in education and social welfare, but it has never constituted a majority or even a plurality in the Kuwaiti system.

Although there are technically no parties permitted in the Kuwaiti Parliament, adherents of the Brotherhood, in addition to other political factions on the right and left of the political spectrum, have formed informal blocs.[9] The Brotherhood, officially represented by the Social

Reform Society,[10] actively supported the presence of American troops during the Gulf War in pushing back Saddam Hussein. This broke from the Brotherhood's international consensus, which generally advocated against the presence of non-Muslim troops or foreign intervention.[11] Unlike in other countries, the Brotherhood's presence in Kuwait is viewed as fairly transparent and pragmatic, and it works with other political interests across a wide range of issues. It seeks to promote religious interests, but within the mainstream of accepted practice and views.[12]

Although the size of Hawaii, Kuwait has the fourth-highest GDP per capita in the world.[13] It lacks the flash and dazzle of Dubai. It will host no World Cups; Parliamentary oversight and careful auditing of spending would preclude the Kuwaiti government from taking on vast global projects. Even in the abeyance of Parliament, the executive is conscious of its population's aversion to ostentation or profligacy. Western-style nightlife is effectively nonexistent; alcohol is not permitted, and life revolves around extended families, who often live in multigenerational houses built around central courtyards that tack on additions as each son starts his family.[14]

When the Kuwaiti men who ended up at Guantanamo left the country in 2001, the country's population was under 2 million. When the last Kuwaiti detainee came home, it had increased to more than 3.5 million and has increased again as of 2024 to more than 4.9 million. Of that 4.9 million, only 1.56 million – or around thirty percent are Kuwaiti citizens, and coveted Kuwaiti citizenship is hard to acquire for people not born to Kuwaiti parents. Although initially settled by desert tribes, Kuwait today is 100 percent urbanized, with Kuwait City accounting for more than 70 percent of the country's population.

Kuwait is a modern and developed country, despite occupying one of the most extreme deserts in the world. Kuwait routinely records some of the hottest temperatures on the globe with the mercury approaching and even surpassing 50 degrees Celsius (122 Fahrenheit) in the summertime. In June 2021, the Kuwaiti city of Nawasib recorded the highest temperature ever measured in a settled place on the planet, reaching 53.2 degrees Celsius (127.8 Fahrenheit).[15] Not surprisingly, Kuwait's growth followed on from the discovery of oil – and the widespread availability of air conditioning.

Kuwait originally developed in the eighteenth and nineteenth centuries as a stop on trading routes, becoming an organized political entity in 1752. The Al Sabah family, who descend from one of the largest tribes in the Arabian Peninsula, was initially chosen by the local residents to rule over merchant disputes in the early nineteenth century, which eventually led to the family's elder to be chosen as the first Emir (or Leader) of Kuwait.[16]

In a tacit agreement between Kuwait society's main stakeholders (especially the powerful merchants from a handful of prominent families), the Al Sabah family rules, but Kuwaitis do not consider the Al Sabahs a "royal family" with a God-given right to kingship. Their power reflects a long-standing societal consensus, limited in its authority by other important institutions. This is a critical distinction in the region. The Al Sabahs exercise important powers, but there is a system of limited but meaningful checks and balances that blends democratic and local political elements.[17]

Kuwait had been something of a global volleyball, batted back and forth among imperial powers playing the Great Game in the region. From 1899 to 1961, Kuwait was mainly a British protectorate, after the then-Emir, Sheikh Mubarak Al Sabah signed the Anglo-Kuwaiti Treaty, which promised British protection in the face of threats from the Ottoman Empire. In 1913, however, the British and the Ottoman Sultan signed (without consulting anyone in Kuwait) the Anglo-Ottoman Convention, which, among other things, made Kuwait an administrative division of the Ottoman Empire.[18] It gave the Emir autonomy over only an eighty square kilometer portion of what had previously been a much larger country. Having agreed to put Kuwait under its imperial wing, the British abruptly left Kuwait to the tender mercies of the dying Sublime Porte when Britain viewed it as in its interests to do so; of course, this was before the discovery of massive hydrocarbon reserves.

Having been abandoned by the British, the Kuwaiti Emir supported the Ottoman Empire, allied with the Central Powers, during World War I, in retrospect a short-sighted move, as the Ottoman Empire was defeated and collapsed in the aftermath of the war. During the war, the British Empire imposed a trade blockade, which heavily damaged Kuwait's economy. After the war, the British reasserted its protectorate status over Kuwait, although Kuwait had not asked to regain any such protection. Unlike other global empires, the British retained their global footprint after World War I, asserting control as they saw fit in Kuwait and the region.[19]

Land disputes between Kuwait and the powerful tribes in the Najd region of Saudi Arabia (around today's Riyadh and the traditional heartland of the Al Saud family) led to further conflict. Saudi-supported militants besieged a key Kuwaiti fortification with the intention of incorporating Kuwait into the ongoing Saudi consolidation of the Arabian Peninsula. Despite supporting both the Kuwaitis and the Saudis at the time, the British eventually came down on the side of Kuwait and ended the threat, but relations between Kuwait and the Al Sauds remained tense. Had Britain chosen otherwise in the Al Sabah-Al Saud dispute, Kuwait would likely never have come into existence.[20]

The Al Sauds imposed a further blockade of Kuwait by land and sea from 1923 to 1927, followed by the Great Depression, which largely destroyed Kuwait's economy yet again, as its main economic driver was international trade. With the discovery of massive oil reserves in the 1930s and the petroleum industry's rapid expansion after World War II, Kuwait took on newfound importance, and Great Britain, its purported protector, tried to take full advantage. Kuwait's oil reserves turned out to be massive, and today, this tiny emirate holds nearly one-tenth of all global oil reserves, projected to last another 150 years.[21] It also produces significant quantities of natural gas. The black gold of the Kuwaiti oil fields has attracted the often-unsought attention of many regional and international powers, again jeopardizing its existence.

On June 19, 1961, Kuwait became fully independent following the agreed termination of the original Anglo-Kuwaiti Treaty. Both the United Kingdom and the United States, however, continued to keep Kuwait close, bound by oil concessions, which brought great wealth to the various British and American producers, with vast royalty rights (but not ownership of the oil) accruing to the Kuwaiti government.

As in other Gulf countries, Kuwait began more aggressively to assert sovereign rights over its natural resources after independence. By 1976, it had achieved full ownership of Kuwait's oil production with its former partners given the right to buy oil from the state at a discount and the Anglo-American multinationals receiving preferences to enter into lucrative technical services contracts.[22] Kuwait had earlier also created the first sovereign wealth fund, the Kuwait Investment Board,[23] which was using its newfound oil wealth to make strategic investments in foreign entities. The government also partnered with Kuwaiti investors to form the Kuwait National Petroleum Company (KNPC) to serve as an integrated oil company, including marketing abroad. In 1980, the State founded Kuwait Petroleum Corporation (KPC) as an umbrella organization overseeing not only domestic oil operations but also an oil tanker company, a petrochemical company, and a foreign exploration entity.[24] Kuwait had overtaken its former partners in hydrocarbon wealth and was leveraging that wealth globally.

Unlike many other resource-based rentier economies, the Kuwaiti government has proved to be a responsible guardian of its immense oil revenues, investing large portions of those revenues in infrastructure and social development. By the mid-1980s, Kuwait was refining four-fifths of its oil domestically and marketing some 400,000 barrels a day, supplying more than 5,000 European retail outlets under the name "Q8." It's management is viewed as world class in training and sophistication.

The Kuwaiti system is headed by an Emir, who is a hereditary constitutional monarch, who in turn appoints a Prime Minister, who appoints a Council of Ministers. The Kuwaiti Constitution guarantees a number of political freedoms, including freedom of speech and association. As a practical matter, these freedoms have ebbed and flowed over the years, depending on the political climate and the government of the time.

There is a unicameral National Assembly also referred to as the Parliament, which has fifty directly elected members in addition to fifteen appointed Cabinet Ministers. Debate among the various factions in Parliament has been aggressive and freewheeling to a degree unique in the region. Prime Ministers are often subject to aggressive grilling by members of the Parliament, akin to Prime Minister's Questions in the UK. Three Prime Ministers, two of whom were members of the ruling branch of the Al-Sabah family, were forced from office after pressure from Parliament and external protest.

The Emir has the power to veto legislation and return it to the National Assembly for revision. If a revised piece of legislation is then passed by two-thirds of the members, it becomes law despite the Emir's veto. There has been significant conflict over policy between the executive and the legislature, and the Emir has dissolved the Parliament pursuant to the Constitution on multiple occasions, leading to eventual new elections. As in many countries, the Parliament is often viewed as a thorn in the side of the executive, and the multiple suspensions of Parliament, including the 2024 suspension, may reflect both impatience with its aggressive approach as well as legitimate concerns regarding corruption and dysfunction.

Participation of the public in elections is high, although legislative gridlock has been a persistent feature of the Kuwaiti system.[25] Scholars of the region view these checks and balances, although limited, as substantive and more effective than in other Gulf states. Whether and how quickly the Emir allows new elections will be watched carefully in the region and elsewhere as a key to the future direction of governance in Kuwait.

Kuwait's law is an amalgam of the French Civil Code (transported with the heavy influence of Egyptian scholars who initially adapted the Code) and Islamic Sharia law. Kuwaiti judges are appointed by the Emir on the recommendation of the Supreme Judicial Council. The Supreme Judicial Council is composed of senior judges from the Ministry of Justice and Kuwaiti lawyers who are previously approved by the Emir.[26] According to the World Economic Forum's 2019 Global Competitiveness Index, Kuwait's judicial independence is fairly good, with a score of 4.6 out of 7 points. It is ranked Number 41 of 180 countries.[27]

Kuwait has been viewed as having a relatively free press, although there have been periodic crackdowns and legal prohibitions imposed. Criticism of religion is not permitted, and journalists are careful with respect to sensitive subjects such as uprisings during the Arab Spring against hereditary monarchy. In the final days of Sheikh Sabah Al Ahmad Al Jaber Al Sabah (2006–2020), further laws restricting press freedom were enacted, and international observers moved Kuwait behind Qatar and the UAE in the Gulf with respect to press freedom.[28]

In sum, Kuwait is a hybrid system, combining various aspects of traditional hereditary governance and democratic republicanism. It is more transparent than most of its neighbors, but it remains a conservative society. It disperses power more widely than others in the region, but the ruling family maintains significant authority. Its government provides prosperity and employment but lacks the economic vigor of its neighbors. Its population is affluent, educated, and well travelled, while retaining strong links to its traditional extended family structure.

What this brief history illustrates is that the Kuwaitis who ended up in Guantanamo did not fit any stereotype of impoverished extremists radicalized by unsupervised, radical Imams calling for anti-Western violence. Whatever such elements existed in Kuwaiti society would have been limited in number and furtive in a highly regulated, monitored, and security-conscious society. As we will see, the Kuwaiti authorities are well aware of the forces in the region and on the internet and monitor and address people whom they view as having "wrong thoughts."

An Indelible Identity Forged in War and Suffering

Despite its long history and economic achievements, Kuwait and the forces that form its national character cannot be properly understood without primary reference to two signal events in its national story: first, the Iraqi invasion of August 1990 and subsequent war of liberation in 1991; and second, the events and aftermath of September 11, 2001.

Kuwait's location, compact size, limited population, tiny military, and remarkably valuable petroleum industry have long made it a compelling target for its larger neighbors. Iraq and Kuwait had squabbled over borders for decades (as did Saudi Arabia and Kuwait), but Kuwait provided valuable support to Iraq during its costly war with Iran in the 1980s. Kuwait also provided critical financing to Iraq, funding military equipment purchases during the eight-year war. The war effectively ended in a stalemate, but Iraq had been bled dry in human and economic resources and had enormous debts, including more than $8 billion owed to Kuwait. Iraq demanded that Kuwait forgive what was owed, but Kuwait declined to do so. As a longtime Middle East hand, Ambassador Richard Murphy said, the Al Sabahs were "methodical bankers," who would never simply write off such a huge debt.[29] Saddam Hussein was both contemptuous and envious of Kuwait, whose wealth from oil had been earned "without sweat." He viewed himself as holding the line against Tehran on behalf of his timid and self-indulgent neighbors in the Gulf.[30]

Iraq began to make threats and accusations, accusing Kuwait of violating Organization of Petroleum Exporting Countries ("OPEC") production quotas, depressing oil prices, and depriving Iraq of needed revenues. Saddam Hussein also accused Kuwait of stealing oil from the Rumayla oil field on the border between the two countries and demanded the return of certain islands held by Kuwait.[31]

Attempts were made to conciliate, but neither the United States nor its allies in the region anticipated a full-scale invasion. Having failed to be given instructions for a clear response to the gathering threat, the newly appointed US Ambassador to Iraq, April Glaspie, met with Saddam Hussein on July 25, 1990. There has been ongoing controversy ever since about what Glaspie communicated and how it was construed by Saddam. Glaspie asked Saddam whether it was not reasonable for the United States to be concerned and to inquire about Iraq's statements that Kuwaiti actions were the equivalent of military aggression and that units of his elite Republican Guard were being sent to the border. Saddam said that these were reasonable requests, but rather than stating his intentions, he asked how the royal families of Kuwait and the UAE could "understand how deeply we are suffering" and that "pensions for widows and orphans will have to be cut."[32]

According to a transcript published in the *New York Times*, Glaspie then told the Iraqi leader:

> But we have no opinion on the Arab-Arab conflicts, like your border disagreement with Kuwait. I was in the American Embassy in Kuwait during the late 1960s. The instruction we had during this period was that we should

express no opinion on this issue and that the issue is not associated with America. James Baker has directed our official spokesmen to emphasize this instruction. We hope you can solve this problem using any suitable methods via Klibi [the Secretary General of the Arab League] or via President Mubarak. All that we hope is that these issues are solved quickly.[33]

Glaspie's cable on her meeting with Saddam reports that President Bush "had instructed her to broaden and deepen our relations with Iraq." Saddam, in turn, offered "warm greetings" to Bush and, she reported, was "surely sincere" about not wanting war.

When the purported transcripts were made public, Glaspie was accused of having given tacit approval for the Iraqi invasion of Kuwait, which began a week after the meeting, on August 2, 1990. It was argued that Glaspie's statements that "We have no opinion on the Arab-Arab conflicts" and that "the [Kuwait] issue is not associated with America" were interpreted by Saddam as giving a green light to handle his disputes with Kuwait as he saw fit. It was also argued that Saddam would not have invaded Kuwait had he been given an explicit warning that such an invasion would be met with force by the United States. Journalist Edward Mortimer wrote in the *New York Review of Books* in November 1990:

> It seems far more likely that Saddam Hussein went ahead with the invasion because he believed the US would not react with anything more than verbal condemnation. That was an inference he could well have drawn from his meeting with US Ambassador April Glaspie on July 25, and from statements by State Department officials in Washington at the same time publicly disavowing any US security commitments to Kuwait, but also from the success of both the Reagan and the Bush administrations in heading off attempts by the US Senate to impose sanctions on Iraq for previous breaches of international law.[34]

Later reporting on the meeting indicated that Saddam had assured Glaspie he did *not* intend to invade and that he referenced his intention to meet the Kuwaiti Emir for further negotiation.

Other observers indicated that Saddam was under no illusions that an American response was likely if he invaded, but he proceeded anyway, believing that his huge army would resist any US response, which in his view would not commit the necessary resources to displace him. In any event, there was certainly ambiguity as to the American position and miscalculation on both sides, leading to tragic results.

It also remains impossible to assess how much of the massive response of Operation Desert Storm was motivated by the desire to liberate Kuwait or instead by the fear that Saddam would then wheel south and invade his much larger and strategically important neighbor, Saudi Arabia. Prior to the invasion, the US military presence in the region was quite limited, and there was concern about whether Gulf countries would accept large numbers of foreign troops. After the invasion, the Saudis moved quickly to obtain a religious *fatwa* from the Grand Mufti, which gave religious legitimation to the liberation of Kuwait and, not coincidentally, to the elimination of a military threat to Saudi Arabia and its oil reserves. The issue of American troops on sacred soil in the Gulf would remain a flashpoint through 9/11 and afterward.

The Iraqi Invasion and Dismantling of the Kuwaiti Nation

Soon after the Saddam–Glaspie meeting, Iraq declared war and overran Kuwait in thirty-six hours, despite courageous resistance from the 20,000-member Kuwait Army. Thousands of Kuwaiti soldiers were believed to have died in this bloody day and a half. Despite its poor economic condition, Iraq maintained a standing army of 900,000 troops, with the ability to quickly mobilize up to 2 million men. Kuwait's entire population was approximately 2 million at the time, of whom only about 825,000 were actually Kuwaitis. In other words, Iraq had more men under arms than Kuwait had citizens, with predictable results.

Iraq annexed Kuwait and declared it Iraq's nineteenth province. There was fierce hand-to-hand combat around the Emir's palace, and the Emir's younger brother was killed. On August 3, the second day of the Iraqi invasion, Kuwaiti radio signed off, "Arabs, brothers, beloved brothers, Muslims. Hurry to our aid."

Iraq immediately took steps to try to wipe Kuwait off the map. Saddam appointed his cousin Ali Hassan Al Majid, known as Chemical Ali for his ruthless use of chemical weapons against Kurds and Shias, as the governor of the new Nineteenth Province. He declared that this new province "must become less developed."[35] Homes were ransacked; virtually everything worth stealing was grabbed by Iraqi troops. Within days, Kuwaiti courts had been "affiliated to the chairmanship" of the Basra, Iraq Court of Appeal; Kuwait no longer had its own legal system. The Kuwaiti dinar, which had earlier been declared at parity with the Iraqi dinar, was abolished, and the Iraqi dinar became the only recognized currency. Kuwaiti establishments and organizations were shut down, and their properties and rights were incorporated into Iraqi administrative structures. The Kuwait Central Bank and Kuwait Airlines were dissolved; Kuwaiti citizens were required to exchange their Kuwaiti identity papers for Iraqi identity papers and Kuwaiti car license plates for Iraqi plates identifying Kuwait as an Iraqi province. Kuwait street names were changed. All references to Kuwait as an independent entity or the old regime were banned from textbooks.[36] From an Iraqi perspective, Kuwait had ceased to exist.

While trying to destroy these indicia of nationhood, the Iraqis, at the same time, treated the Kuwaitis with terrible violence, and there were massive violations of human rights. Many thousands of Kuwaiti military personnel were captured and held without adequate food or medical care in the brutal Iraqi summer heat. Civilians were arrested in huge numbers and sent to Iraq and imprisoned on a variety of trumped-up charges.

Family members and friends were often arrested and imprisoned when the Iraqis could not locate the person who had been targeted for arrest. Arrested Kuwaitis were subject to repeated coercive interrogations, severe beatings, and frequent torture. They were denied lawyers, and their families were not told where they were or if they were alive.[37] Overnight, a prosperous and tightly-knit society was brutalized and undone.

The UN Special Rapporteur found widespread and grisly torture of thousands of Kuwaitis:

> While most victims of torture were men between 18 and 40 years old, elderly men were also reportedly tortured, as were women and allegedly even children.
>
> The methods of torture and cruel, inhuman or degrading treatment were manifold. The most common method was heavy beatings on all parts of the body including sensitive parts; instruments used included sticks, metal rods, clubs, whips, rifle butts and steel cables. In some cases beatings of this kind caused severe injuries. Often beatings included falaqa [beating of the bottom of the feet].
>
> Electro-shocks (the application of electricity to sensitive parts of the body, including ears, tongue, fingers, toes and genitals) were also reported to have been commonly used: There were numerous accounts of psychological torture, including threats to torture or rape relatives, forcing persons to watch executions or torture including rape of other detainees or even of relatives, mock executions or threats of execution. Another frequent form of torture was suspending detainees, sometimes for prolonged periods, by the feet, the arms or the waist; often they were beaten while suspended.
>
> The Special Rapporteur received evidence of cases of burning, normally with cigarettes but in some cases with boiling water or domestic appliances. Pulling out of nails was another form of torture repeatedly used. Other methods used included sexual torture. Female detainees were raped and both men and women suffered from the insertion of bottle necks,

sometimes broken. Because many victims of sexual torture were reluctant to reveal their experiences, no statistical figures are available. Severe mutilations were less frequent; however, among those executed many bodies showed severe mutilations. According to photographic evidence, torturers resorted to gouging out eyes, cutting off ears or pouring acid onto the face or parts of the body.[38]

"This Shall Not Stand": The First President Bush and the Liberation

Hussein had badly misgauged the resolve of the Kuwaitis and of regional and global allies. The invasion quickly led to an embargo and sanctions, followed by the first President Bush organizing a massive US-led "Coalition of the Willing," which began combat operations in January 1991, and ended with a massive Iraqi defeat and withdrawal six weeks later. Approximately 400,000 people fled Kuwait to Jordan, Saudi Arabia, Europe, and elsewhere, but many more stayed and formed an active resistance to aid coalition forces.[39]

As Hussein retreated from Iraq in January and February 1991, the abuse of civilians intensified, including mass arrests, summary executions, and widespread destruction of infrastructure. As Iraqi troops left Kuwait in the last week of February, they set fire to multiple government buildings, including the National Assembly and the Foreign Ministry, and a number of luxury hotels; the Sheraton Hotel was built back exactly as it had been before, with pictures of the burnt-out shell displayed throughout the public areas.

As a final wanton act, the Iraqis set Kuwaiti oil wells on fire and destroyed oil field infrastructure. The oil wells burned for ten months, leaving thousands of lakes of oil and an environmental disaster. These fires damaged or destroyed approximately 85 percent of the wells in every major Kuwaiti oil field. It was estimated that the ignited wellheads burnt through between 4 and 6 million barrels of crude oil and between 70 and 100 million cubic meters of natural gas per day. The fires were visible from space. The total amount of oil lost was estimated at 1 billion barrels, amounting to $157.5 billion at the then-world price of oil.[40]

Iraqi authorities ordered highly publicized executions of suspected resistance members during the last days of the war. The exact number of those killed by Iraqi forces in January and February has never been determined. The Iraqis were thoroughly defeated, but they would not leave before taking revenge on innocent Kuwaiti victims.

The 1990 invasion was a collective trauma that profoundly affected, and continues to affect, the psyche of the country. Kuwait had always been a small emirate surrounded by larger neighbors, but it had been a deft and generous regional player. Kuwait had diversified into Europe; it had close relations with the United States, and its wealth and diplomatic savvy were viewed as bulwarks for the "Sunni crescent" that ran across much of the Gulf. Kuwait was a supporter of Palestinian rights and housed and employed approximately 400,000 Palestinians, around 20 percent of the population;[41] Kuwaitis were shocked and outraged when certain Arab nations and Palestinian groups, including the Palestinian Liberation Organization, supported the Iraqi invasion. Only twelve of the twenty-one Arab League members supported a resolution condemning the invasion. Kuwait had provided significant funding and support to its neighbors. Yet, Kuwaiti society could be overwhelmed and Kuwaiti sovereignty taken away in a matter of hours, and some of its erstwhile friends did not come to its aid.

For Kuwaitis, the question of "What happened to you and your family during the war?" was crucial. Did you stay and fight? Did you assist the US military, who saved the country from Iraqi depredation? Did you try to support Kuwait from abroad? Did you lose family or livelihood? Or did you collaborate with the puppet government set up by Iraq? Who were you and what did you do, or not do, for your country at this existential moment? The drama of Iraqi destruction followed by American liberation was burned into the collective memory of Kuwait. Kuwaitis knew who supported their nationhood (and who did not) at the existential moment, and the United States was at the top of that list of supporters; it saved Kuwait. This central principle of national memory created both shock and anxiety a decade later – after 9/11 – when a dozen Kuwaitis were deemed to be mortal enemies of their country's liberators.

The Aftermath of 9/11 and the Challenge for Kuwait

Kuwait faced only bad choices after 9/11. President Bush had drawn a line in the sand. His father had saved the country. The Kuwaiti government's first instinct after 9/11 and the subsequent invasion of Afghanistan and capture of detainees was to do nothing and send the message to other young people in Kuwait: This can happen to you; you too can end up in Guantanamo Bay. The detainees were initially singled out as bad examples to the young people of Kuwait before they had received any process to find out whether they had done anything wrong.

Many of the Kuwaiti detainees had families who depended on their monthly salaries from the government. The government directed that the detainees be summarily fired for unexplained absence; their salaries were stopped, and the government refused to provide any support to the families. The detainees and their families were cut off in those early days by a shaken and cautious Kuwaiti government.

While the families and the Core Team were trying to figure out what to do in this unique situation, there were now hundreds of men held in chains thousands of miles away, including the twelve Kuwaitis. Who were they? What was happening to them? How were they being treated? Was the United States trying to figure out who was who, or did it have a different agenda?

While the legal landscape was being transformed in Washington, the detainees knew almost nothing of what was going on in the United States for years. But these men knew very well that they were being treated like terrorists, they were being degraded and abused, and they were trapped into participating in repeated and senseless interrogations and sham hearings that had the purpose of keeping them where they were indefinitely. It was only after litigation that was not decided by the Supreme Court until 2008 – litigation for which the Core Team was a principal architect and a Kuwaiti detainee was a named plaintiff – that these men finally had at least some opportunity to tell their stories to US courts rather than to Pentagon and US National Intelligence officials who knew what results they wanted to reach.

3

Strategizing in a New World: Navigating the New Paradigm

By early spring of 2002, there were more than 300 men imprisoned; by year's end, more than 600, and the population peaked near 700 in the spring of 2003.[1] They could not speak with their governments or families. They were guarded by a hastily assembled force consisting primarily of young national guard reservists, almost none of whom could communicate with detainees in their own languages, an estimated thirteen of which were spoken by detainees.[2] But as their days went by in a welter of uncertainty, repeated interrogations, and abuse, the world of their captors was rapidly changing.

The United States, the greatest military, economic, and political power in world history, had been shocked and humiliated. The threat of terrorism had created panic, rage, and resolve; there was strong pressure to retaliate by any means conceivable and to prevent further attacks. Guantanamo became the crucible to determine whether the United States would adhere to the principles of the rule of law or whether it would lash out and make new enemies while forfeiting its moral authority.

This is not a legal treatise, but the story of these men cannot be told without some understanding of the complex and novel issues of law and politics swirling in the United States unbeknownst to the detainees. Did these men have any rights? What, if anything, should or must the United States do to sort the genuine terrorists from the men who happened to be in the wrong place at the wrong time or who, at worst, were cannon fodder fighting against a superpower invasion that they could never have anticipated? How long could they be held? Could they be held forever? Could they be forcibly interrogated or even tortured for actionable intelligence? How would the "new paradigm" affect the American rule of law and the presumption of innocence with respect to these men? There were only questions and more questions, and very few answers, when the families of the twelve detainees came together to form the Family Committee in early 2002.

Even as threats receded over time, the power of 9/11 to terrify and to justify indiscriminate torture did not fade away. The Bush administration, having been warned multiple times of the Al Qaida threat prior to September 11, and having failed to heed that threat, now needed to show its toughness and competence in dealing with the aftermath. The September 11 attacks were seen as another Pearl Harbor, yet even more furtive and nefarious. This time, Muslims rather than Japanese became the presumptively suspicious "other." Politicians tried to stoke and capitalize on those fears. American society seemed not to demand effectiveness in combating future terrorism, but rather to revere leaders who, having failed to act effectively beforehand, now channeled rage and a thirst for revenge.

The ethnocentrism against foreigners, especially foreigners not of European origin, began to rear its head once again, despite President Bush's statements immediately after 9/11 that Muslims and Islam were not collectively to blame. The rest of his administration and much of American society plainly did not get the message. Suddenly, Muslims were being profiled, surveilled, stopped at airports, wiretapped, and often arrested and held as material witnesses until charges could be developed. Islamophobia, despite protestations to the contrary, became ingrained in American national life, where it remains today, decades later, in various guises.

Kuwait was not going to turn this battleship of paranoia and xenophobia around. Its only real option was to try to persuade the courts that this was a matter of basic rights guaranteed to everyone and required neutral fact-finding by independent judges. The Family Committee wanted, first and foremost, to find out whether their sons were being held on some legitimate basis. The detainees should be given fair and proper hearings affording due process; as long as there were such hearings, the Family Committee would accept the results. Not surprisingly, the families did not believe their sons had committed terrorist acts; if they were innocent, they should be sent home.

The Family Committee Chair, Khalid Al Odah, made his first call upon learning there were twelve Kuwaitis at Guantanamo to Abdul Rahman Al Haroun (ARH), a cousin and dear friend, who was the founder of International Counsel Bureau, a leading Kuwaiti commercial law firm. He had an excellent understanding of the culture and legal system of the United States, at least the United States that he had known prior to 9/11. But he was a business lawyer, without any background in criminal or international human rights law.

ARH immediately reached out to his close colleague, William Brown, an American lawyer who had practiced in New York and Washington, DC, before relocating to the Gulf, first to Abu Dhabi and then to Kuwait.

Brown, who spoke in the folksy tones of his native South Carolina, loved Kuwait and the Kuwaitis – their work ethic, their family values, and their candor. He spoke often of his Kuwaiti "brothers," of whom ARH was his closest one. Brown too was a business lawyer; he was not a litigator and also had no background in public international law or human rights.

ARH went right to the point and told Brown he wanted to ask a question, and it would be all right if Brown answered no. He asked if Brown would work with him on behalf of the Family Committee – figuring out first why these young men were being held, and what should be done to get these boys home if, as they believed, they were not terrorists.

Brown asked why he would possibly say no to such a request. Mindful of the political atmosphere, ARH answered, "because it's your country." Brown responded, "That's why I'll do whatever I can to support you and Khalid in your efforts to get justice."[3] Both ARH and Brown had enough common sense to know that the cause of the Kuwaiti detainees, or any of the detainees, would not be a popular one in the legal profession, in the halls of the US government, or, indeed, with governments anywhere reluctant to take on the United States. They could not anticipate the full force of the hostility that would be directed at them and at Guantanamo lawyers generally.

Brown cautioned that American justice was slow and expensive. If the Family Committee could "stay in the game," he was confident that due process and justice would prevail and their families would get their boys back. Little did he know it would take 5,000 days to accomplish that mission. Nor did he know that the legal, political, and diplomatic struggles ahead would take much of their time on a daily basis for all of those days. The Family Committee had the will, but not the money, to stay in the game, but ARH and Brown were committed to the justice of their cause. It was some years before any appreciable funding from the Kuwaiti government flowed, and that money went to pay US lawyers, not the strategists who were directing the entire process.

With ARH's concurrence, Brown contacted Marcia Newell in Washington, DC, who worked with and was trusted completely by Brown and ARH. Newell knew exactly how Washington worked, as well as how to organize and manage large projects. She knew the bureaucracies at Defense and State and the legal market. She had spent decades as a legal recruiter and legal project manager. She was also close to the families of both ARH and Brown. Newell was immediately on board. With Newell strategizing the Washington bureaucracy as well as organizing the legal teams; Brown managing a careful and sophisticated US legal strategy; and

ARH coordinating at the highest levels of the Kuwaiti government and working with the families, each brought unique skills and experience to the project. The Core Team had been formed and would persevere until the last Kuwaiti had come home. But they needed a strategy and US lawyers to execute it.

There were no guideposts and no funding, and the Core Team did not know if help – financial or diplomatic – would ever be forthcoming from the Kuwaiti government. It was entirely possible that taking on this cause at this time would adversely affect their careers and their reputations. Representing Guantanamo detainees in the shadow of September 11 was not something that anyone was putting in their brochures or on their websites. It became trendy only years later.

ARH knew some of the families, but neither he nor the rest of the team knew the backstory of any of the twelve Kuwaiti detainees. Their families all said their sons were innocent, but that is nearly always the case when family members are incarcerated. The Core Team would need to find out. The Core Team also knew that an initial essential tactic would have to be litigation to sort out the legal rights and remedies available in the United States; in any event, there were few other options.

Meanwhile, the Core Team understood that it also needed to try to obtain the support of the Kuwaiti government. This too would not be easy or quick. The Kuwaiti government's initial view was similar to the view taken by every other country: We don't support terrorists; we have no interest in repatriating terrorists, and if these men are terrorists, which we must preliminarily assume based on the US actions, then they deserve whatever punishment they receive.

The Emir of Kuwait (at the time H. H. Sheikh Jaber Al Ahmed Al Sabah) and the then-Foreign Minister (Dr. Sheikh Mohammad Al Sabah) were willing to engage the full weight of the government, but only if they could be convinced that they were not being asked to bring back terrorists or create security risks to the United States or Kuwait. At the outset, they were highly skeptical. The Family Committee and the Core Team were on their own.

The Core Team tried to move quickly to figure out whether the Kuwaitis had been wrongly detained and, if so, to engage litigators and put together legal claims as quickly as possible for filing in the United States. ARH's law firm, International Counsel Bureau, agreed to make a down payment to litigation counsel in the United States from its own funds. The two constants in the strategy were straightforward and modest: first, the detainees should be given a fair and proper hearing; and second, there should be no "mission creep," addressing broader policy issues that went beyond justice for these men, such as whether Guantanamo should be shut down or whether indefinite detention without trial was ever permitted. They were committed to these men, not to abstract causes.

Although they could not know for certain what each man had done or not done, the Core Team was able to ascertain relatively quickly that it was likely there were no high-level terrorists in this group. Most of these men had gone just before or just after September 11 to do charity work. While the US government had decided these were Al Qaida "cover stories," there was long experience in Kuwait and elsewhere of young men going to poor Muslim countries and digging wells, building schools, teaching Arabic, the language of prayer, to non-native Arabic speakers (like those in Afghanistan or Pakistan) or instructing Muslims in countries where people knew relatively little about the articles and practices of their common faith.

Even if some may have flirted with radicalism, none of the detainees would conceivably have been privy to any plotting of the September 11 attacks, which had occurred over a period of years by a small cabal in Afghanistan. Kuwaitis would generally have been unlikely in any event to have had any sympathy for the aims and methods of Al Qaida, which had supported Saddam Hussein in the First Gulf War. Everyone in Kuwait knew people who had been killed or injured by the Iraqi invasion; supporters of that invasion were still anathema in the country. And Al Qaida clearly had placed a target on the politically more moderate regimes in the region like Kuwait. Kuwaiti society was the antithesis of the nightmarish vision of Al Qaida.

Some of the foreigners in Afghanistan may have been given rudimentary training in firearms, as Afghanistan was also a violent place with ongoing conflict between the Northern Alliance and the Taliban over control of the country. They were strangers at risk in a strange land. And now the United States had been attacked, and its focus was on Afghanistan. These men needed to get out, and they needed to do so quickly. There were bounties on their heads. Former Pakistani President Musharraf confirmed, in his 2006 memoir, that, in return for handing over 369 terror suspects to the United States, the Pakistani government "earned bounty payments totaling millions of dollars."[4] According to a report prepared by Seton Hall University Law School, only 5 percent of Guantanamo detainees were actually captured by US forces and 86 percent of the detainees were handed over to the United States for bounties.[5]

Although the Core Team was aware that there was a high probability that many of these men were legally innocent or, at worst, low-level combatants, now that they were detained, no one wanted to hear arguments about innocence. The crisis in America was both legal and political, and there seemed to be no obvious way to proceed.

There were so many novel and complex questions without clear answers. The Law of War permitted one side to hold enemy combatants of the other for the duration of the war. But was the "Global War on Terror" a war? Where was the battlefield? Who was the enemy, and how did one define an enemy combatant? When did this war start? How would it end?

While it often has been assumed that foreigners detained by the US authorities were guaranteed certain core constitutional rights, it was a somewhat unsettled question as to whether foreign nationals outside the territory of the United States had any rights at all. Guantanamo Bay was selected by the Bush administration precisely because it wanted to argue it was a legal void, so the military could detain without any oversight from the US courts.[6] The US government knew that if the detainees had been brought to the United States, all constitutional protections would apply; it hoped that the Constitution would be left behind entirely when the US military chose a site on the far eastern shore of Cuba. The Constitution, the Bush administration argued, was not a backpack that traveled with American troops. Its remit stopped at the water's edge. Nor, invoking the formulation of Justice Robert Jackson, was the Constitution "a suicide pact," reflecting the ingrained view of the Bush administration that 9/11 threatened the continued existence of the United States.[7]

The Family Committee would need to go to court, but it was not at all clear that US courts would or could do anything for them. They had to try. While lower courts might be less inclined to issue judgments in favor of Guantanamo detainees, many decisions had been overturned by the Supreme Court in the end. William Brown pointed out to ARH and Marcia Newell and the various legal teams that *Brown v. Board of Education* (the case that found segregated education unconstitutional) had initially been decided *against* the students, until the Supreme Court issued a 9–0 decision striking down its earlier decision in *Plessy v. Ferguson* permitting "separate but equal" schools. But the interval between *Plessy* and *Brown* was nearly sixty years. The detainees would be dead by then. They could not wait to be vindicated by history.

Other more recent precedents involving detention were even less promising. The detention of American citizens of Japanese ancestry as enemy aliens during World War II is now widely viewed as a historic injustice, but the Supreme Court upheld these detentions in *Korematsu* and companion Japanese internment cases, a great stain on the court's moral standing. *Korematsu* was only rejected by the Supreme Court nearly three-quarters of a century later in 2018, ironically in its decision approving a Muslim ban.[8] There was no way to know whether Guantanamo would be another *Brown* or another *Korematsu*. And US law regarding rights often distinguished between citizens and noncitizens. None of the men brought to Guantanamo were US citizens.[9]

Guantanamo presented new challenges as to whether this was a matter for the judicial branch at all. The executive branch claimed plenary power in dealing with foreign affairs and national defense. It also asserted plenary power to decide who could be brought into the United States. Courts were reluctant to act in these core areas of executive functioning. Would courts decide that detention at Guantanamo was a "political question," not susceptible to resolution by the judiciary, or would the government claim that facts about Guantanamo detainees and their actions were "state secrets" that could not be litigated at all in US courts? Was there a role for law here at all?

Despite the forbidding legal landscape, litigation was the only apparent route. A US litigation team needed to be put together that was effective, respected, and could move quickly. There are, of course, no shortages of lawyers in the United States, particularly in Washington, DC. Marcia Newell began to probe her broad legal networks.

Amazingly, virtually all of the major firms in Washington and New York expressed zero interest in early 2002 in taking on the Kuwaiti detainees as clients. To be sure, funding was uncertain. But many law firms simply declined outright, suggesting that their partners were against such a representation on moral grounds. Other firms pointed vaguely to conflicts such as having defense industry clients, although none of these would have been actual conflicts in representing detainees against the US government. Firms spoke of "reputational risk." Still other firms demanded nonrefundable multi-million-dollar retainers, which the Family Committee did not have, and these firms no doubt were aware that these fee demands would be the end of the discussion. One major firm declared something new in the area of legal ethics: "a psychological conflict."[10]

Newell spoke to *ninety-three* law firms. Ninety-two of them turned down the assignment.[11] At this point in time, Big Law did not see these cases as the *Brown* or *Korematsu* for the twenty-first century, raising new issues of human rights and due process. For the legal profession in the early days, there were precious few profiles in courage.

The Core Team also knew that they needed frontline litigators in the United States who could work effectively as a group and not be jostling for position or the last word on strategy. US lawyers needed to understand that the Family Committee members were taking great personal risks in bringing any lawsuits, and the advocacy would need to be managed through the Core Team, both to avoid creating risk for these families in Kuwait and to maintain the decorum and professionalism that the Kuwaiti government would expect. This was not a simple or easy assignment for any US lawyer.

In early April 2002, Newell reached out to Tom Wilner of Shearman & Sterling. Shearman had represented Citibank and other major financial institutions and industrial companies for decades. Wilner had practiced law for more than thirty-five years, leading the firm's international trade practice. Shearman's initial assignment was limited: ascertain whether it agreed with the Core Team that the Kuwaiti detainees were not terrorists and that there was a strong basis to conclude they were wrongly held.

Wilner was not then a human rights lawyer, but he was shrewd and smart as a strategist. He had not had experience in Kuwait specifically or the Middle East generally. But he was a tough, aggressive litigator both in court and out, who was used to being the team leader in every team in which he was involved. He had confidence in his own judgment and rarely deferred to the judgments of others. The balance between the necessity for self-confidence and good teamwork is a delicate one, which litigators often struggle to achieve. Wilner had more difficulty than many.

Years later, Wilner gave an extensive interview to the Columbia University Rule of Law project, which displayed both his strengths and weaknesses for this assignment, his effectiveness and fearlessness in early days, as well as his stubbornness and reluctance to work within a disciplined team structure and to avoid the limelight, factors that unfortunately but inevitably led to his replacement four years later.[12]

When presented with the case, Wilner firmly believed that the rule of law was at stake, echoing the initial views of the Core Team:

> Another theme is the story of how the hysteria of 9/11 caused the country to lose its way and lose it for a pretty long time. For a long time, I have always expected that we had checks in our society that would stop real excesses. Maybe I was naïve about that, but I was surprised at the way the press did not work as a check. They really, by and large, did not question the administration. There was no opposition party willing to stand up; the law schools and student bodies were silent at the time. People didn't give a damn.

He indicated that he had not previously paid much attention to Guantanamo until he was approached by Marcia Newell. It was indicative of the atmosphere that a tough and skeptical lawyer like Wilner was initially supportive of US policy:

I first became aware of Guantánamo shortly after it opened in January 2002. I saw these guys in orange jumpsuits being crowded into cages in Guantánamo and my first reaction was, "Thank god we got these guys, these guys who did this horrible thing to us." That was the way it came across to us. Then I did not really think that much about it until about March [2002]. In March I was contacted by a woman, a headhunter in Washington, on behalf of some Kuwaiti families to see if I would be interested in representing them.

Wilner joked that he knew he was not anyone's first choice:

I found out that they had actually approached Warren Christopher, the former Secretary of State, at O'Melveny & Myers, and he had turned them down. They had approached Lloyd Cutler, at Wilmer Cutler, and he had turned them down as well. I do not know whether they approached others – I think they might have – and they finally got down to me. [Laughs]

So they came to me. I looked at it and said, "Sure." I didn't see any problem with it at the time. Part of the very carefully drawn retainer agreement said that if we found out that any of these guys were terrorists we could drop out.

When he first broached the matter with his partners, he indicated that his role was to ascertain whether the Kuwaiti detainees were guilty or innocent.

So, I put in a conflict check. There was no conflict. The main office of the firm is in New York, as was the head of the litigation department. He did call me to ask me what it was about and I told him, "We have been retained by these Kuwaiti families to try to find out where their kids are." He said, "Sounds interesting." And I didn't think of it as a controversial sort of thing. I really didn't.

After visiting the detainees in Guantanamo in April 2002, the Shearman team recommended beginning a civil case in the United States. They shared the view of the Core Team that it did not appear that any of these men were terrorists. The Shearman litigation team was formally engaged in late April 2002. At that point, a great deal of conflict arose within Shearman management. Wilner, to his credit, stuck to his guns and offered to leave the firm. The offer was declined, but the representation remained controversial.

There was broad agreement that the case should be brought and argued with legal skill and zeal but that it should not degenerate into a political diatribe against the Bush administration or its overall policies. That would not be productive for any diplomatic breakthrough or make release more likely. And while developments in the case could be discussed in the media, media relations needed to be managed with extreme care. The messaging needed to avoid sensationalism and conflict that often occurs in reporting on legal cases, especially cases about the rights of accused terrorists. This was a time when major publications were largely lionizing their sources in the Pentagon and the CIA and showing little curiosity about the detainees' histories.

The case was filed in May 2002. Other public interest lawyers had previously filed habeas corpus cases, which claimed that the detainees should be released immediately. The case brought on behalf of the Kuwaiti detainees was more modest. It was a civil action asking only for a declaration under the Constitution that they had basic due process rights.

The Family Committee complaint was filed with Khalid Al Odah as "next friend" of his son Fawzi as lead plaintiff because Fawzi could not review and approve it. He did not know that he would be a named plaintiff in a landmark Supreme Court case just two years later. The complaint alleged that the detainees were in Afghanistan and Pakistan as volunteers providing humanitarian aid; that local villagers seeking bounties seized them and handed them over to United States forces; and that they were transferred to Guantanamo Bay between January and March 2002. The Al Odah plaintiffs claimed a denial of due process under the Fifth Amendment of the US Constitution and arbitrary and unlawful governmental conduct under the Administrative Procedures Act. They sought an order that they be informed of any charges against them, requiring permission to consult with counsel, meet with their families, and prompt hearings. The suit did not ask for immediate release. The Core Team and the litigators wanted to distinguish their cases from the others and sought more limited relief, knowing that no court would order these men released, at least not in the foreseeable future.

The Rights of Foreigners Outside the United States

The government responded that because the detainees were not US citizens and were held outside the United States, they had no rights whatsoever and no rights to go to a US court for any purpose, whether to assert habeas rights to be released or merely to seek a declaratory judgment that they have a right to a hearing and access to the outside world. The Bush Department of Justice was playing hardball. Guantanamo was a lawless enclave, as the Bush administration had planned in choosing to incarcerate these men there. The Bush Justice Department based its argument primarily on *Johnson v. Eisentrager*,[13] a 1950 Supreme Court case that involved Germans convicted of war crimes in Nanking, China, for assisting the Japanese after VE Day but before the surrender of Japan. These German prisoners had been tried by an Allied military commission in China and then imprisoned in the Landsberg Prison in Germany. One of these prisoners filed a writ of habeas corpus before the US Supreme Court, challenging the right of a US military commission to convict him.

The Supreme Court refused to grant relief, as these prisoners were found not to have had sufficient US contacts to permit access to US courts. The court held, "[T]hese prisoners at no relevant time were within any territory over which the United States is sovereign, and the scenes of their offense, their capture, their trial and their punishment were all beyond the territorial jurisdiction of any court of the United States."[14] Moreover, "trials would hamper the war effort and bring aid and comfort to the enemy."[15] Of course, by this point, World War II had been over for five years.

The *Al Odah* team fought to distinguish *Eisentrager*, arguing that the German petitioners were "enemy aliens" who had the rights of Prisoners of War and had been given full trials with multiple procedural protections before allied officers. The Kuwaiti detainees were not nationals of a country that was or ever had been at war with the United States, and they had not been charged with any war crimes against the United States or indeed charged with anything at all. They had been given no hearings whatsoever to determine what they may have done or not done.

The *Al Odah* district court, nevertheless, dismissed the case, finding that foreign detainees held by the United States at its naval base offshore had no right of access to US courts.[16] The Kuwaiti detainees appealed to the D.C. Circuit Court of Appeals, which affirmed in an opinion that was remarkable for its unquestioning affirmation of the executive's ability to impose indefinite detention without charge, evidence, or hearing.[17]

The Court of Appeals dismissed the notion that Guantanamo Bay was under the complete and total control of the United States and therefore effectively was US territory. Responding to the point that the United States could indict and try individuals for crimes committed at Guantanamo under its special maritime and territorial jurisdiction, it held that the applicability of that jurisdiction did not mean that the United States was sovereign at Guantanamo. Cuba, of course, was not sovereign at Guantanamo either, so, in effect, there was no sovereign at Guantanamo.[18]

While conceding that the United States was not at war with Kuwait or other detainee nations, the D.C. Circuit concluded: "Nonetheless the Guantanamo detainees have much in common with the German prisoners in *Eisentrager*. They too are aliens, they too were captured during military operations, they were in a foreign country when captured, they are now abroad, they are in the custody of the American military, and they have never had any presence in the United States."[19]

The narrower course taken by the *Al Odah* plaintiffs was irrelevant: "They cannot seek release based on violations of the Constitution or treaties or federal law; the courts are not open to them. Whatever other relief the detainees seek, their clams necessarily rest on alleged violations of the same category of laws listed in the habeas corpus statute, and are therefore beyond the jurisdiction of the federal courts."[20]

The D.C. Circuit held bluntly: "The law of the circuit now is that a 'foreign entity without property or presence in this country has no constitutional rights, under the due process clause or otherwise.'"[21]

Had one of them owned a house or a business in the United States, the result might have been different.

Thus, for this bleak moment in 2003, the Bush administration plan to create a "legal black hole," where detainees had no enforceable rights in US courts, had succeeded. The Guantanamo detainees were told that *all* courts were completely closed – they would have no hearing to determine whether they were in fact rightly or wrongly held; they would have no right to be informed of the charges or evidence against them; they would have no right to counsel; they would have no right to meet with their families. They would have only what the US executive branch decided was appropriate for "the worst of the worst" under the new paradigm.

What next? The US Supreme Court hears very few cases. Each year, petitioners from Courts of Appeals file around 8,000 petitions for certiorari, that is, for the case to be heard by the Supreme Court. The Court generally grants certiorari in about 1–2 percent of those cases. And while the Supreme Court may take cases with great public significance, it is also easy for the Court to duck difficult issues by declining to hear them. The chances of the Supreme Court wading into a case that raised the specter of 9/11, terrorism and the rights of the men in the orange jumpsuits, whose pictures had been displayed throughout the world, were not high. But the Core Team decided that it had to try, and the US legal team filed a petition for certiorari. And to everyone's surprise, the Supreme Court granted it.

The Kuwaiti detainees' case was consolidated with a petition filed by Shafiq Rasul, a British detainee (and later my client), and they were argued together in early 2004. Of course, every advocate wants to argue in the Supreme Court, especially in a generational case like the Guantanamo detainees' case. Wilner had never argued there, and he very much wanted to do so. If he could not, then he thought the case should be argued by a leading human rights practitioner like Anthony Amsterdam of NYU Law School. But the Core Team wanted an experienced appellate advocate with a style and approach that was more formal and scholarly; in effect, an advocate like the Solicitor General who argues the government's position in the Supreme Court and has (with certain exceptions) come to be trusted by the Justices to say what the law is without excessive topspin on the argument.

The Core Team approached former Circuit Judge and Attorney General (under President Jimmy Carter) Griffin Bell, but his firm said it had a conflict. After interviewing a number of other advocates, the Core Team settled on Judge John Gibbons, a retired Judge of the Third Circuit Court of Appeals based in Philadelphia. He had been an appellate judge for more than twenty years and had written more than 800 opinions. A New Jersey Republican, he had been appointed by Richard Nixon to the appellate court. Gibbons' style was low-key – to many Guantanamo lawyers overly so – but he was known to the Justices as a former judicial colleague and someone whose arguments would be measured and based in the case law. The Supreme Court treated him with deference and respect. The briefing and the argument were carefully argued without flights of rhetoric. Many criticized Judge Gibbons as lacking flash or sparkle; Gibbons was trying to present a technical legal case, not a cause. He was doing exactly what was required. And he won.

On June 28, 2004, the Supreme Court overruled the Court of Appeals by a 6–3 margin, with Justice Stevens writing the majority opinion.[22] The Court not only affirmed that the judiciary had an essential role in reviewing the actions of the executive in the War on Terror, but it held that Guantanamo detainees would have access to the US courts. The attempt by the Bush administration to create a lawless enclave where men would languish without trial indefinitely had failed at the final hurdle. Habeas corpus – the right to challenge detention – is a right granted by statute as well as by the Constitution. Reflecting the cautious approach of the court, Justice Stevens specifically considered only the statutory habeas question, so that he did not need to confront directly whether a constitutional right to habeas applied to foreign detainees.

The court's opinion was consistent with the arguments that the detainees had been making for two years:

> Petitioners in these cases differ from the *Eisentrager* detainees in important respects: They are not nationals of countries at war with the United States, and they deny that they have engaged in or plotted acts of aggression against the United States; they have never been afforded access to any tribunal, much less charged with and convicted of wrongdoing.[23]

The court also dispensed with the fiction that Guantanamo Bay was a death star; it was under the complete control of the United States and therefore functionally part of the United States for purposes of determining the right to habeas corpus.

> By the express terms of its agreements with Cuba, the United States exercises "complete jurisdiction and control" over the Guantanamo Bay Naval Base. Petitioners contend that they are being held in federal custody in violation of the laws of the United States. No party questions the District Court's jurisdiction over petitioners' custodians. Section 2241 [the federal habeas corpus statute] requires nothing more. We therefore hold that Section 2241 confers on the District Court's jurisdiction to hear petitioner's habeas corpus on challenges to the legality of their detention at Guantanamo Bay.[24]

With respect to whether detainees had specific constitutional (as opposed to statutory habeas) rights, the court decided to leave that issue for another day.

Post-Rasul/Al Odah Defiance

When Pyrrhus defeated the Romans in 279 BC, he suffered such heavy losses that Plutarch wrote, "one other such victory would utterly undo him."[25] Thus, the term Pyrrhic victory, which fits the legal triumph in *Rasul/Al Odah*. On that heady day in late June 2004, the team could not anticipate that this victory would be thoroughly undermined and that the team would still be fighting more than a decade later.

The Core Team directed that individual habeas actions immediately be filed on behalf of the Kuwaiti detainees in the federal district court in Washington, DC. But how would these proceedings be managed and under what legal standards? The legal victory was sweet, but the devil was in the details, and the Bush administration officials, which controlled those details, were no angels.

What Process Was Due: The Post-Rasul/Al Odah Stonewalling

Despite the Supreme Court ruling, neither the Bush administration nor Congress was ready to concede that the United States was holding many innocent people. Real evidentiary hearings in US courts would no doubt have revealed that the Bush administration and Congress already knew that the detainee population would yield no actionable intelligence and housed no senior terrorists.

The United States had another problem that needed to be covered up. There had been widespread torture, not only at black prisons or in camps in Afghanistan or Pakistan but at Guantanamo as well. A team at the Justice Department prepared the so-called torture memos. They advised the Central Intelligence Agency, the United States Department of Defense, and the president on the use of "enhanced interrogation techniques" – mental and physical torment and coercion such as binding in stress positions, cramped confinement (placing the detainee in a dark, tight space for hours or days at a time);[26] slapping in the face,[27] prolonged sleep deprivation,[28] walling (being pushed face first "quickly and forcefully" against a flexible wall), and waterboarding or simulated drowning[29] – and stated that such acts, widely regarded as torture, were legally permissible under the Authorization for the Use of Military Force passed by Congress for use during the "Global War on Terror." According to these Department of Justice memos, "cruel, inhuman, or degrading" treatment is not torture. They concluded that torture only consists of acts that inflict severe pain that results in "serious physical injury, such as organ failure, impairment of bodily function, or even death"; that prolonged mental harm is harm that must last for "months or even years"; that criminal "prosecution under Section 2340A [the torture statute] may be barred because enforcement of the statute would represent an unconstitutional infringement of the President's authority to conduct war"; and that "under the current circumstances, necessity or self-defense may justify interrogation methods that might violate Section 2340A." A March 13, 2003, legal opinion written by John Yoo of the Office of Legal Counsel at the Department of Justice, opined that laws related to the use of torture and other abuse did not apply to agents interrogating foreigners overseas.[30]

The torture memos had legitimated and set the stage for barbaric acts at Guantanamo and elsewhere. Indeed, when General Geoffrey Miller was sent to run Guantanamo in November 2002, he was instructed to implement interrogation on a massive scale, using the "Special Enhanced

Interrogation Techniques" authorized by Secretary Rumsfeld. In August 2003, he was transferred from Guantanamo to Abu Ghraib prison in Iraq to "GTMO-ize the facility," leading to the photographs of abuse of prisoners seen around the world.[31] Torture and abuse as an adjunct to interrogations became standard operating procedure for the Bush administration, and the US government had a powerful incentive to keep it quiet as much as it could. As the United Nations Special Rapporteur on counterterrorism and human rights found in calling for criminal prosecutions, there was a clear policy orchestrated at a high level within the Bush administration, which allowed it "to commit systematic crimes and gross violations of international human rights law."[32]

While affirming the right of detainees to have access to the courts, the Supreme Court also let stand a decision by the Court of Appeals in a case that I and my firm brought that held that torturing of detainees was not clearly prohibited under law and therefore the Secretary of Defense and the officers in the chain of command had qualified immunity from liability for ordering torture.[33] While the Supreme Court had struck a blow for judicial review of detention at Guantanamo, it would not condemn torture as an absolute prohibition; indeed, the prohibition against torture remains unresolved as of this writing as a matter of established legal principle.

In July 2004, a week after the *Rasul/Al Odah* decision, the Department of Defense announced that it would comply with the Supreme Court ruling by creating Combatant Status Review Tribunals (CSRTs) to review the case of each detainee and determine whether he was properly classified as an enemy combatant. The administration was hoping to neutralize the impact of the *Rasul/Al Odah* decision and see whether some new variety of "due process lite" might satisfy the judiciary. There would be no lawyers representing detainees at the CSRT hearings; each would have a military officer appointed as a personal representative, but that military officer was not a lawyer and was not even tasked to be an advocate for the detainee. His or her job was to explain the proceedings to the detainee and comment on the evidence as he or she saw fit, whether favorably or negatively. In effect, the detainee's own representative could tell the CSRT that the man he represented was a terrorist and should continue to be held. And in certain cases, they did.[34]

The CSRTs were not bound by the rules of evidence; the government's evidence was presumed to be "genuine and accurate." Only witnesses who were "reasonably available" could be presented. Of the 393 unclassified CSRT summaries produced, it appears that not a single live witness other than the detainee himself or a detainee informer was called either by the government or by a detainee. The detainee could not see classified information, which could be provided to the "personal representative," who would be entitled to comment on it to the tribunal, although outside the hearing of the detainee. The proceedings would not be public. As human rights lawyer Joseph Margulies wrote, the CSRT process was a system that "forces an alien prisoner unfamiliar with our justice system and held incommunicado to disprove allegations he cannot see, and whose reliability he cannot test, before a military panel whose superiors have repeatedly pre-judged the result, all without counsel."[35]

Between July 2004 and March 2005, the Department of Defense conducted CSRTs for 558 detainees, averaging more than five per day. Most hearings took only a few minutes, and many detainees did not want to submit to the gauntlet of body cavity searches and shackling to be moved to attend a proceeding that gave them little hope of success and where there was suspicion the hearing would seek to gather incriminating evidence against them. As one detainee told the CSRT tribunal, "This is not a court; it is just hocus pocus."[36] He had a point. Just 38 of the 558 detainees were found to have been classified as enemy combatants in error, although even this finding did not result in release. This hastily created process in which the government was both prosecutor and decision-maker, not surprisingly, yielded a confirmation of its own initial conclusions in more than 93 percent of cases and zero relief. This 93 percent affirmation of enemy combatant status was all the more incredible given that multiple senior officers and law enforcement personnel at Guantanamo had stated their views years before that the bulk of detainees should not have been there.[37] But whatever the officers on the ground who were with these detainees thought, the Department of Defense officers constituting the CSRTs knew that their job was to find enemy combatants, not to conduct genuine factual hearings. The US government claimed to be complying with the letter of the *Rasul/Al Odah* decision, which was highly doubtful, and certainly ignored its spirit. In the meantime, the United States was helping itself to more years of insulation from meaningful review, as any challenge to the CSRTs would have to inch again through the courts.

Congress Seeks to Cut Out the Courts

Congress quickly joined the executive in trying to emasculate the habeas rights just declared by the Supreme Court, passing the Detainee Treatment Act (DTA)[38] in 2005, which purported to eliminate all statutory habeas jurisdiction for detainees. Since Congress had passed the habeas statute and the Supreme Court said the right to the hearing arose under this statute, Congress simply got rid of it and thereby legislatively eliminated what the detainees had fought for years to obtain.

The DTA stated that it applied to strip the court of jurisdiction of any habeas claim "on or after the effective date" of the Act, but it said nothing about prior pending proceedings. This was likely the result of poor draftsmanship, as there was no legislative history that indicated any intent to allow prior pending habeas petitions to continue in tandem with CSRT determinations. Indeed, the legislative history suggested the contrary – no federal court habeas hearings at all. But detainees' counsel saw an opening in the sloppy language of the DTA that could at least preserve existing statutory habeas proceedings, which appeared a better prospect than bringing brand new proceedings to seek yet another Supreme Court hearing to request the declaration of a constitutional right to habeas corpus, which the court had explicitly declined to decide in *Rasul/Al Odah*.

The DTA also took some cautious steps to address the widely reported issue of cruel and inhuman treatment and torture at Guantanamo. The Act set the Army's standards of interrogation as the standard for all agencies in the Department of Defense. It prohibited all other agencies of the US government, such as the CIA, from subjecting any person in their custody to "cruel, inhuman, or degrading treatment or punishment." However, the Act did not provide detailed guidelines that spelled out what they meant by that phrase and how it affected already approved "enhanced interrogation measures."

The DTA did cite the US Army's Field Manual on interrogation as the authoritative guide to interrogation techniques but did not cite a specific edition of the Manual, which is controlled by the Department of Defense, and thus the executive branch controls whether a given technique will be permitted or banned. And Congress had amended the anti-torture provisions to permit the Department of Defense to consider evidence obtained through torture of Guantanamo Bay detainees and prohibited detainees from raising claims of torture in US courts. So, the apparent imposition of limits was effectively toothless virtue-signaling and created no enforceable rights for detainees to protect them from torture.

Once again, the detainees challenged the government's attempt to deprive them of a fair hearing and the rights granted to habeas defendants, arguing that the language prohibiting claims on file "on or after" the effective date of the DTA only prohibited new petitions and did not foreclose petitions that were already pending. The government again fought back, arguing that the purpose of the DTA was to bar all statutory habeas petitions from being heard in the federal courts – past, present, or future. Once again, the detainees won and the government lost. The Supreme Court in *Hamdan v. Rumsfeld* took the case and held "that omission [of pending proceedings] is an integral part of the statutory scheme."[39] The Supreme Court ducked the constitutional argument that Congress' jurisdiction-stripping of the courts raised separation of powers questions and instead just looked at the fact that the statute did not by its terms address pending cases and therefore should be presumed not to have intended to bar them. This was simple statutory construction. If Congress wanted to eliminate all statutory habeas cases, it could easily have said so, and it did not.

But Congress and the Bush administration were not going to let the Supreme Court have the last word on rights for alleged terrorists. A few months after the Supreme Court construed the DTA to allow pending petitions to continue, Congress passed the Military Commissions Act (MCA), which made clear its intent was to quash *all* habeas petitions from Guantanamo detainees. The amendment "shall apply to all cases without exception, pending on or after the date of the enactment of this Act."[40]

This remarkable tit-for-tat between the branches of the US government was not yet over.[41] Now the question was squarely presented as to whether Congress could strip the US courts of all jurisdiction and so eliminate the right to habeas corpus under the Suspension Clause of the US Constitution.[42] Fawzi Al Odah, joined by an Algerian detainee, Lakhmar Boumediene, filed yet another case, this time raising the previously undecided issue of whether detainees had constitutional rights, including the right to habeas corpus. Once again, the detainees lost at the trial and appellate levels and filed a petition with the Supreme Court. This time, the court denied the petition. There would be no Supreme Court vindication of constitutional habeas rights. Another dead end.

The Supreme Court almost never changes its mind on whether or not to grant certiorari, but shockingly, two months later it reversed its earlier denial and granted the petition in June 2007, for hearing during the next term. This was the first time in almost forty years that the court had revisited a denial and then granted review.[43]

Although the Supreme Court did not state its reasons, in the interim between the initial denial and the subsequent grant of certiorari, Fawzi Al Odah's legal team had obtained a remarkable affidavit from a senior military officer actively participating in the CSRT tribunals, Lt. Colonel Stephen Abraham. Abraham's affidavit pulled back the curtain of the

CSRT process and made clear that the US government was playing games with the judiciary and deliberately providing the mere illusion of any meaningful process. Abraham wrote in his sworn declaration about the conduct of the hearings: "What were purported to be specific statements of fact lacked even the most fundamental earmarks of objectively credible evidence." He asserted that the office charged with collating evidence was "incapable of collecting or competently analyzing much of the relevant information about the detainees held by the government" and relied "mainly on detainee informants" and "failed to make any effort to investigate whether outside evidence corroborated these statements from other detainees. Nor were detainees able to obtain evidence from outside witnesses at their CSRTs."[44]

"Due process lite" was a sham. It was impossible to know with certainty why the Supreme Court changed its mind, but the blunt public statements of a senior military officer with knowledge of the process were likely to have made continued confidence in the CSRTs as the sole legal remedy for detainees untenable.

Once again, Fawzi Al Odah, along with his fellow detainee, Lakhmar Boumediene, was heading to the Supreme Court to litigate whether the United States had provided sufficient due process protection and, if not, whether detainees had a right under the Constitution to habeas corpus in the US federal courts. On June 12, 2008, more than six years after their arrival and nearly four years after it had upheld the statutory right to habeas, the Supreme Court, in a 5–4 decision, *Boumediene v Bush*, found a right under the US Constitution to habeas corpus for all detainees held at Guantanamo.[45]

The CSRTs created under the DTA were found to be woefully inadequate. The Court held that Guantanamo had de facto sovereignty over Guantanamo, which was sufficient to accord at least certain constitutional rights to detainees in US courts, including the right to habeas corpus. Justice Kennedy, writing for the majority, explained that the political branches may not "switch the constitution on or off at will."[46] The court was further concerned that years had gone by with no meaningful relief:

> The cases before us, however, do not involve detainees who have been held for a short period of time while awaiting their CSRT determinations… In some of these cases six years have elapsed without the judicial oversight that habeas corpus or an adequate substitute demands… While some delay in fashioning new procedures is unavoidable, the costs of delay can no longer be borne by those who are held in custody. The detainees in these cases are entitled to a prompt habeas corpus hearing.[47]

Once again, Fawzi Al Odah and his co-detainees had gone to the Supreme Court and won. Fawzi's father, Khalid, exulted to the media, "[A]fter more than six long and painful years, justice for our family is finally within reach."[48] Praise for the decision initially came from across the political spectrum. The *Washington Post* called it a "welcome victory for due process and the rule of law" and called for "robust rights" for the detainees in their habeas proceeding, including "the ability to challenge the evidence against them."[49] And conservative academic Richard Epstein called the decision "a rejection of the alarmist view that our fragile geopolitical position requires abandoning our commitment to preventing Star Chamber proceedings that result in arbitrary incarcerations."[50]

But there were clouds on the horizon. The *Boumediene* decision was 5–4, and the dissents were predicting disaster. Justice Scalia wrote ominously: "The game of bait-and-switch that today's opinion plays upon the Nation's Commander in Chief will make the war harder on us. It will almost certainly cause more Americans to be killed."[51] And the week after the decision, Attorney General Michael Mukasey signaled that he would not be reading the decision broadly. He said that *Boumediene* did not require the executive to "simply release [detainees] to return to the battlefield," while reiterating the view that many of the remaining detainees, despite no charges against them, "pose an extraordinary threat to Americans." He continued, "These are dangerous people who pose threats to our citizens and to our soldiers."[52] Even if the judiciary found there was no basis to hold them, detainees would not necessarily be released by the executive. Once again, the United States would use the inertia of the judicial process and the "worst of the worst" propaganda to straitjacket due process and keep prisoners for additional years. The Supreme Court provided enough additional wiggle room to give the lower courts and the executive branch the power to ensure that Fawzi Al Odah and others still had multiple years ahead of them at Guantanamo.

4

The Rules of the Road: The Lower Courts Define a Narrow Path

The *Boumediene/Al Odah* decision once again spoke in lofty terms, while deferring to the lower federal courts to define the process. The court wrote, "We make no attempt to anticipate all of the evidentiary and access-to-counsel issues that will arise during the course of the detainees' habeas corpus proceedings."[1] It also deferred to the intelligence process, despite the clear abuses that had been shown through the years of litigation. "We recognize, however, that the government has a legitimate interest in protecting sources and methods of intelligence gathering; and we expect that the District Court will use its discretion to accommodate this interest to the greatest extent possible."[2]

Writing for the court, Justice Kennedy viewed the balancing here as one which the lower courts could and would do with fidelity to the principles articulated by the Court:

> It bears repeating that our opinion does not address the content of the law that governs petitioners' detention. That is a matter yet to be determined. We hold that petitioners may invoke the fundamental procedural protections of habeas corpus. The laws and Constitution are designed to survive, and remain in force, in extraordinary times. Liberty and security can be reconciled; and in our system they are reconciled within the framework of the law.[3]

But the four dissenting Justices had laid down an ominous marker that would inform the process and that would be echoed in conservative media. The *Wall Street Journal*, in response to the decision, echoed Justice Jackson's dictum that "the Constitution is not a suicide pact," but adding, "about Anthony Kennedy's Constitution, we're not so sure."[4]

With the issue joined between the majority's ringing but standardless endorsement of the rule of law and the conservatives' dire warnings, the Supreme Court returned the cases to various federal district judges in the District of Columbia, which had mostly been deciding cases in a very cautious manner for the previous six years and, when going outside that very limited framework, were often smacked down with aggressive opinions from their Court of Appeals, the D.C. Circuit. While the D.C. Circuit was bound by the decisions of the Supreme Court, it had made its ideological disapproval of the Supreme Court's Guantanamo jurisprudence clear, and it also knew that it was likely that the Supreme Court would be taking few, if any, additional Guantanamo cases over the next few years. This left the D.C. Circuit as effectively the last word on issues that would arise in administering the Guantanamo habeas process. That appellate court would construct a set of evidentiary hurdles and rules that would eventually lead the habeas process to yet another dead end, dismissing only the most baseless cases, and even then, not effecting the release of a single detainee through judicial order.

Nevertheless, as the government was compelled to present its evidence in support of continued detention, even under favorable standards, it was forced in many cases to concede that it had no real support for many of its most serious charges of affiliation with terrorism. Even traditionally pro-government district judges, many of them former prosecutors, expressed concern, even anger, about the presentations made by the government. Allegations in multiple cases were withdrawn, and, not infrequently, the government repatriated detainees rather than continuing to try to establish a basis for continued detention. So, while appellate courts may have erected hurdles to success, the very fact of judicial scrutiny, under any standard, served to filter out many of the most egregious cases.

Standard and Burden of Proof

The first critical issue was who bore the burden of proof in the habeas hearings and under what standard of proof. While these evidentiary distinctions may appear technical, they were the filters through which judges would view the evidence presented, and certainly in close cases, the breadth of the designated filter could make the difference between the granting or denial of the petition for release.

In criminal cases in the United States, the government is constitutionally required to prove guilt beyond a reasonable doubt. This was consistent with the common law tradition expressed through the familiar formulation of Blackstone, "it is better that ten guilty persons escape than that one innocent suffer."[5] Was that the standard to be applied to the habeas corpus petitions of detainees, especially given that they already had been incarcerated for up to six years and had never been subject to trial, let alone criminal conviction? The one Supreme Court case directly on point[6] interpreted the habeas statute as requiring that evidence establish the basis for continued detention beyond a reasonable doubt. It was clear, however, that courts would not follow that precedent. Detainees' counsel needed to press for a standard of proof that had some reasonable chance of being adopted.

Other Supreme Court precedents in related contexts involving the deprivation of liberty had applied the "clear and convincing evidence" standard,[7] which is evidence that "is highly and substantially more likely to be true than untrue; the finder of fact must be convinced that the contention – in this case, that there is a basis for detaining the detainee – is highly probable."[8]

There was ample precedent and logical support for applying the clear and convincing evidence standard at Guantanamo. Presumably, after all this time, all these interrogations, all this investigation, the government could come up with something clear and convincing to justify keeping a detainee at Guantanamo.

In the age of the Global War on Terror, however, the US government would never concede that it was better that ten possible terrorists go free rather than one innocent man be detained; indeed, it would likely not even agree were the numbers reversed. And as we shall see, many judges made clear that they would not apply normal evidentiary standards; indeed, the appellate court, traditionally not an evaluator of the weight of evidence, intervened in multiple cases to substitute its judgment of the evidence for that of the district court that actually heard it. Nor would the new Obama administration hold itself to the "clear and convincing evidence" standard. Its attachment to executive discretion may have been different in degree, but not in kind, from that of the Bush administration.

The new administration's Department of Justice (and security apparatus) understood that it had to concede *some* fact-finding role for the judiciary but that its burden should be minimal. The government's initial position was that it should only have to put forth "some credible evidence" that a habeas petitioner meets the proper detention criteria, after which the burden should shift to the petitioner to rebut it with more persuasive evidence.[9]

"Some credible evidence" is one of the least demanding standards of proof. It is often used as a legal placeholder to avoid irrevocable danger or to preserve the status quo until a controversy can be brought into a legal process with formal fact-finding. The "some credible evidence" standard does not require weighing conflicting evidence and demands only the bare minimum to support the allegations without reference to contrary exculpatory evidence, which might be overwhelming. In effect, the government was arguing that if the government had *any* nonfrivolous evidence of membership in or support for Al Qaida or the Taliban, it was up to the detainee to prove that he was not a terrorist.

Realistically, a detainee, incarcerated at Guantanamo and with limited understanding of the evidence against him, much of which was classified and unavailable, had essentially no change of meeting the burden of proving that there was no credible evidence against him. If a detainee had counsel, that counsel could review classified evidence, but could not discuss it with or show it to his client. And with respect to certain classified evidence, even the detainee's security-cleared counsel could not review it, and it would be shown in secret to the judge. Thus, the "some credible evidence" standard could be met by an evidentiary showing that neither the detainee nor counsel had ever seen and knew nothing about, other than that it satisfied a district judge that the charges were not wholly baseless.

Detainee's counsel knew from the CSRTs and the prior Administrative Review Boards (ARBs) that most of the "evidence" that the government had compiled to date was in the form of intelligence assessments of various levels of comprehensiveness and reliability. These dossiers included certain limited biographical information, paraphrased statements allegedly made by detainees, often filtered through translators, and conclusions made by interrogators. Most often, the key evidence was statements made by other detainees or confessions that may have been obtained through torture and later retracted.

Presentation of legal evidence and compilation of intelligence are very different processes. The standard for what is put in an intelligence report is of a very different level of reliability, and once in the report, such statements were almost never removed or qualified, even if the statements were inherently incredible or interrogators decided that the informer was unreliable. The intelligence analysts were being pressured to produce information and results quickly, and many of the interrogators had limited experience in interviewing witnesses or in understanding the circumstances in which these men were captured.

If the burden was on the government to prove its case by clear and convincing evidence, and the government would be relying on the same purported materials that it did in the non-adversary CSRT and prior Administrative Review Board (ARB) proceedings, it was likely that it would lose many of the habeas proceedings before a neutral federal judge, and that it would become public that the United States had been detaining hundreds of people without justification. If the standard was "some credible evidence," there would be no real weighing or testing of the facts. The standard of proof imposed would have significant consequences, both for the likely outcomes of the proceedings and the public perception of the competence with which the "Global War on Terror" was being waged.

The district courts considering Guantanamo cases acted with characteristic caution on the burden of proof. They rejected both the government's "some credible evidence" position and the detainees' "clear and convincing evidence" (or, in a few cases, a "beyond a reasonable doubt" position). The district courts showed an unusual degree of consensus in adopting a "preponderance of evidence" standard – that is, more probable than not – in assessing whether there was a proper basis for an individual to be detained under the executive's detention power. Ultimately the Obama administration supported this standard. Of course, whether a judge views a case as 51–49 percent in favor of the detainee, or 49–51 percent, is a matter of effectively unreviewable discretion. The standard also insured that detainees could be held indefinitely – even for life – in close cases.

The D.C. Circuit made clear to the district courts that under whatever standards were technically in place, it would be cutting no slack in its review of the burden of proof issue. In *Al Bihani v. Obama*,[10] the detainee, who was found to have been a cook for an Al Qaida-affiliated unit fighting with the Taliban, challenged the district court's denial of habeas corpus, arguing that "the prospect of indefinite detention in this unconventional war augurs for a reasonable doubt standard or, in the alternative, at least a clear and convincing standard." The panel rejected this argument, not only finding that the preponderance of the evidence standard was constitutional, but strongly suggesting, despite it not being argued by the government, that even a lesser standard would meet constitutional muster:

> We emphasize our opinion does not endeavor to identify what standard would represent the minimum required by the Constitution. Our narrow charge is to determine whether a preponderance standard is unconstitutional. Absent more specific and relevant guidance, we find no indication that it is.[11]

Continuing its discussion in a footnote of what it said it was *not* deciding, the court added:

> In particular, we need not address whether some evidence, reasonable suspicion, or probable cause standard of proof could constitutionally suffice for preventative detention of non-citizens seized abroad who are suspected of being terrorist threats to the United States ... cf. Anti-terrorism, Crime and Security Act, 2001, c. 24, §§ 21, 23 (Eng.) (adopting a reasonable suspicion standard in Britain; later overturned as inconsistent with European Union law).[12]

By citing an English statute imposing a very low standard in terrorism cases, the D.C. Circuit unmistakably hinted to the government that it would look favorably on a burden of proof requirement *less* than a preponderance of the evidence. It was particularly ironic that the D.C. Circuit, whose hostility to arguments based on foreign law was well known, cited an English statute that appeared to suit its views that there could and should be a lower standard of proof in terrorism cases. Even more unusual, when the case was reheard en banc (an unusual procedure involving all the judges on the court rather than the usual panel of three), the D.C. Circuit rejected the detainee's claim that the war powers granted to the executive were "limited by the international laws of war."[13] Here, the Obama administration had conceded that international law *does* apply to limit its executive powers. The D.C. Circuit dismissed the government's "eager concession" as warrant[ing] no deference from this court." Foreign and international laws were fine when they supported a restrictive approach to the habeas rights that the D.C. Circuit begrudgingly had to enforce but were anathema when they constrained the executive, even when the executive conceded those constraints applied. The court had no patience for a more conciliatory Obama administration.

The next year, the D.C. Circuit, frustrated by what it viewed as a continuing lax approach by the Obama administration with respect to its evidentiary prerogatives, pushed even further. In Al *Adahi v. Obama*,[14] Senior Judge Randolph, perhaps the most consistently anti-detainee judge, openly expressed doubt that the preponderance of the evidence standard was appropriate and launched a broadside on the Supreme Court's detailed historical analysis of habeas corpus law in *Boumediene*, stating that the D. C. Circuit was "aware of no precedents in which eighteenth century English courts adopted a preponderance standard." Not content to leave the issue there, Senior Circuit Judge and fellow conservative Laurence Silberman went even further in his contempt for the Supreme Court's jurisprudence, making clear that he and his fellow appellate judges viewed the "preponderance of the evidence" standard as a foolish and largely irrelevant formality. In a remarkable concurring opinion in *Abdah (Esmail) v. Obama*,[15] Judge Silberman wrote:

> In the typical criminal case, a good judge will vote to overturn a conviction if the prosecutor lacked sufficient evidence, even when the judge is virtually certain that the defendant committed the crime. That can mean that a thoroughly bad person is released onto our streets, but I need not explain why our criminal justice system treats that risk as one we all believe, or should believe, is justified. When we are dealing with detainees, candor obliges me to admit that one cannot help but be conscious of the infinitely

> greater downside risk to our country, and its people, of an order releasing a detainee who is likely to return to terrorism. That means that there are powerful reasons for the government to rely on our opinion in *Al-Adahi v. Obama*, which persuasively explains that in a habeas corpus proceeding the preponderance of evidence standard that the government assumes binds it, is unnecessary – and moreover, unrealistic. I doubt any of my colleagues will vote to grant a petition if he or she believes that it is somewhat likely that the petitioner is an Al Qaida adherent or an active supporter. Unless, of course, the Supreme Court were to adopt the preponderance of the evidence standard (which it is unlikely to do – taking a case might obligate it to assume direct responsibility for the consequences of *Boumediene v. Bush*, 553 U.S. 723 (2008)).[16]

The game was up. Judge Silberman had declared that the preponderance of evidence standard would *not* be honestly applied by his court and that he also knew the Supreme Court would not make it do so because, in his view, it was too cowardly to assume the burden of potential consequences. There would be a different standard for detainees. He then went on to explode the myth that *any* of this litigation would actually lead to detainees being released through judicial order:

> Of course, if it turns out that regardless of our decisions the executive branch does not release winning petitioners because no other country will accept them and they will not be released into the United States, then the whole process leads to virtual advisory opinions. It becomes a charade prompted by the Supreme Court's defiant – if only theoretical – assertion of judicial supremacy, see *Boumediene*, 553 U.S. 723, sustained by posturing on the part of the Justice Department, and providing litigation exercise for the detainee bar.[17]

While after much litigation, the preponderance of the evidence standard remained technically in place, the D.C. Circuit made clear to its district courts that in close, and even not-so-close cases, the appellate court would overrule a district court if in its view it is "somewhat likely," even if not more likely than not, that a detainee was a supporter of or part of Al Qaida, the Taliban, or "associated forces." This was an unprecedented and jaw-dropping attack by a lower federal court on the Supreme Court. No one was getting out of Guantanamo because of a judicial decision.

The D.C. Circuit also established that, whatever the government's evidence, the reviewing court not only may but *should* consider a detainee's lack of credibility during prior interrogations at Guantanamo as a factor in favor of the government, even if the government's affirmative evidence is lacking. In reversing the district court's granting of a habeas petition in *Al Adahi v. Obama*, the court found the absence of credibility findings about statements made by the detainee "[o]ne of the oddest things about this case" and noted that Al Qaida training manuals "[put bluntly, the instructions to detainees are to make up a story and lie."[18] In other words, courts could conclude that if a detainee says he was *not* affiliated with Al Qaida, that may be evidence that he *is* part of Al Qaida and executing the Al Qaida playbook. Once again, there were no right answers.

While a witness who testifies will generally have his credibility evaluated, Guantanamo presented a more difficult case. Given the years of interrogations, many coercive, virtually every habeas factual return contained statements of the detainee, sometimes multiple statements and some statements that were contradictory over time. Thus, even if the government put in no other evidence, if it could point to earlier statements made by a detainee without counsel and under unknown conditions, even if the detainee himself said nothing at the hearing, this could be a basis for finding that the witness was not credible, and on this basis, his petition for habeas could be denied.[19]

Evidentiary Presumptions

Having effectively hollowed out the preponderance of evidence standard, the D.C. Circuit then considered how various types of evidence should be considered and admitted. In *Latif v. Obama*,[20] the D.C. Circuit adopted a "presumption of regularity" regarding government intelligence reports. This meant that the district court should assume the accuracy of the government record. While the majority opinion suggested that this was effectively ministerial – "[t]he presumption of regularity – to the extent it is not rebutted – requires a court to treat the Government's record as accurate; it does not compel a determination that the record establishes what it is offered to prove" – it was a significant development in the evidentiary calculus applied in Guantanamo habeas litigation, given that (i) a large proportion of the evidence submitted by the government in its factual returns was reporting of statements allegedly made by the detainee himself or by other detainees eager to curry favor in their own cases; (ii) such statements were often made in the witness' own language and then translated by translators, who often spoke a different dialect, or were not terribly good translators or wanted to be helpful to their interrogator-partners; and (iii) these translations or statements were generally not transcribed verbatim or in their entirety, leaving significant discretion to the person actually writing the report as to what to include or exclude or how to paraphrase what he or she understood a witness or translator to have said.

While a detainee could claim that the statement made by another detainee was not true or that it failed to accurately relate some statement that he allegedly had made, the detainee had very limited ability to claim years after the fact that the interrogator or the translator was wrong or incomplete. Those who had experience with the way these cases had been prepared knew that virtually every dossier was inaccurate, incomplete, or erroneous in material ways.[21] But it would be an uphill battle to prove it. In his dissent to the D.C. Circuit's decision imposing a presumption of regularity, Circuit Judge Tatel warned:

> [T]he Report at issue here was produced in the fog of war by a clandestine method that we know almost nothing about. It is not familiar, transparent, generally understood as reliable, or accessible; nor is it mundane, quotidian data entry akin to state court dockets or tax receipts. Its output, a redacted intelligence report, was, in this court's own words, "prepared in stressful and chaotic conditions, filtered through interpreters, subject to transcription errors, and heavily redacted for national security purposes." Needless to say, this is quite different from assuming the mail is delivered or that a court employee has accurately jotted down minutes from a meeting.
>
> * * *
>
> Given the degree to which our evidentiary procedures already accommodate the government's compelling national security interests by admitting all of its evidence, including hearsay; given the heightened risk of error and unlawful detention introduced by requiring petitioners to prove the inaccuracy of heavily redacted government documents; and given the importance of preserving "the independent power" of the habeas court "to assess the actions of the Executive" and carefully weigh its evidence. I find this court's departure from our practice deeply misguided.[22]

The majority's granting of a presumption of regularity for intelligence documents put forward by the government – when numerous courts had found consistent and potentially case-dispositive irregularity – allowed a habeas petition to be denied solely on the basis of a single intelligence report of dubious accuracy or reliability.

Admission of Hearsay

While the Federal Rules of Evidence prohibit the admission of hearsay (out-of-court statements made by the declarant), other than if within certain limited exceptions, the D.C. Circuit nevertheless declined to make the Federal Rules applicable with regard to hearsay. Thus, a district court had broad discretion to admit any evidence that it chose to, including multiple hearsay (A said X to B who said it to C who repeated it to D, who testifies as to what A said), and to "give it the weight it deserves." Different judges, however, will react to the reliability of hearsay in different ways depending on a wide variety of factors, leading to potentially dispositive rulings based on how a specific judge reacts to interrogator reports or the statements of jailhouse informants.

Habeas cases have no juries, and district judges are experienced in evaluating the probative value of all types of evidence, including hearsay, but it is not so simple to separate the role of judge as trier of law and of fact. Once the government tries to admit hearsay, it is not possible to "un-ring the bell," in that the judge has already seen the evidence. In a jury trial, the information is never presented to the trier of fact. Many judges have indicated reluctance to rely on certain hearsay statements, especially statements made by informants, and have taken pains to indicate that their decisions were not based on such statements. But even experienced judges cannot reliably perform the cognitive feat of completely ignoring statements that have been presented, even if they can claim to ground their decisions on other evidence.

The hearsay issue arose concretely in Guantanamo cases in very important ways. There were frequently inconsistencies between a set of inculpatory admissions during early interrogations and later exculpatory recantations. Of course, the often-unstated issue in cases involving inconsistent hearsay statements that were later recanted was whether the evidence was acquired by torture or coercion and, if so, whether it should be admitted. This is more than just a technical question of assessing the reliability of the statement; it is also a question of acute moral hazard. If the interrogator thinks he may get a tortured confession into evidence, his incentive structure is clear.

Evidence Tainted by Coercion or Torture

It is no longer seriously denied by US government officials and contractors that detainees were tortured, both at Guantanamo and before they arrived there, while held at various "dark prisons" in Afghanistan, Thailand, and Europe.[23] According to the Justice Department's Office of Inspector General, FBI agents filed multiple complaints regarding mistreatment of detainees at Guantanamo by military interrogators. In a 2004 email, an FBI agent described detainees chained in stress positions in extreme temperatures, left for up to twenty-four hours without food and water, urinating and defecating on themselves. One detainee was described as "almost unconscious on the floor, with a pile of hair next to him. He had apparently been literally pulling his own hair out throughout the night."[24]

For years, the US government indulged in the Orwellian fiction that detainees were simply subject to "enhanced interrogation," not torture. The photos at Abu Ghraib destroyed that euphemistic lie. And for the first time in October 2021, Supreme Court justices in the oral argument in Abu Zubaydah's case against certain psychologist contractors, who oversaw interrogation at a dark site in Poland, freely used the term "torture." Several Justices, beginning with Justice Amy Coney Barrett, repeatedly called the treatment that Abu Zubaydah endured (*inter alia*, waterboarded more than eighty times) torture, plain and simple. As Justice Barrett said, "it's not a secret that he was tortured."[25] Abu Zubaydah remains at Guantanamo as of October 2025.

In 2006, when President George W. Bush first acknowledged the existence of black sites, he said, "I want to be absolutely clear with our people and the world: The United States does not torture. It's against our laws, and it's against our values."[26] This was not true, at Guantanamo and elsewhere. In 2014, President Barack Obama acknowledged this, saying blandly,[27] "we tortured some folks." President Trump has said he believes "torture worked" and supports its use.[28]

Aggressive interrogation accompanied by torture was a standard feature of operations at Guantanamo from late 2002 through much of the Bush administration, justified by various memoranda from the Department of Justice, which were later withdrawn with a clear order against torture issued by President Obama.

Presumably, the justification for such techniques was not pure sadism, but the expectation was that torture during interrogations would lead to confessions and those confessions could be used as reliable evidence that could be used for intelligence purposes as well as a basis to continue detention. There is ample literature suggesting that, as a general matter, a person who is tortured will say whatever he believes the torturer wants to hear,[29] but there remained the question for courts whether evidence obtained from torture, even if reliable or corroborated, should ever be used.

The cases regarding coerced confessions of Guantanamo detainees are complex and contradictory. No federal judge stated flatly that evidence obtained from torture will be admissible provided it is reliable, but numerous courts have hovered around the issue of admissibility in less egregious cases. Courts reviewing evidence where a detainee claims it has been obtained by torture or coercion needed to resolve three principal questions: First, in what circumstances is a statement inadmissible solely because it was coerced, even if its reliability can be corroborated? Second, given that virtually all detainees claimed mistreatment, and mistreatment appeared to have been systematic as a matter of policy, what factual inquiry should be conducted into individual claims of mistreatment? And third, if a prisoner is tortured, does that make all future statements inadmissible or is there a de facto limitation period after which the torture should be ignored?

The district courts indicated discomfort with evidence that had unambiguously been obtained with physical coercion, and, indeed, the US government stated in a number of cases (post-Bush administration) that either it would "not proceed in a case because the detainee was tortured, or it would not seek to rely on any confessions of a tortured detainee." All of the district court judges indicated in general terms that physical coercion *can* require exclusion of statements derived from abuse or even taint subsequent statements, but the guidance was by no means categorical or consistent.

Few judges accepted that years of indefinite detention and solitary confinement coupled with repeated interrogations, even if not physically coercive, in and of themselves, raise issues of voluntariness. The D.C. Circuit avoided the issue, although certain of its rulings suggest that it would find a lack of voluntariness in very few circumstances. It appears that while an individual judge may believe he or she has preserved his or her own moral compass, it is impossible to know what, if any, role a judge's knowledge of a coerced confession played in his or her decision that such evidence will not be relied on, or whether the judge conveniently excludes the coerced statement while relying on other purportedly independent evidence to sustain continued detention.

In *Khalifh v. Obama*,[30] Judge James Robertson wrote that he would not admit evidence that was the product of mistreatment but that he did not need to resolve the issue of whether Khalifh was tortured or whether to admit confessions obtained under coercion because he could resolve the case without such evidence. He held that he could decide the case by setting aside the statements that occurred within the "window of alleged mistreatment," from late 2004 to early 2005, because "none of the statements from the window period [were] necessary for the government to prove its case in toto."

The import of the opinion is that evidence obtained during the period of active torture may not be admitted (although Judge Robertson did cite certain "window period" testimony that was corroborated) but that evidence obtained at other times, even shortly after a period of torture, would not be tainted by the prior physical abuse. He found that the petitioner was a part of Al Qaida and associated forces based largely on confessions outside the "window period" and denied the petition. The decision is troubling on at least two grounds: First, it assumes that the unreliability of evidence obtained by torture only applies in a limited time frame and ignores the cumulative and post-trauma impact of torture on a detainee; and second, it allows a judge to assert that he or she has been able to ignore the evidence procured by torture and relied on other matters, which is impossible to know other than on the judge's say-so.

Unfortunately, no consensus has emerged with respect to just what this modified approach to voluntariness actually requires. In theory, judges might draw that line anywhere along a spectrum that ranges from admitting evidence otherwise reliable that is obtained through unambiguous torture, through cruel, inhuman, and degrading treatment, and on to still-lesser forms of coercion that may be lawful but that exceed the baseline level of coercion inherent in long-term detention at Guantánamo. Alternatively, the courts might draw lines according to some more objective measures, such as whether or not the methods employed were within a certain time frame, either singly or cumulatively. Of course, the best way both to mitigate torture and avoid having to delve into its impact in individual cases is to reject any evidence procured through torture, coercion, or in breach of the Army Field Manual or the Geneva Conventions. The courts were unwilling to do so.

In *Al Rabiah v. Obama* (discussed in detail in Chapter 7), Judge Kollar-Kotelly found that after innumerable interrogations that yielded no confessions, the government then appointed a new lead interrogator who employed a three-pronged approach. Al Rabiah was told that if he confessed he would be allowed to return to Kuwait; if he did not, he would remain in Guantanamo forever; and he would continue to be abused until he did confess. The court found that the lead interrogator used tactics that were prohibited by the Army Field Manual and the Geneva Conventions and excluded all inculpatory statements that were made under coercion, as well as subsequent confessions, despite noting:

> As a legal matter, it is certainly true in the criminal context that coerced confessions do not necessarily render subsequent confessions inadmissible because the coercion can be found to have dissipated. Nevertheless, the Court must consider the "totality of the circumstances" in order to determine whether there exists evidence from which to find that there was a "clean break" between the coercion and the later confessions.[31]

The D.C. Circuit did not opine directly on the ruling since the government did not appeal its loss in *Al Rabiah*. But it signaled a general unreceptiveness to Geneva Convention claims in *Al Adahi*, which dismissed the petitioner's argument that his interrogation statements should be suppressed because they were gathered in violation of Geneva Convention provisions that require that individuals "shall in all circumstances be treated humanely." The court held that the Geneva Conventions were not incorporated into US domestic law and, even if they had been, they were not self-executing and, therefore, did not give rights to individuals: "Even if the Convention had been incorporated into domestic U.S. law and even if it provided an exclusionary rule, Congress has provided explicitly that the Convention's provisions are not privately enforceable in habeas proceedings."[32] In other words, the Geneva Conventions were enforceable only to the extent that the executive chose to accept their provisions. A detainee had no right to prevent evidence obtained by torture from being used against him. The ban on torture and inhuman treatment did not give detainees a right to seek exclusion of evidence.

Other judges in the district court indicated unease regarding coerced confessions but failed to articulate bright-line exclusions of all coerced evidence. In *Ali Ahmed*, Judge Kessler stated that the witness's testimony had "been cast into significant question, due to the fact that it was elicited at Bagram amidst actual torture or fear of it."[33] She concluded that "[a]ny effort to peer into the mind of a detainee at Bagram, who admitted to fearing torture at a facility known to engage in such abusive treatment, simply does not serve to rehabilitate a witness whose initial credibility must be regarded as doubtful."[34] She was highly dubious about receiving testimony from a tortured witness in any circumstances, but not categorical.

Judge Hogan in *Anam* discussed in detail the severe and unrefuted allegations of government abuse made by the petitioner in Afghanistan and Pakistan, before his transfer to Guantanamo. The government then tried to introduce twenty-six statements made by the petitioner at Guantanamo. Judge Hogan excluded twenty-three of the twenty-six, but admitted three statements and found that there was a basis for further detention.[35] He identified the conditions that, in his judgment, could make statements tainted and inadmissible:

> Factors guiding a court's inquiry include "the time that passes between confessions, the change in place of interrogations, and the change in identity of the interrogators." Additionally, criminal courts "may take into consideration the continuing effect of the prior coercive techniques on the voluntariness of any subsequent confession." The burden is on the government to demonstrate that each subsequent confession was not a product of coercion.[36]

While finding that his initial confessions at Guantanamo just after arriving from Afghanistan would not be admitted, the court did find that statements made in ARB and CSRT proceedings approximately two and three years after his arrival at Guantanamo were sufficiently remote from the trauma of his abuse in Afghanistan and Pakistan and initial treatment at Guantanamo that they could be admitted against him.[37] Here again, a district judge was making ad hoc determinations about admission of confessions based on his impressionistic judgment of the likely lingering effects of torture on subsequent statements.

While the Court of Appeals was erecting high hurdles to success, the habeas hearings themselves were nevertheless proving highly embarrassing to the government, even under those standards. Forced at last to show its hand, the government needed either to concede it had very low cards indeed or to try to build a case with evidence that it knew would never be accepted in a normal case. Often in weak cases, the government quickly sent men home when district judges looked with skepticism or outright contempt at the cases that the government was presenting against men who had been in detention for many years. I will deal in Chapters 8 and 9 with the specifics of Fawzi Al Odah and Fayiz Al Kandari's hearings, which I conducted on their behalf, but will describe here some of the government's disastrous showings in early cases when put to its proof.

The habeas hearings were governed by a single case management order which was put in place for all habeas cases by Judge Hogan, a well-respected, experienced Republican appointee. The order directed trial court judges to make habeas corpus cases their top priority. "The time has come to move these forward," Judge Hogan ordered. "Set aside every other case that's pending in the division and address this case first."[38] In the first hearing before Judge Hogan, when the Justice Department said it needed eight additional weeks to add to its initial evidence, Judge Hogan said, "If [the evidence] wasn't sufficient then they shouldn't have been picked up."[39] In the end, in many cases, extra time was not going to help the government.

The first group of cases brought by the *Boumediene* group of petitioners was heard by an arch-conservative but iconoclastic Republican appointee, Judge Richard Leon. He promised shortly after the Supreme Court's *Boumediene* decision in the summer of 2008 that his twenty-four cases would be decided by Christmas. Despite having held these men for six years based on these allegations, the government quickly dropped its claims that the six *Boumediene* petitioners had plotted to blow up the US embassy in Sarajevo, as well as the claim (based on information from an unnamed informer whom the government itself had called a liar) that one of the petitioners had military training in Afghanistan and worked for a charity later designated as a terrorism sponsor. In one set of hearings, the core of the government's case collapsed. Judge Leon noted:

> While the information in the classified intelligence report ... was undoubtedly sufficient for the intelligence purposes for which it was prepared, it is *not* sufficient for the purposes for which a habeas court must now evaluate it. To allow enemy combatancy to rest on so *thin* a reed would be inconsistent with the Court's obligation ... to protect petitioners form the risk of erroneous detention. (Emphasis in original)[40]

He granted five of the six petitions, and the men were quickly repatriated by executive action. The sixth petition, which was originally denied, went to a panel of the D.C. Circuit, which dismissed it, noting that since the hearing, the government's claims that this petitioner was in touch with "a senior Al Qaida facilitator" and had rendered support to Al Qaida had been dropped.[41]

Other cases had similar collapses. One detainee had been linked to a dirty bomb, but those allegations were withdrawn just before the deadline for turning over exculpatory evidence. Judge Emmet Sullivan, another tough, experienced judge, said the government's actions "raise serious questions in this court's mind about whether these allegations were true" and warned, "Someone is going to rue the day these allegations were made if they turned out to be unfounded."[42] While the government continued to argue that it had proof of a dirty bomb plot, it appeared from documents turned over by the British government that the detainee had been tortured at a secret CIA prison in Morocco. The United States dropped the charges and quickly sent the detainee to the United Kingdom in early 2009.[43]

Twenty-two Uighurs, a Turkic-speaking ethnic group from western China who fled oppression and established lives in Afghanistan years earlier, were also handed over to American troops and sent to Guantanamo.[44] There was no real doubt that most of these men were simply merchants fleeing the bombing and that several others had received military training from the East Turkestan Islamic Front (ETIF), which was seeking to liberate Uighur lands from China. The ETIF had not been listed as a terrorist entity at the time the men were captured, but the *Washington Post* reported that ETIF was later added at the request of the Chinese government, allegedly as part of an agreement for China to support the Iraq war.[45] A 2008 report by the Inspector General of the

Justice Department found that American military interrogators collaborated with visiting Chinese officials at Guantanamo Bay to implement a sleep deprivation strategy for interrogating Uighur detainees.[46] This was realpolitik at its most contemptible.

Two Uighurs were found by CSRTs not to be enemy combatants in March 2005, but were not told of this finding, and the government did not inform the judge in the habeas proceeding until four months later. Three others were also found not to be enemy combatants. All five were released to Albania, but not until May 2006, after more than four years at Guantanamo. As for the seventeen other Uighurs, a habeas petition was filed shortly after the *Boumediene* decision in 2008, which the government opposed. A week before a scheduled hearing on their enemy combatant status, the Justice Department filed with the court a statement that the seventeen were "no longer enemy combatants," a de facto admission that the government had no basis for detention. The district judge ordered that the detainees be brought to his courtroom in Washington, writing:

> There comes a time when delayed action prompted by judicial deference to the executive branch's function yields inaction inconsistent with the constitutional imperative. Such a time has come in the case of the 17 Uighurs in Guantanamo Bay, Cuba. [B]ecause separation of powers concerns do not trump the very principle upon which this nation was founded – the unalienable right to liberty – the court orders the government to release the petitioners into the United States.[47]

The D.C. Circuit granted an emergency stay to prevent the transfer, and the Supreme Court granted certiorari. The US government stated it was trying to find countries to resettle the Uighurs, and so the Supreme Court did not hear the case. Ultimately, the remaining Uighurs were resettled, but over a period that dragged on until 2013. These Muslim victims of Chinese oppression spent years – some more than a decade – enduring Guantanamo when even the government had to concede there was never any conceivable basis.

Other detainee habeas cases revealed similar abuses by the Department of Defense in continuing detention. In January 2009, the petition of Mohammed El-Gharani was granted, as Judge Leon found that the only evidence offered was that of two other detainees whose credibility was either directly called into question by the government itself or had been characterized as having been "undermined," with stories "plagued with internal inconsistencies," including an allegation that El-Gharani "was a member of a London-based cell."[48] His lawyer, Clive Stafford Smith of Reprieve pointed out that El-Gharani was a Chadian national who had grown up in poverty in Saudi Arabia, had never been to London, and was eleven years old when he was alleged to have been part of this cell. He was arrested at the age of fourteen. The Department of Defense alleged he was a twenty-six-year-old Al Qaida financier and never bothered to get his birth certificate.[49]

Stafford Smith, who represented dozens of detainees, was the target of authorities at Guantanamo, and El-Gharani was alleged to have been tortured to extract a confession implicating his lawyer in suicides of detainees.[50] Detainees had been interrogated at length trying to establish a tie between Stafford Smith and the suicides.[51] In a letter to the Associated Press, Stafford Smith wrote: "The interrogator said I told my clients to kill themselves, and word was passed to the three men who did commit suicide." It was a lie.

One of the leading chroniclers of abuses at Guantanamo, Andy Worthington, described the torture El-Gharani endured at Guantanamo in an effort to extract a confession implicating Stafford Smith in the suicides, including:

- sleep deprivation;
- having a cigarette extinguished on his body;
- being suspended by his arms, with his feet hanging free from the floor, for extended periods of time; and
- having a soldier hold his penis in his hand, hold a pair of scissors, and threaten to cut it off.[52]

After the collapse of yet another government habeas case, El-Gharani was repatriated to Chad, after more than seven years in custody.

In another habeas case, Judge Kessler granted habeas to a Yemeni, Alia Ali Bin Al Ahmed, also a teenager, when the source of information against him was again detainee informers, principally the same detainee that Judge Leon found "cannot be credited," while another had exhibited mental health problems.

The government did not appeal the finding, and Al Ahmed remained for another four months after Judge Kessler's order, seven years in all. Indeed, the government argued after its evidentiary presentation fell apart that Al Ahmed may have been wrongly captured, but in seven years of captivity, he may have become embittered and therefore now posed a future danger if he was released as a result of his experience of being wrongfully incarcerated at Guantanamo.[53] Thus, trauma imposed by the United States became a reason for continued detention by the United States.

Judges continued to show frustration with the government's habeas cases. In the case of Ayman Saeed Batarfi, a Yemeni doctor, Judge Sullivan issued an order to show cause why the government should not be held in contempt for failing to disclose exculpatory information. He found that the government had improperly withheld psychiatric records about one of the unreliable story-spinning informers who testified against multiple witnesses. He denounced what he called the government's attempts "to hide relevant evidence," which he called "fundamentally unjust, outrageous and will not be tolerated." He threatened, "someone's going to pay a price ... I'll tell you quite frankly if I have to start incarcerating people to get my point across, I'm going to start at the top." He referenced the diplomatic process in resettling detainees as "a travesty ... a horror story," saying "I'm not going to buy into an extended indefinite delay of this man's stay at Guantanamo."[54] A week before the scheduled hearing, the US government approved Batarfi's release through the Periodic Review Board (PRB) process, although it took another eight months before he left the prison. The Periodic Review Board process, described in later chapters, proved a useful safety valve to send back detainees without further exposure to government incompetence or misconduct.

In Mohammed Jawad's habeas case, the USG sought to rely on confessions, which it subsequently conceded had been obtained through torture and should be suppressed. Judge Huvelle denounced the case as "unbelievable," "an outrage," and "in a shambles." She found that these coerced confessions were "90 percent of the case." She granted habeas and ordered him released within the next two months. He was repatriated by the executive less than a month after her ruling.[55]

A year after the *Boumediene* decision, District of Columbia federal district judges had granted habeas relief to twenty-six petitioners and denied relief in only five cases. By contrast, the CSRT process had yielded a 93 percent rate for continued detention. Before actual judges in the first year, 83 percent of the habeas petitioners had their petitions granted. Of the twenty-six whose petitions were granted, nine had been sent home, and seventeen remained detained, as the USG had made clear that it would not release a petitioner because of a decision by a federal judge. This would happen only if the United States decided that it had sufficient security guarantees from a receiving country to do so. As a Department of Justice lawyer told one federal judge who was lambasting the weakness of the government's case, "We are not going to release anyone if it would endanger national security."[56] Even if courts found no justification for continued imprisonment, the Justice Department would still invoke national security in the wake of an evidentiary presentation that grossly failed to support the premise. This was not the immediate post-9/11 Bush–Cheney–Rumsfeld administration. This was the Obama Justice Department. As Jonathan Hafetz wrote in his superb book on habeas corpus post-9/11, "Even as Obama spoke about the need to restore the rule of law and to return to constitutional principles, he preserved many of his predecessor's policies, tinkering at the edges but leaving the core intact. He had moved to adopt and institutionalize many of Guantanamo's key features."[57]

After that first year, the D.C. Circuit began to crack down on the evidentiary and procedural rules, as well as to second-guess the factual determinations made by the district court. The statistics radically shifted. Of the next twenty-eight cases decided, only six petitions were granted and twenty-two were denied.[58] The cases were not presented in order of severity, but were based on judicial schedules. Yet the ominous warnings by the D.C. Circuit turned an 83 per cent success rate into a 21 per cent success rate over a period of months.

5

Twelve Men

The previous chapters have described a legal landscape that was profoundly changing. The goal of the Family Committee and the Core Team had seemed straightforward and modest – get hearings for the men detained so that the innocent could be released and the guilty could be convicted and sentenced. Yet as the years went by, this simple objective kept receding into the distance. The Geneva Conventions and Army Regulations required prompt hearings to prevent erroneous detentions during military operations. In the wake of 9/11, civilian officials vetoed the implementation of this required process.[1]

It took more than six years to determine that the detainees had any rights at all under the Constitution in a US court. Congress and the Executive had worked to frustrate the Supreme Court at every turn. And once that right was established, the D.C. Circuit further frustrated these goals by putting obstacles in place that greatly reduced the prospect of successful habeas petitions. Judge Silberman put the dirty little secret of the entire legal infrastructure into public view. The process was a "charade"; "regardless of our decisions the executive branch does not release winning petitioners because no other country will accept them and they will not be released into the United States."

While this exercise in frustration was playing out among the branches of the US government, hundreds of men were living through the Guantanamo gauntlet, subject to repeated but fruitless interrogations, enhanced interrogation techniques amounting to torture, separated from families, without charge, without a timetable, and without hope of release. The United States knew fully that it had mainly nobodies, and the very few "high-value detainees" were held in black prisons offshore until they were brought to Guantanamo in 2006 and segregated in another facility in solitary confinement where they remain.

Over the years, the United States began to release men from Guantanamo. Logistically and operationally, the military could not house and guard and feed and provide medical care for nearly 800 men. It did not have the personnel, the language skills, or the trained interrogators to continue the day and night enhanced techniques. And it was incredibly expensive. As a matter of pure operational feasibility, men had to be released. Some were released because their governments were supporting the "War on Terror" as well as the Iraq War, which was going badly. Secretary of State Powell was receiving insistent demands for releases and kept pressing his staff to find countries willing to take detainees and to press the defense and intelligence establishment to agree.[2] Many releases were based on where the detainees were from rather than what they may have done.

Four British detainees were released in March 2004, approximately two years after their capture. Working with my colleague and friend, Michael Ratner, the visionary human rights lawyer and founder of the Center for Constitutional Rights (I later served on its board at Michael's request), we brought a civil case against Secretary Rumsfeld and the officers in the chain of command at Guantanamo for torture and abuse. The case, brought in October 2004, a few months after their release, was one of the first accounts of the industrial torture process ongoing at Guantanamo. I spent many hours debriefing the four young men, and despite the detailed descriptions of fruitless torture, it led to little change. The complaint, however, was an early window into what hundreds of men were still experiencing and tracked closely with later accounts by the Kuwaiti detainees and others.

The Tipton Lads were three young men, ranging in age from nineteen to twenty-four at the time of capture, who had been born and raised in the small industrial town of Tipton in the West Midlands. All came from families of Pakistani extraction. When I met with them, each was dressed in Nikes and athletic gear, and one wore a backwards baseball cap. All were "football mad." They were not viewed as particularly devout and admitted to drinking, clubbing, and smoking weed as teenagers.[3] They told the story of being English-speaking young Brits in an environment full of Arabic, Pashtun, and Urdu speakers, most of whom had grown up in highly sheltered environments. When they heard that these sheltered men were being shown pornography and being sexually approached by female service members, they joked about why they were not getting that treatment.

In September 2001, one of the lads, Asif Iqbal traveled to Pakistan to get married. His long-time friend, Ruhal Ahmed, traveled from England in October to serve as his best man. Shafiq Rasul was at the same time in Pakistan visiting his family with the expectation of continuing his degree course in computer science; this was common for British nationals of Pakistani descent, as the cost of courses was a small fraction of those offered in the UK. Prior to the wedding in Pakistan, in October 2001, they crossed the border into Afghanistan. Years later, Rasul and Iqbal admitted on a British television program that they had visited a Taliban training camp and fired AK-47s. Rasul explained:

> Being in Afghanistan, we were at that age where ... seeing a gun ... you'd never seen a gun in the UK ... you want to hold it. You want to see what it's like. But we were never there to do any training. That's what, that's what, we were just there. We held it to see what it was like. That's how we've explained it. But it has been taken out of context, saying that "Oh, these guys from the UK, they were at that age, 9/11 had just happened, and they were there for terrorist training." But, but – that's not the case. That's not what happened.[4]

Captured by a notorious Uzbek warlord, they were handed over to US forces along with many others. No US forces were present when they were captured or had any knowledge of what they had been doing. They were taken to the notorious Sherbegan prison, where they were held for a month under appalling conditions. In late December, the International Committee of the Red Cross visited and told them that the British Embassy was aware of their situation and that embassy officials would soon be in contact. But US Special Forces arrived, and they were placed under US custody, stripped in the freezing cold of the Afghan winter, bound and interrogated. They were threatened with beatings and death, punched, kicked, slapped, and struck with rifle butts repeatedly. They were then flown to Kandahar, where everyone was systematically and violently beaten. When they identified themselves as British, American soldiers insisted that they were "not white," but "black," and so could not be British.

Arriving in Guantanamo, they were beaten and kicked, threatened with death, not allowed to pray, and their Qurans thrown on the floor or in the toilet. They were interrogated around the clock, held in isolation, in complete darkness, injected with undisclosed drugs, held in conditions of great heat during the day and freezing cold at night, subject to music playing at ear-splitting volume and chained in the "short-shackle" position so that they could not move, soaked with high pressure hoses in their cells (also soaking their Qurans). They were later paid compensation by the British government.

Carol Rosenberg, whose reporting first for the *Miami Herald* and then the *New York Times* was and remains unparalleled, visited Shafiq Rasul in 2023. He has rebuilt a quiet life:

Today, Mr. Rasul, 45, lives with his wife, their two children and his widowed mother in the same rowhouse along Victoria Road in Tipton, England, where he was raised. Two of his brothers live with their families in adjoining houses in the former factory town of brick buildings and bygone canals. A soft-spoken man, Mr. Rasul describes himself as a homebody who earns a living by servicing natural gas home heating systems for a locally based national firm.[5]

Rasul regrets as a folly of youth the trip to Afghanistan that he took "out of curiosity." "There was a bit of naivete," he told Carol Rosenberg.

Jamal Al Harith's path was quite different and ended in tragedy. His parents had emigrated from Jamaica as part of the Windrush generation and settled in Manchester, where he was born Ronald Fiddler in 1966. He became a web designer and converted to Islam in 1991. He began an internet relationship with the daughter of an Australian Senator and travelled to Perth in early 2000 to meet her. The relationship did not work out, and he returned to Manchester.

He told me that he then travelled to Pakistan intending to attend a religious retreat sponsored by Al Tabligh, a global Islamic religious revival group, and arrived there on October 2, 2001. He was told to leave the country because of animosity toward foreigners and the British in particular. He planned to travel overland by truck through Iran and Turkey and back to the United Kingdom. His truck was hijacked in Northern Pakistan at gunpoint by Afghans, who forced him into a jeep, which crossed into Afghanistan, where he was handed over to the Taliban. He was beaten repeatedly by Taliban guards, interrogated, and accused of being a British spy and held in isolation. After the US invasion began, he was released into the general prison population, and when the Taliban fell, he and others were told they could leave. The International Committee of the Red Cross (ICRC) told him to remain where he was, and they would contact the British Embassy to fly him home.

When American Special Forces arrived, he felt that he had been saved and that his ordeal was over. Special forces questioned him, and the ICRC reiterated that he would be flown to Kabul and then home. Two days before the scheduled flight, American soldiers told him, "You're not going anywhere. We're taking you to Kandahar."[6] He told me he received abusive treatment similar to that of the Tipton Lads.[7]

When I saw Jamal in 2004, he was mature and measured. He was more than a decade older than the Tipton Lads. He was back in Manchester but had difficulty finding work. He married and had five children. He had received approximately 1 million pounds from the British government as a settlement for British involvement in his mistreatment. His wife said that he was not an extremist and "posed no threat" after his release in 2004, but that his views became more extreme after seeing "atrocities committed by the regime in Syria."[8] He left the UK in 2014 and joined ISIS. His wife said that her husband was "ideologically opposed to suicide attacks," but committed to the war in Syria. In February 2017, he detonated a car bomb at an army base near Mosul in Iraq. He was fifty years old. After his death, his family issued a statement, saying: "The Jamal they knew up until 2001 when he was taken to Guantanamo Bay would not have become involved with a despicable organisation such as so-called Islamic State. He was a peaceful and gentle person."

They believed he was utterly changed by the physical and mental cruelty and the inhuman treatment he endured for two years at Guantanamo. A cousin offered that they never understood his conversion, that he came from a "normal Jamaican family." "He was just a bit of a silly boy. There was never anything mentally wrong with him – the only thing I can think is that he was brainwashed."[9]

So who was Jamal Al Harith? The romantic who went halfway around the world to meet an Australian woman he met online? The religious pilgrim seeking to deepen his faith in Pakistan, only to find himself in the middle of a war, first a prisoner of the Taliban and then the United States? An extremist when he went to Pakistan? The calm man who sat with me for many hours and recounted his ordeal? A man who lived a quiet life in Northern England with a wife and children for a decade before the Syrian massacres led to his joining the most violent of Islamist groups? A man who never recovered from being tortured at Guantanamo? A silly boy or a hardened extremist? Or was he all of those men?

This book is primarily about the Kuwaiti group of detainees. But the British detainees provide an interesting counterpoint and should have been the detainees who attracted the best treatment. They were native English speakers; they were nationals of America's closest ally; and they would have had far more in common culturally with the men guarding them than any of their detainees. Tony Blair was pressing for their release when he spoke to President Bush. Their nationality got them out early, but every one of the detainees appears to have received similar abuse.

*****

We will now turn to the twelve Kuwaitis. The Kuwaiti detainees had little in common other than their nationality. Many came to know each other closely over the years, living together, eating together, praying together, and constructing support networks so that each Kuwaiti could tell his family about the others during the monthly calls that began around 2008 and periodic letters, if any substance remained after the censors got through with them. This community enabled the Family Committee as well as individual family members to provide news and hope to the other Kuwaiti detainee families.

In this chapter, we look at the personal histories of the Kuwaiti detainees. What kind of lives did they live before they came to Guantanamo? How and why had they been captured? What happened to them at Guantanamo? What sort of hearings did they have before the Defense Department? What relationship did the presentations in those hearings, where they had no lawyers and no meaningful due process, bear to the detainees' actual stories? When and why were they released? And, to the extent that their histories can be traced after their releases, what have their lives been like since they were released from Guantanamo?

Gaining the release of these twelve men was a long political and legal process. But most of all, it was a process that involved real men who had lived real lives before being thrown into a nightmarish world without end. This chapter tries to understand those twelve individual lives. Some were more willing to share their stories than others, so each of these portraits is different based upon what they went through, what was learned about them through various administrative records and court proceedings, and their varying comfort levels in reliving some of these events and having their stories told.

In November 2021, we brought together five of the eleven surviving detainees at ARH's offices in Kuwait City. Many of them had not seen each other in years, after spending seven days a week in close quarters for a decade or more. Abdullah Kamal Al Kandari, Fayiz Al Kandari, Fawzi Al Odah, Omar Rajab Amin, and Abdulaziz Al Shammeri sat around a conference table for hours. Khalid Al Odah, Fawzi's father, also joined the meeting, as well as the Core Team, the three people who had devoted fourteen years to getting these men out of Guantanamo. In September 2022, Omar, Abdullah, Fawzi, and Fayiz met again with ARH and me in Kuwait.

At first, we went around the table and each one of these men spoke individually, but the conversation was halting. After some time, the conversation began to flow, with each man sharing memories and discussing shared experiences as well as what it was like when they came home. They spoke of how well they worked as a group. They shared humor and a keen sense not just of the horror of their experience, but its absurdity. They spoke of the cynicism of USG measures, how the worst of the torture subsided after the early years, but it continued in subtle ways and became largely psychological.

Many of the Kuwaitis were leaders of the hunger strikes. Their force-feeding was accomplished with maximum pain; the many hunger strikers were chained to six-point feeding chairs, with the widest nasal tubes shoved aggressively through their noses and down their throats, or with painful suppositories inserted rectally. Videos were taken of the force-feeding. They have been and remain classified, although it is difficult to know why scenes of wanton cruelty committed by US troops present national security issues. I was one of the few with a security clearance for the injunction hearing on force-feeding that I conducted on behalf of the detainees, and I was permitted to see them. They were horrific and remain lodged in my memory.

All of the detainees from Kuwait, except Fayiz Al Kandari, had been shipped by plane to Guantanamo from the US detention facility in Kandahar. They had been in Kandahar for between one and two months, detained outdoors with razor wire at their heads and feet. It was winter and Kandahar was freezing; the average low temperature in December through March is in the low 30s (around 0 centigrade). They wore jumpsuits with no coats. They were beaten viciously and constantly. There was a particularly violent Egyptian interrogator who repeatedly asked them throughout the long interrogations. "Are you Al Qaida?" "No." Beating. "Are you Taliban?" "No." Beating. "Are you a Jihadi?" "No." Beating. There were no correct answers. Day after day for weeks on end.

Our discussions in Kuwait not only revealed horror stories, but also brought home that what kept most of these men going over all these years was their shared faith and sense of community. In the end, they were proud of their strength and stamina. They endured the torture and humiliation, emerging with their dignity. Here, then, are their stories.

Omar Rajab Amin

Omar Rajab Amin was among the first prisoners brought to Guantanamo Bay, on January 12, 2002, and one of the older Kuwaiti detainees. He was born in Kuwait City on June 14, 1967. A graduate of the University of Nebraska-Lincoln, he speaks fluent English. His training was in agricultural engineering, and he worked in the Kuwaiti Ministry for Social Affairs in the Section on Agriculture. He supervised the planting and maintenance of a major complex in Kuwait City for the elderly. He had a wife and three children, and his wife was pregnant with a fourth child when he left for Afghanistan.

Omar had been in Afghanistan on a charity mission when the United States attacked the Taliban in October 2001, and he fled to Pakistan, where he was captured in December 2001. Although handed over to the Americans in Pakistan, he was flown back to Kandahar in Afghanistan. He felt fortunate not to have been sent to Bagram, which his fellow detainees told him was the worst in the degree and constancy of physical abuse. His interrogators told him "You are going somewhere 'far away,'" but did not tell him where he was going. He had no communication with his family for months until he finally could write and receive a few letters.[10]

When Omar arrived in Guantanamo, he was told he had been sold by the Afghans. When his guards learned that he had lived in Nebraska and graduated from the University of Nebraska-Lincoln, it spread among the guards who would shout at him as a constant refrain, "The Cornhuskers are losing. The Cornhuskers are losing."[11] Omar was sent to Camp X-Ray, where he lived in the open air for four months. Because he spoke English, he was frequently called on to assist as an interpreter.

Omar was and remains deeply troubled by the deliberate disrespect shown toward Muslim religious practice and especially the guards' treatment of the Quran. One of the Arab translators gave a small Quran to another prisoner. "Why are you taking this piece of shit?" one of the guards shouted. Military Police often searched the cells of the detainees and threw Qurans roughly on the floor. Cells were hosed down, and Qurans became soaked. Omar was angry and felt humiliated by the treatment of the Holy Book, as did many of the men. While detainees were allowed to pray, they were frequently and deliberately interrupted during prayer. Guards chose that time to kick in cell doors for inspection or to make deafening noises in the corridor. During Ramadan, the guards would not provide food before sunrise, tossing in a meal tray that would remain in the cell during the day, while the detainees could not eat.[12] They would need to wait until sundown. The month of Ramadan, requiring fasting during the daytime, moves through the seasons, and so the length of the fast varies; when they first arrived in 2002, it began in November, but from 2008 to 2015, Ramadan began during the much longer days of summer.

Omar was dragged out of his cell on regular occasions by the Immediate Reaction Force (IRF), six guards who seized prisoners and threw them face down onto the cement floor. Omar once took three stitches to his head when he was smashed into the vents during an IRFing. Virtually every detainee was IRFed on multiple occasions. This happened frequently when detainees on hunger strike declined to come out of their cells to be force-fed. Like many of the detainees, Omar was also subject to the "Frequent Flyer Program." He was transferred from cell to cell every hour, twenty-four hours a day, for an entire month.[13]

And it was not only the guards who were aggressive and violent. Interrogators also used physical violence, and there were interrogators from multiple countries who came through Guantanamo. Omar recalled Spanish, French, Jordanian, and Egyptian interrogators questioning him, and a number of them were physically violent.

Omar's Journey to Afghanistan

What was Omar doing in Afghanistan in 2001? The nearly irrebuttable presumption by the Department of Defense (DoD) with respect to virtually all of the detainees was that they were there to support Al Qaida or the Taliban, and they all had been trained to make up a story about volunteering. The Defense Department categorically ignored the long history of Gulf men doing charity work and the individual histories of particular detainees, well before September 11.

Omar had a long and verifiable record of doing charitable projects in conflict zones. He had gone to Bosnia with the Kuwait Joint Relief Committee (KJRC), which provided assistance to the thousands of Bosnian children orphaned in the wake of Serbian massacres of Muslims. He remained in Bosnia during the war and visited periodically until 2000, traveling back and forth between Kuwait and Bosnia, with official leave obtained each time from his employer, the Ministry of Social Affairs.

The KJRC was a major Kuwaiti NGO coordinating relief through Bosnia during the war and thereafter. It included sixteen Kuwaiti organizations, charities, and public sector entities that, for more than twenty-five years, have done charitable relief work in war zones and areas of natural disasters. The KJRC sought to unify relief efforts and assistance, working with, among others, the United Nations High Commission for Refugees. "There was so much need; so much need." Omar recalled with emotion.[14]

With respect to Omar, the USG could have easily checked with the Kuwaiti Ministry regarding his long experience in doing charitable work and his leadership position in Bosnia. In the upside-down world of Guantanamo, however, telling the truth about why you were in Afghanistan was received as evidence of guilt. Omar's true story, backed up by a documented history of similar work, was received as an Al Qaida cover story and supported a finding of his being an enemy combatant.

Omar would spend nearly five years in Guantanamo. Yet he was one of the lucky ones. Omar was repeatedly interrogated for over three years about a wide range of allegations from a variety of unidentified sources. Finally, he was brought before a CSRT, one of the mechanisms adopted by the USG to provide the appearance of due process, before it was struck down by the Supreme Court, as discussed in Chapter 3. Despite not having counsel or access to evidence or a neutral tribunal, Omar tried to defend himself before the panel of military officers. All of the evidence that he saw in a truncated charging dossier (later obtained and released by WikiLeaks) spoke of "suspected" or "possible" affiliation. This was enough to convince the DoD that it should continue to hold him.

The dossier referenced his experience with the KJRC in Bosnia and stated that the KJRC provided support to families of former mujahideen. Of course, with so many massacred in this genocide, no doubt there were men killed fighting the Serbian ethnic cleansing, leaving countless widows and children in desperate need of basic support. That was what Omar was doing as he had done many times before.

During Omar's CSRT, the Defense Department described the KJRC as "being tied to Al Qaida," without specifying any actual connections. Numerous relief organizations from all over the world were working together, including the KJRC, trying to prevent the wholesale slaughter of Bosnian Muslims by Serbian death squads, a cause that, after significant delay, the USG also embraced by bombing Serbian positions. In his testimony before the CSRT, Omar pointed out that during the six years he worked as director of the KJRC's work in Bosnia, he enjoyed a close working relationship with the American military there.[15] The KJRC continues to perform vital functions in conflict zones to this day.

Omar begged to know what the evidence against him might be. At one point, he asked the tribunal, "Is it possible to see this evidence in order to refute it?" No, he was told. The evidence was classified; he could not see it for reasons of national security. An unclassified summary of evidence called him a "terrorist financier." He was alleged to have met with Osama Bin Laden in 1999 and 2001 and given him large amounts of money.

Omar had never met Osama Bin Laden then or at any time, and there was no evidence ever presented that he had. Omar was never in Afghanistan in 1999 or until October 2001, by which time Bin Laden was on the run; Bin Laden could not and did not travel outside Afghanistan after 1996. One alleged informer source said Omar "looks like an Afghan individual once seen in an Al Qaida guest house in Kabul."

Omar is not an Afghan and Afghanistan is a country of 46 million people from many different ethnic backgrounds, so it is unclear what it means to "look like an Afghan." Omar said:

> One time, the interrogator had a document in his hand and was reading from it and said that I was a member of the Mujahideen Brigade in the Bosnian army from either 1992 to 1993 or 1993 to 1994. I answered him by asking him if he knew where I was in 1992. I told him I was in Nebraska and I was graduating.

One of Omar's professors and his academic advisor at the University of Nebraska, Dr. Jack Schinstock, an associate Dean in the College of Agricultural Sciences, recalled Omar fondly and said in an interview that Omar had missed a year of school – in 1990–1991 – when Iraq invaded Kuwait and Omar was in Kuwait and forced into hiding. Little did Omar know it would not be his only encounter with a war involving the United States.

When meeting with Omar in November 2021, we told Omar that Professor Schinstock had reached out to help him and had provided a letter in support of Omar to the CSRT.[16] We showed him a copy of the letter. Omar Amin, a pious and stern man, now with a long white beard and wearing a white ghoutra (headdress) without an igal (the black band that usually goes around the ghoutra)– which is emblematic of people of very strong faith – said he never knew that Professor Schinstock had tried from Nebraska to secure his freedom. Omar broke down in tears.

Omar left Bosnia in 2000, returned to Kuwait, working again for the Kuwaiti Ministry of Social Affairs. He requested and was granted an approved leave of absence and went to Afghanistan in immediately before the US bombing campaign began on October 7, 2001. He was obviously not privy to US war plans; he, of course, knew about September 11, but had been told that most of Afghanistan was quite far away from the battlefront in the civil war between the Taliban and the Northern Alliance and that the need for relief was greater than ever.[17]

Omar went to Afghanistan seeking to establish a relief NGO with support from the United Nations and funds from friends and family in Kuwait. He testified that he had no association with Bin Laden or any weapons training and never engaged in any fighting. There was no evidence offered to the contrary. Things became so bad in Kabul after the bombing started that Omar was advised as a foreigner to leave the city. He fled without retrieving his passport. He walked to the border and was arrested in mid-December by Pakistani patrols and transferred to US custody in Peshawar, Pakistan. As so often the case, he was never observed by US forces doing anything.

The USG stated in its secret detainee assessment, which was never shown to Omar, that its purpose for transferring Omar to Guantanamo was to "find out about the inner workings of governmental ministries in Kuwait," which had coordinated efforts with the KJRC in Bosnia and Croatia, as well as to find out about "the refugee community between 1993 and 1999 in Bosnia and Croatia," and to "interrogate him about connections between the KJRC and Al Qaida," connections which the US assumed without evidence.

In other words, Omar was brought to Guantanamo in 2002 because the US wanted to interrogate him coercively about an ally, Kuwait, and its official activity in Bosnia in the early to mid-1990s, obtain other information about the Balkans, and explore some purported connection between a Kuwaiti government-supported entity coordinating charitable relief and Al Qaida. What he might have known, if anything, could have been learned in an afternoon, but Omar spent five years being interrogated.

In concluding that Omar was an enemy combatant and needed continued detention, the US stated as its principal reason that many managers and staff of Islamic NGOs "have been suspected of aiding mujahideen in those countries." The mujahideen in Bosnia were trying to prevent ethnic cleansing, mass rape, and genocide (as was the United States eventually), and the NGOs were providing support to their families; yet years later it connoted terrorist activity that purportedly presented a danger to the United States.

The CSRT viewed Omar's narrative as Deputy Director of the KJRC Sarajevo branch as "empty" and devoid of detail about his responsibilities and the people with whom he worked. It viewed his trip to Afghanistan as a cover to support jihadist activities. Because he did not give interrogators enough information that they found useful, they concluded that he must have been supporting terrorism in Bosnia, and since that what was he did in Bosnia, he could not have had another valid reason to have gone to Afghanistan. Thus was the logic of CSRT determinations.

He was "assessed to be an Islamic extremist" who used his management position with KJRC for over six years in Bosnia and Croatia to "help facilitate mujahideen activity." The CSRT also found that he was "associated" with a major Kuwaiti financier of terrorism, but the identity of that financier and the nature of that association were never stated to Omar or disclosed in any unclassified documents.[18]

Omar was said by a source of "undetermined reliability" that a certain Kuwaiti was a terrorism financier, and Omar had been at the home of this person on several occasions. He could not refute these allegations because he did not know whose home he was supposed to have been at, when he was supposed to have been there or what the basis was for calling him a terrorist financier from a source that even the Defense Department did not find to be reliable.

With respect to Omar's trip to Afghanistan in October 2001, the USG believed he "possibly accompanied a group of six Kuwait Nationals" to Afghanistan and that group "possibly brought funds to a charity."[19] The nationals were not named nor was the charity. The CSRT report stated that Omar may have "possibly assisted in delivering funds" to the director of Al Wafa, a charity not designated as Al Qaida-controlled until after Omar left Kabul.

The secret dossier compiled for Omar's CSRT also noted, "During a Kuwaiti delegation visit in January 2004, the Kuwait State Security Service interviewed Omar" and, according to the US dossier, "The KSS believed Amin was not dangerous and would release him directly if he was returned to Kuwait." Yet, despite the judgment of the KSS, a reliable allied intelligence service, that he did not present a security risk, this was ignored by the CSRT in ordering continued detention.

After the persistent diplomacy of the Emir, Omar was finally released from Guantanamo and transferred to Kuwait on September 14, 2006. Kuwait was forced to agree that if the United States had sufficient evidence in its possession and provided it to the Kuwaiti prosecutors, it would try him in Kuwait. At the request of the US, Omar was charged in Kuwait with joining Al Qaida and engaging in activities harmful to relations with a friendly country. The United States declined to provide a single piece of evidence. He was acquitted of all charges in March 2007.

As mentioned earlier, Omar had three children when he left. His wife was pregnant, and a fourth child was born while Omar was at Guantanamo. His wife kept Omar alive to his children, talking about Omar to them every day and always bringing them to the phone when he was allowed a rare phone call through the ICRC. When he returned home, they were very shy and cautious, but they knew who he was through their mother's devoted efforts.

Omar's last child was four years old when she first met her father. She and her siblings asked him questions about Guantanamo, and he told them that he had been detained while doing good works for poor people. They were proud of their father and, after a few awkward weeks, they became and remain a close and loving family.

Omar lives quietly in Kuwait today with his family. He does not speak to the media. He is retired from his position at the Social Affairs Ministry, where he returned after his acquittal in 2007. Omar speaks quietly and calmly about his life and his ordeal. Regarding Guantanamo, he says he does not complain about it. "It happened; life goes on; I try to forget about it." He says he is full of forgiveness. "I have known many Americans in my life," Omar says, recalling his years in Nebraska. "Americans have been very kind to me." His issue, he says, is with the Bush administration that detained and abused so many Muslims. He tries consciously to move past the memories of Guantanamo. He has no nightmares about his time there. "It is in the past."[20]

Khalid Abdullah Mishal Al Mutairi

Khalid Abdullah Mishal Al Mutairi was twenty-six years old when he was captured near the Pakistan-Afghanistan border in November 2001. He was brought to Guantanamo Bay on February 9, 2002, and kept at Camp X-Ray until he was moved to solitary confinement at Camp Delta when it was completed at the end of April 2002. He was released after more than seven and a half years at Guantanamo, on October 9, 2009, and repatriated to Kuwait. While at Guantanamo Bay, he was found to be an enemy combatant, first in 2004, then again in 2007, and in 2008, based on DoD dossiers that he did not see. He was recommended for continued detention on all three occasions.[21] He was one of four detainees who were actually given a habeas corpus hearing before a federal district court, which held there was no basis for his continued detention; he was released shortly thereafter.[22]

Had the Supreme Court not granted every detainee the right to an expedited habeas corpus hearing in the 2008 case brought by Fawzi Al Odah, and Lakhmar Boumediene, Khalid could well have been a forever prisoner at Guantanamo based on DoD's self-evaluation of its own purported evidence. It was only when Khalid was finally able to get before a neutral judge did the USG's case unambiguously and rapidly unravel.

Khalid's History and Its Bizarre Reflection in His CSRTs

According to the DoD dossier, Khalid had nine years of formal education in Kuwait before dropping out of high school in 1993. From 1993 to 2000, he had worked as a clerk in the Civil-Incident Police Division of the Kuwaiti Ministry of Interior. His father had also worked in the Ministry of Interior; his brother was a major in the Kuwaiti military, and another brother attended university in the United States. The dossier reported that

Khalid requested numerous leaves of absence from the police division to help his family financially over many years, well before 9/11. During his absence from the police division, he made money by buying and reselling cellular phones and incense throughout the Middle East and Asia.

In December 2000, Khalid resigned from his police job and applied for a position within the Ministry of Social Affairs. It is not clear from the records whether he ever obtained this job. What is clear is that shortly after September 11, he left for Afghanistan. All of this background was accurate as far as it went. What was remarkable was how the government distorted this banal recitation of a minor civil service career punctuated by intervals as a small trader into something sinister.

CSRT Proceedings

Khalid told his interrogators that he went to Afghanistan to build a mosque, after meeting and becoming friendly with Ali Fahim, a Kuwaiti national, whom Khalid had hired as a carpenter to do a renovation project at his home. He said that he told Ali Fahim at that time that he planned to build a mosque in Afghanistan at some point, and they stayed in touch over the next few years. In the spring of 2001, Khalid called Ali Fahim and told him that he had decided to build the mosque for charity, and they agreed to go together to work on the project. Shortly thereafter, in September 2001, but before September 11, Khalid made travel arrangements to go to Afghanistan to work on building the mosque.

Khalid left Kuwait with $15,000 in US currency on a flight to Mashad, Iran, which was the closest and one of the most common entry points for men from the Gulf to get to Afghanistan prior to 9/11. He met Ali Fahim and the two travelled to Nimruz on the Afghan-Iranian border. In Nimruz, Khalid gave Ali Fahim $2,000 to provide clothes to refugees huddled on the border. Khalid also traveled to Kabul to offer assistance through the Al Wafa organization. Khalid stayed in Kabul for approximately six weeks. During this time, Khalid learned that he could construct the mosque for $9,000 and gave Ali Fahim that amount to find a team to build the mosque. He also donated $1,000 to an Al Wafa doctor to help build a school.

Khalid learned of the fighting reaching Kabul and wanted to leave Afghanistan. On the day before his departure, Khalid testified that his passport and his remaining $3,000 were stolen. On November 17, 2001, Khalid and Ali Fahim fled to a small village near Khost, Afghanistan, and stayed at the home of Ali Fahim's friend for four or five weeks.

Afterwards, they paid an Afghan guide to take them across the Afghanistan-Pakistan border.

The group crossed the border in the Nangarhar region of Pakistan in mid-December 2001. Their Pakistani contact gathered the group along with others in a mosque, where Pakistani forces were waiting and immediately arrested them. Pakistani authorities transferred Khalid to US custody on January 2, 2002.

The CSRT dossier and board effectively credited none of Khalid's story and portrayed Khalid as a hardcore, high-level Al Qaida operative. The DoD stated that Khalid had "acknowledged a long-term association with UBL [Usama Bin Laden] and jihad and he is assessed to have participated in hostilities against US and Coalition forces." Those charges were based solely on the report of an interrogator who said that Khalid had shouted out hysterically during a prolonged aggressive interrogation that he had the

> "honor of being [UBL's] humble servant," and Detainee added he (detainee) was in Afghanistan fighting with "Shaykh" UBL in 1991. Detainee noted he is ready to stay at JTF-GTMO for 100 years, even if he is innocent, he will not reveal any information about the Taliban or al-Qaida. (Analyst Note: Detainee's loyalty to UBL indicates he would continue to support al-Qaida and other extremist organizations if released).

The interrogator also reported that Khalid told him:

> He stated that he wished to be called Osama bin Laden ... ISN 213 [Khalid's identification number by which all detainees were known and addressed]] stated he was an enemy of America because Americans had told him so. Americans had cursed his parents. Prior to the war, he'd had no problem with Americans. But due to the situation at Guantanamo Bay, Cuba, and his detention, America had made him their enemy ... He stated that with all this legal process being so useless, he might as well be Osama bin Laden, since he was never going to be freed from US custody.[23]

This was part of an interrogation where the translator according to the habeas court's finding was goading Khalid, and the government then relied on these provoked statements during this interrogation to support its view that Khalid not only was pro-Bin Laden, but had fought alongside Bin Laden in Afghanistan in 1991.[24]

The DoD neglected to perform the most basic arithmetic to reach the conclusion that Khalid was sixteen years old in 1991. Nor did the dossier consider that the Iraqi invasion of Kuwait was ongoing at the time, and so the notion of a sixteen-year-old leaving his country and his family to go to fight in a civil war in Afghanistan was not credible and without any corroboration.

The government also relied on a series of other documents, which it called "Al Qaida documents," to support the conclusion that Khalid had a starring role at Tora Bora. First, it relied on his visit to Al Wafa charity because Al Wafa was listed as an Al Qaida-affiliated charity by the United States. Al Wafa was not listed by the US until the day that Khalid arrived there, and the news was highly unlikely to have made it to Kabul (eight hours ahead) or to Khalid on the date of his arrival. The government also asserted Khalid had trained at an Al Wafa training camp, although it provided no evidence in the CSRT and conceded at trial that the camp itself was "nascent."

Khalid was also implicated for being affiliated with numerous radical groups in Pakistan and elsewhere, but almost all of that information came from other detainees. The interrogators eagerly lapped up even the most far-fetched stories of what Khalid and numerous others allegedly confessed to them. Khalid lashed out and said he supported Bin Laden, that he was Bin Laden, that he always would be. That was plenty for the DoD; case closed for seven and half years. The judge's evaluation in the habeas hearing of the evidence against Khalid, discussed in Chapter 6, showed how a real judicial official, as opposed to non-lawyer soldiers whose careers depended on their bureaucratic cooperation would view such vague and improbable snippets.

Fouad Al Rabiah

Fouad Al Rabiah, unlike most of his fellow Kuwaitis, was not a young man when he was detained in Afghanistan in late 2001 and brought to Guantanamo in early 2002, where he was held for eight years. Fouad was forty-two years old, married with four children and had enjoyed a successful and well-established career when he went to Afghanistan. He spent his early years in Egypt, where his father was posted as a Kuwaiti diplomat. He attended the Air Service Training Technical School in Scotland, graduating in 1981 with a Bachelor's Degree in Engine and Air Frame Maintenance. In 1981, Fouad began working for Kuwait Airlines, which was at the time the premier airline in the region.

From 1985 to 1988, Fouad attended Embry-Riddle Aeronautical University in Daytona Beach, Florida, where he earned a second Bachelor's Degree in Professional Aeronautics and a Master's of Business Administration in Aviation. Fouad and his wife traveled extensively in the United States. He spoke fluent English and viewed himself as a great friend of America. He returned in 1988 to Kuwait Airways and served as a senior aviation engineer.

Not only was Fouad an experienced engineer, he also had a long and honorable record in philanthropy. As the DoD catalogued, he had for years traveled to impoverished and war-torn countries to provide material relief and spiritual guidance to those in need. During the month of Ramadan in 1991, Fouad took time off from work to collect goods for Kurds in Northern Iraq, who were being brutalized by Saddam Hussein in the wake of the First Gulf War. In 1994 and 1995, he took another leave of absence from Kuwait Airways to travel to Bosnia as a volunteer for the Revival of Islamic Heritage Society, a group that works in countries where Islamic practice had been suppressed or ignored, as it had been during the recently ended Communist era in Yugoslavia.

In 1998, he traveled to Kosovo to work as a volunteer for the Kuwait Red Crescent. The Kosovo war saw another ethnic cleansing, as a million Kosovar Albanian Muslims were forced from their homes by the majority ethnic Macedonians, with mass migration of refugees. The Kuwait Red Crescent provided integrated aid to refugees on a massive scale. In April 2000, Fouad once again obtained leave from Kuwait Airways to go to Bangladesh to provide kidney dialysis equipment to a hospital in Dhaka.[25]

There was never any question then as to whether or why he went on these relief missions. This was all documented, and he had the means and the commitment to make a difference in various places that desperately needed relief. But that was a different time, before September 11. Before humanitarian activity in support of threatened and displaced populations became equivalent to support for terrorism.

In July 2001, Fouad went to Afghanistan for ten days on a visit related to Afghanistan's refugee problems and disastrous medical infrastructure. He returned in October, entering Afghanistan through the most common entry point in Iran. "The day that I went into Afghanistan is the day the [American] bombing started. Of course, this is all documented because I had the stamp," Fouad said.[26] The US authorities took his passport and saw that this was indeed the fact. But when the bombing started, the Iranians closed the border, so Fouad, like so many others, decided he could only leave Afghanistan from Kabul through Pakistan, and he wrote a letter to his family about the situation, asking them to let Kuwait Airways know that he may be delayed in returning to work.

Fouad did not fit the profile of a warrior. He said at the time he weighed 108 kilograms (237 pounds) and could not see at night; he was ill-suited physically for any exertion on the harsh Afghan terrain. On December 25, he was captured in a village outside Jalalabad, Afghanistan. The villagers handed him over to the Northern Alliance, who tortured him. The Northern Alliance sold him to the Americans for $5,000. He was then sent to Bagram Air Base.

Fouad was told at Bagram that they were preparing for his transfer back to Kuwait, but that he would first need to be taken to Kandahar. He spent two and a half months in Kandahar, where again he was brutally tortured by American interrogators. A report by Human Rights Watch in 2004 on Kandahar confirmed "Abuse of detainees was an established part of the interrogation process."[27]

Fouad said he had convinced himself in thinking the US military would contact Kuwait and send him back home. "What first comes to anyone's mind is that once a citizen of any particular nation travels abroad ... when a problem takes place, the logic dictates that he should be handed to his native country of origin and not to be extradited to a third-party nation. That's what anyone in their sane mind would think," he said.[28] But by the time he was led to the plane in Kandahar, Fouad knew from listening to the English being spoken by his captors that none of the detainees would be going home.[29]

Fouad arrived in Cuba on May 1, 2002. Remaining positive, he thought the place was "heaven" compared to his detention in Afghanistan. Camp Delta had just opened, and the camp was clean. It was not blistering hot during the day and freezing at night like in Afghanistan. They were allowed to shower. He was told that none of the detainees would be held at Guantanamo for more than six months, which he now understands was a tactic to mislead him.

"The first year in Cuba, I left my cell ... for recreation only 24 hours for the whole year." He passed his time reading the Quran. He spent a lot of time in isolation. He said early on he was told by a woman working at the camp, "We have nothing against you. We know nothing about you, but the President said, 'there is no innocent [person] in Cuba.'" She told him: "You cannot leave here, so confess to something so we can charge you, sentence you and you go home. But if we don't charge you and sentence you, you are not leaving." Fouad rightfully thought this made no sense and that he was not going to go along. "I said this is absurd ... that was way in the beginning and then they changed the tactics and started the torture." He reported, "I was threatened by two major things." First, they asked: "Would you like to go home a drug addict? Then they threatened to send me to a place where I would 'disappear.'" He understood they were telling him he could be injected with addictive substances or killed, and no one would know what happened to him.[30]

The United States would not consider that Fouad's visit to Afghanistan in October 2001 was consistent with a long history of applying his skills and resources as a manager and relief volunteer in Muslim countries in crisis. As with all of his previous volunteer travels, he requested and was granted leave to go to Afghanistan by Kuwait Airlines. To the United States, Fouad was not an "aid worker caught up in the front lines of the United States' war against Al Qaida," but instead was someone who went to Afghanistan in October 2001 "as a devotee of Osama Bin Laden, who ran to Bin Laden's side after September 11th."[31]

The United States convinced itself that what it wished was true: that Fouad Al Rabiah was an important and senior figure in Al Qaida. Its dossier contained thirteen pages of alarming allegations:

> Detainee is an Al Qaida member who met with Usama Bin Laden (UBL) at least four times, and gave him a $1 million US contribution During a July 2001 meeting, detainee .... [and a colleague] visited UBL at his home. UBL greeted them by name, and they discussed issues relevant to UBL, and prayed and ate together.
> According to admitted Al Qaida member and explosives trainer, Tariq Mahmud Ahmad al-Sawah, detainee attended a dinner with UBL and other senior Al Qaida members including Khalid Shaykh Muhammad, aka (KSM), Sayf al-Adel, and UBL driver Salim Ahmed Salim Hamdan. At this dinner, EG-535 stated that detainee handed UBL a large briefcase with approximately $1 million.
> Detainee provided support to the Taliban and Al Qaida on the Bagram frontline, before going to fight at Tora Bora, where he was placed in charge of logistics.
> Detainee was possibly the Emir (leader) of the al-Faruq training camp in the early 1990s and reportedly commanded frontline fighters during the period following the Soviet withdrawal from Afghanistan. Detainee may have provided training to some of the individuals involved in the 11 September 2001 terrorist attacks.
> Detainee probably attended training at one or more of the Al Qaida affiliated training camps and resided at several Al Qaida guesthouses.
> Detainee has associated with numerous Islamic extremists over the past 20 years, including former and current JTF-GTMO detainees.
> Detainee has worked since the 1980s on behalf of several non-governmental organizations (NGOs) known to support terrorist organizations, and has visited numerous countries in this capacity.[32]

These were serious allegations, all of which appear to have been made by the same person, Tariq Al Sawah, the Egyptian bombmaker and tireless informer, who was plied with separate quarters, a reclining chair, a television, and unlimited McDonalds, ballooning from 180 to 420 pounds.[33]

Based on these allegations, in October 2008, after more than six years at Guantanamo, Fouad was charged by the Office of Military Commissions. He was supposed to be one of the dozen or so detainees who would be tried by a military tribunal. He was charged with conspiracy to commit terrorism and attack civilians and providing material support for terrorism. He was exposed to the possibility of a life sentence or even capital punishment, if a death had resulted in the commission of these crimes. Fouad was now really being viewed as "the worst of the worst."

What was the evidence? The interrogators told him they had a two-page document found at Tora Bora, which Fouad was accused of writing, and which said that Fouad, under the alias "Abu Abdullah," along with his son Abdullah, were the leaders of an attack in Afghanistan in the wake of the Soviet withdrawal in 1991. To be sure, Fouad was often called Abu Abdullah because his oldest son was named Abdullah. That is his "kunya," a common way of identifying fathers of sons in Muslim countries. But not only was Fouad not the only Abu Abdullah in that part of Afghanistan, his son Abdullah was one year old in 1991, presumably not of an age to accompany his father into battle against the Soviet Union. And ten years later, Abdullah Al Rabiah, now eleven, would come up again as somehow having been with his father in Afghanistan when alleged terrorist acts were committed. If the United States had simply done the arithmetic, it would have made clear that Tariq Al Sawah's information was not conceivably accurate. But doing the arithmetic would yield the wrong answer. Al Sawah's reporting on more than 150 detainees is a through line in the CSRT determinations, along with a few other unfettered informers.

The United States was also certain that Fouad had been in Afghanistan in July and October 2001, not to continue his longstanding conflict zone relief work, but to support Al Qaida and the Taliban. Fouad was interrogated by his own count more than 200 times. "Lots and lots of torture."[34] He eventually confessed to anything and everything his interrogators said about him, which is what happens sooner or later with repeated torture.[35]

As Fouad was preparing to defend the charges in the Military Commission, potentially on trial for his life, the Supreme Court decided *Al Odah/Boumedience*, which could well have saved him. His case was also assigned to Judge Colleen Kollar-Kotelly, who presided over all four of the Kuwaiti habeas proceedings. We will review Fouad's remarkable hearing and the court's habeas decision in Chapter 6. Suffice it to say that a dossier that placed him at Bin Laden's side with a suitcase full of money quickly evaporated into the ether. There was no money, no dinner, and no meeting between Fouad Al Rabiah and Usama Bin Laden. There was only torture and lies.

Abdulaziz Al Shammeri

Abdulaziz Al Shammeri was part of the group of five Kuwaitis released quite early, and he was repatriated to Kuwait on November 2, 2005. He was a young and well-regarded Islamic scholar who worked at the Ministry of Islamic Affairs in Kuwait. He had a wife and two children, who were six and two at the time of his detention.

Planning to further his training in Islamic law, Abdulaziz had applied to a Master's program at a leading Egyptian university shortly before he left Kuwait for Afghanistan. He was twenty-eight years old. When he left Kuwait in the middle of October 2001, he had never been to Afghanistan before.

The United States determined that he was an enemy combatant and a member of Al Qaida, citing three principal reasons:

1. The detainee traveled from Kuwait to Iran and then to Afghanistan soon after September 11, 2001.
2. Detainee was arrested by the Pakistani Army while attempting to cross into Pakistan from Afghanistan without identification documents.
3. One of the detainee's known aliases was on a list of captured hard drives associated with a senior Al Qaida member.[36]

The CSRT concluded that he had become a member of the Taliban judiciary. The designation did not consider that Abdulaziz had never been to Afghanistan before or had any training in legal practice before arriving in mid-October for a short visit; that he did not speak any local language; that dozens were arrested at the same place and in the same way; and that, with respect to an alias, the designation failed to say what his alias might be (possibly another kunya – the father of his oldest son's first name) or that there were three Al Shammeris at Guantanamo and the DoD appeared confused or indifferent as to which Al Shammeri may have been listed on a hard drive.

At Guantanamo, Abdulaziz was questioned numerous times, and he answered questions freely. The accusation that he was a judge in the Taliban regime was presumably made because of his sharia background. He also was accused of making bombs because they found in his notes a number of equations, not to make bombs – he had no training whatsoever in engineering or physics – but because he was an expert in the Islamic law of inheritance and had been preparing diagrams for division of assets depending upon various complex family configurations as part of his scholarly work.

Abdulaziz was beaten viciously at Kandahar. At Guantanamo, he was deprived of sleep to the point that he was hallucinating. He was also given pills to take for his hallucinations but refused to take them. In 2004 and 2005, he joined a hunger strike and was force-fed and hospitalized.

In September 2004, Abdulaziz had a ninety-minute hearing before a CSRT. He submitted a statement and answers to questions sent to his family; he participated in the hearing, but no witnesses were called, and he did not have a lawyer. His colloquy with the panel of three military officers would have been funny if his liberty was not at stake, and his relentlessly logical responses had not been entirely futile and disregarded.

With respect to the allegation of Al Qaida affiliation, he made clear that it was neither accurate nor logically coherent. The CSRT decision quotes Abdulaziz:

> "This accusation does not have anything to support it, but it is merely words with no evidence to prove it." The Detainee went on to say that he journeyed to Afghanistan to teach and to help the needy and that he had thought that the fighting would be far away from where he was going. However, once he arrived in Afghanistan and the Taliban fell from power, "every Arab in Afghanistan was wanted dead or alive." I heard they had started buying Arabs and selling them, so I became afraid at hearing this news so I decided to escape quickly. That's why I could not return to my luggage.[37]

Abdulaziz also could not figure out why the fact of traveling to Afghanistan after September 11 would necessarily have been to support Al Qaida. He tried to reason with the panel:

> How can it be that travel to a large country with millions of people is travel for Al Qaida, which does not even represent 1% of that number or population? For is a person who traveled to China considered a communist? And is a person who traveled to Iraq considered loyal to the Baath Party? So, how did you make the fact that I traveled to Afghanistan an accusation that I am a part of Al Qaida? As for the fact that I traveled from my country, Kuwait, after the events of September, this is a very natural thing. These events, the events of September, occurred in America. So the chaos and confusion was not present anywhere but America only. But as for the rest of the countries in the world, the situation was very normal. People were going about their routine lives.[38]

Abdulaziz also pointed to the fact that he had sent his application to Egypt for his Master's degree in order to begin his studies the next term, confirming his intention to stay for a brief period.[39]

> If you want to verify this point, you can get in touch with your embassies in Kuwait and they will get a hold of the Ministry of Higher Education in Kuwait and they will give them receipts or documents that will show that I had registered with them and was waiting for my acceptance into that university. I also presented my paperwork in order to improve my position at work from a teacher at Dar Al Quran, which is a part of the Ministry of Islamic Affairs and Charity, to a teacher at the Institute of Applications after I was sent by the government to obtain a Doctorate Degree.[40]

No such verification was sought. Similarly, he testified he crossed the border without his passport because he wanted to get out of Afghanistan as quickly as possible, not to fight:

> And then what is the relationship between my crossing the border and Al Qaida? Is everyone who crossed the border at that time a person who is loyal to Al Qaida? Those are words that cannot be said, for when Iraq invaded my country, Kuwait, and men and children and women were escaping to Saudi Arabia, Jordan, and Iran, we did not see anyone arrest them and tell them you are followers of Saddam Hussein. Knowing that they were crossing over at the border stations secretly and without travel documents, and those countries' authorities would not arrest them but would help them and construct medical tents for them to treat them in. Under those circumstances no one asks for documents because the circumstances are not normal in that part of the world. And then let's assume that I made a mistake in this matter, I mean by my crossing the border without identification documents. The known procedure in a situation like this in all countries in the world is to detain me until the Pakistani authorities could find out my identity and country then send me back to my country. Not to turn me over to the American authorities, as a member of Al Qaida and the Taliban.[41]

The panel asked, "Why did you pick September of 2001 to travel to Afghanistan?" He responded: "It's just like I told you, because of the trouble that was over there; to help. You know that charity organizations, they only go to places where there is trouble or need. They don't go to any other countries. The situation in Afghanistan was not dependent on the events of September."[42]

To the USG, the thought of going to a conflict zone was inherently suspicious and going to teach impoverished refugees about their religion even more so. Abdulaziz's wife confirmed in a statement

> that he went to Pakistan to help and aid the poor people after he learned that [there were] a lot of refugees coming toward the borders of Pakistan from Afghanistan, and he always thinks of the others suffering and always try to help them. So he left Kuwait on a short vacation (2 Weeks) to help those poor people and come back very shortly.[43]

At one point, Abdulaziz is quoted in the hearing report. "I just want to say that it is my nature to smile. I am always smiling, so it's nothing out of the ordinary. Don't think it is anything else."

Those who have met with Abdulaziz to talk about his life after Guantanamo confirmed that "he is a ... very funny man who smiles without interruption." He smiled amiably throughout our time together in Kuwait. The report noted, "Detainee had been smiling throughout the proceedings."[44] The Guantanamo (GTMO) decision-makers wanted to see pained contrition, not lighthearted calm in the face of adversity.

Despite the lack of any objective evidence other than his movements into and out of Afghanistan and his possible inclusion on an undisclosed and undescribed hard drive, Abdulaziz was not taken back to Kuwait for more than three and a half years.

Abdullah Kamal Al Kandari

Abdullah Kamal Al Kandari, who calls himself Abdullah Kamal Al Hashem, was a member of the Kuwaiti national volleyball team and a manager at the Kuwaiti Ministry of Electricity and Water, where he oversaw water projects. Born in 1973, he was twenty-eight when he went to Afghanistan in September 2001, alarmed at the refugee crisis and hoping to assist. He asked for and was granted a ten-day leave from the Ministry to do charity work in September 2001. He had three children at the time and a fourth on the way, who was born while he was in captivity. He was planning to come back to his job as a project manager at the ministry and to rejoin the national volleyball team after the two weeks; that plan was delayed for five years.

Abdullah was captured in late December 2001 in Pakistan after crossing the border; his details taken down; and he was held at the same place with so many others and then sent to Kandahar. He was brought to Guantanamo in May 2002 and released in the fall of 2006.

Abdullah was assessed by the USG to be a leader of the Tabligh organization in Kuwait, which the US Defense Department asserted was an organization that collected money for Usama Bin Laden through a sheikh at a local Kuwaiti mosque. The Tabligh organization is an established organization with branches all over the world. It began more than half a century ago as an Islamic revivalist organization. It is avowedly apolitical.[45] Nevertheless, the USG noted that certain extremists had started with Tabligh activities, and therefore, it views it as "a gateway for terrorism," whatever that strange metaphor is meant to convey.[46]

The United States viewed Abdullah as having links to Al Qaida and having attended a speech by Bin Laden. He was also said to have "affiliation" with the Al Wafa Charity and connections to other Al Qaida members. In addition to these allegations, the DoD also put forward some of the allegations common to many detainees that in its view indicated terrorist support, including staying in a guest house in Kandahar and allegedly being trained in a Libyan-supported camp. He was said to have received paramilitary training, and it was alleged that Kuwaiti intelligence sources had provided information that he had jihadist ties.[47] While the quality of this information is uncertain, the dossier regarding Abdullah was actually much more detailed than those of others, yet he was one of the first Kuwaitis repatriated, suggesting either that the USG did not have confidence in the information or its process for repatriation was wholly random.

Abdullah was also wearing a Casio F-91 watch at the time of his capture, a cheap and common digital watch, which the USG believed had been used to detonate improvised explosive devices. Abdullah told me that he bought the watch in Kuwait, before he ever went to Afghanistan. As an active athlete on a national team, he needed a cheap watch with a timer and stopwatch that was water resistant. He was shocked that the watch would be seen as connected to bomb detonation or Al Qaida. He said it was common for people in Kuwait to have Fossil or Casio digital watches like the one he wore, because they had an app that automatically showed the direction of Mecca for prayer. He said that if he had known that the watch was viewed as commonly used as a detonator for bombs, "I would have thrown it away. I am not stupid."[48] Abdullah also told the CSRT that there were four Muslim chaplains at Guantanamo, all of whom wore the same Casio watch pointing toward the Qibla at the Grand Mosque in Mecca.[49]

For his hearing before an ARB (a procedure that predated the CSRTs and provided even fewer protections) in the spring of 2005, Abdullah provided a personal statement.[50] He stated he had brought $15,000 with him, his own savings and funds from friends, to help refugees. At the time of his capture, he had retained $2,000 to get home. He has used the rest to buy supplies. The USG viewed such significant sums of cash as indicative of terrorist purposes.

Abdullah also told me that the Muslim chaplains at Guantanamo were treated as highly suspect by the military chain of command. He said that many of the chaplains told the detainees that they sought psychological treatment from the stress of seeing Muslim men being abused for being Muslim. Many of them left the military. He told the story of an African-American Muslim chaplain named Hamza who told his commander, "This is not a war against terror. It is a war against Islam." His commanding officer told this chaplain that it would be better for him to resign from the military.[51]

Abdullah related that another chaplain called Yusuf, who was relaxed and interacted well with detainees, was accused of working with the detainees against the United States, and he also resigned. Abdullah was apparently referring to Captain James Yee, a Chinese-American convert to Islam who took the Arabic name Yusuf. Lee had received commendations from his superiors at Guantanamo for his work as chaplain. Yet returning from duty to the United States in 2002, he was arrested when a US Customs Agent found a list of Guantanamo detainees and interrogators. He was charged with multiple crimes including espionage. He was kept in solitary confinement for seventy-six days at the Naval Brig before charges were reduced and then dropped. He was later reinstated, then charged again, and ultimately discharged. His military career was over.[52]

Abdullah related that interrogators told him, "We have a program here. In three years, you lose your mind."[53] He was told the only way out was to confess. He was told that if he did not confess to being a terrorist, he would be sent to be interrogated by certain guards who had been on duty in Manhattan on September 11. Abdullah said the detainees all felt that the guards had a green light to do whatever they wanted to the detainees without consequence.

When Abdullah asked under what name he was listed in the computer, as there were multiple Al Kamals and confusion as to who he was, the CSRT panel would not tell him. "The problem is the secret information; I can't defend myself."[54] He said that if he was listed as Abdullah Kamal, it would be because he was prominent in Kuwait under that name because of his participation on the national volleyball team. But he would be known by friends and family as Abu Suleiman after his oldest son. He made clear that he was well known and well integrated in Kuwait with a wife and children. He and his wife together earned approximately $4,500 per month in 2001; he and his family received many benefits and he was untaxed, so it was easy to save money, and he was eager to participate in the traditional practice of charity for the poor. He was happy and satisfied with his life. "I'm going to be Al Qaida? I'm not stupid, and I'm going to do this against the biggest country in the world America?"[55]

"They don't have any evidence against me, to put me here," Abdullah said to the panel. "I don't have a choice, God is well here, so I'll be patient. Why did they put me here like this?"[56]

The tribunal ruled that Abdullah was an enemy combatant.

After his release in 2006, Abdullah revealed that he had been subjected to brutal beatings and harassment that appeared to have nothing to do with intelligence gathering. He told *Al Jazeera* when asked what his children know about the years he spent in jail, "I don't like to tell them about the torture," he said. He also tried not to think of them when he was away. If he had thought of them, "I will be crazy … so you try to read the Quran more and memorize the Quran."[57]

He told me that at one time, he had an allergic reaction and was bleeding all over his body. A nurse came and asked whether he had any allergies. He said yes; he was allergic to fish and eggs. For the next three years, he was given fish and eggs at lunch and dinner nearly every day, which he exchanged with other prisoners.[58]

Abdullah returned home nearly five years after his departure to three young children without any memory of him and a fourth, now past four years old, who had never met him. His parents had grown terribly weak and debilitated during his absence. He was kept in a rehabilitation facility at the Kuwaiti Central Prison for five and a half months, while the Kuwaitis, at the request of the United States, took steps to prosecute him. The United States provided no evidence; there was no other evidence from any other source showing any wrongdoing and he was released, which angered the American authorities. Coming home, he said, was "a gift."[59] After a long and difficult process to reconstruct and reintegrate his family, he had four more children. He now lives with his family of ten in a new home paid for by the Kuwaiti government.

Adel Zamel Abd Al Mahsen Al Zamel

Adel Zamel Abd Al Mahsen Al Zamel was captured in late 2001 in Afghanistan and brought to Guantanamo Bay in May 2002. He was one of the older detainees, thirty-eight when captured. He was one of five detainees repatriated in the early group in November 2005. Adel Zamel had traveled to Afghanistan in 2000 and became the manager of the Kabul office of the Al Wafa Humanitarian Organization, the organization that was later listed as being controlled by Al Qaida. He left Al Wafa in August 2001, after a dispute with his supervisor. He told the CSRT panel that he was unhappy with the purchasing of supplies and food and equipment and that Al Wafa was not getting high-quality goods; he suspected corruption, and he confronted the supervisor about the waste of charitable donations that were so needed for relief. Adel Zamel told the

CSRT about his views regarding the operation of the charity and his confrontation with the head of the organization:

> I told him that this is not your money, not my money. This is good people's money you have to care and be careful with it. And be careful of long-distance phone calls because the young people call for hours and call their families overseas and everywhere, I get angry. And I told him that this is good people's money and collected for the mosque to give it to the poor. We don't allow strangers to come and waste it like that, so he got real angry with that. He entered my house while I was absent and he go through my stuff and my wife's stuff and this made me real angry ... And then he said he did not want anyone to come and work for him except for people from Mecca. So after all of my hard work he wanted to kick me out, so I leave.[60]

The DoD asserted instead that he left Al Wafa because he had been somehow alerted in advance to the attacks of September 11. It presented no evidence to that effect, at least in the unclassified portion of his hearing.

The DoD also asserted that he had been one of the founders of Al Wafa, although Adel Zamel emphasized that he was only an employee. What he knew about its activities and sources of funding in his capacity as office manager is unknown, and the United States did not present any evidence of any knowledge by Al Zamel of Al Qaida control or activity on behalf of Al Qaida. It is hard to know all these years later what Al Zamel saw, whom he met and what he understood about his employer. Adel Zamel vociferously denied knowledge of Al Wafa being related to Al Qaida or the Taliban. He viewed himself solely as being involved with refugee relief work in Kabul. He also denied membership in any extremist organization.

While in Afghanistan, Adel Zamel became friendly with Suleiman Abu Ghaith, who emerged after September 11, 2001, as an aggressive and militant spokesperson for Al Qaida. Adel Zamel admitted helping Abu Ghaith get his family out of Afghanistan. Adel Zamel testified he had no previous knowledge of any role of Abu Ghaith as spokesman for Al Qaida or otherwise being connected to the group until he saw Abu Ghaith on television after the 9/11 attacks. Again, there is no way to know what he knew or believed about Abu Ghaith at the relevant time, but Adel Zamel's early release again suggests either a lack of confidence in those allegations or incompetence.

The US DoD considered Adel Zamel "a Takfiri [i.e., so doctrinaire on religious matters that he would declare those who disagreed with him as non-Muslims], but [he] would not be considered a Jihadist as he doesn't have the fortitude to risk his own life for a cause." In other words, a basis for his detention was his purportedly extreme religious views, but the government viewed him as not willing to undertake any actions in support of those views. It also noted that Adel Zamel had allowed Fayiz Al Kandari to stay in his house for a week. The DoD report then stated, "Fayiz Al Kandari was the legal advisor for, and close friend to, Usama Bin Laden." As will be seen, Fayiz Al Kandari, the last Kuwait detainee released, also had no training in law, and was never the friend of Bin Laden (there is no evidence he ever met him) or legal advisor to anyone. The DoD appeared to have the firm if inexplicable view that Bin Laden had the need for significant legal services in rural Afghanistan, even if the purported advisors were not lawyers.

The DoD also suggested that Adel Zamel was suspected of wrongdoing by the Kuwaiti authorities for actions taken in Kuwait. It noted:

> [H]e was invited to the house of a man involved in the October 2002 attack on U.S. Marines on Faylaka Island, Kuwait. The detainee possessed the telephone number of an individual in Kuwait who was shot and killed in October 2002 after he killed a U.S. Marine in Kuwait. The detainee has been investigated by Kuwaiti authorities of being involved with the Takfir movement. The detainee had a history of extremist vigilante activity. The detainee is considered a hard-core extremist.[61]

Of course, Adel Zamel was at Guantanamo in October 2002, so even if he had been invited to the house of a man involved in the Faylaka Island attacks, such an invitation would have necessarily been issued before he left Kuwait in 2000, and the attacks were two years later. Similarly, if he had a phone number of someone else involved in the attack, that phone number would also have been in his phone well before the Faylaka attacks, while Adel Zamel was at Guantanamo and without a phone (cell phones did not work at Guantanamo in any event). He does not appear to have been asked whose number it was or why he might have had it.

While the dossier contained information about the Al Wafa charity, which might well have usefully been followed up, the Defense Department chose not to delve into those facts, instead throwing out vague allegations, like he knew people who were later implicated in crimes or he had extreme religious beliefs but no will to act on them. The alleged but unspecified "history of extremist vigilante activity" does not refer to any specific acts and is indeed inconsistent with the conclusion that he would not have risked his own personal safety for any ideological or religious cause. The evaluation of Adel Zamel as "a hard-core extremist" is, again, a label without substantive content and appears to assert a right to detain because of a person's views rather than their actions.

The DoD recommended continued detention because of a certain vagueness in his timeline as to when he had entered and left Pakistan and because of alleged evidence from the Kuwait Security Service that he had been a member of the Takfir Al-Hijra group and had close relationships with other members of the group. The DoD recommendation stated that he had been convicted in absentia and sentenced to one year in prison by a Kuwaiti court based on alleged affiliations with the Takfir group and unnamed extremists.

There was actually some factual underpinning to this allegation, but it had nothing to do with terrorism. When he was sent to Guantanamo, Al Zamel was wanted in Kuwait on criminal assault charges related to an incident where a female college student had been confronted and assaulted by a group of men for purportedly inappropriate conduct and attire. Al Zamel testified he had not touched the woman, let alone struck her, but one of the men in the group did indeed strike her after the group had seen her acting in what they said was an inappropriate way with another man. Al Zamel was tried in absentia relating to this incident and served out his sentence when he returned to Kuwait from Guantanamo. This was a very troubling, intolerable altercation, reflecting a level of intolerance not often seen in Kuwait. But it hardly involved terrorism.

Adel Al Zamel's case remains puzzling. In many ways, the DoD viewed his case as significantly more serious than numerous others. It had more confirmed facts than many other cases, especially with respect to his employment at Al Wafa and the link to Suleiman Abu Ghaith; it is highly likely that he would have lost a habeas case based on these facts alone but he was released years before the habeas hearings took place. One potential key to why he was released after three and a half years in Guantanamo Bay while others were kept much longer may be related to his treatment while at Guantanamo.

Al Zamel was repatriated in 2005 and was acquitted of terrorism charges in short order by Kuwait because the USG again provided no evidence for a trial. Shortly thereafter, Al Zamel was interviewed by McClatchy News Service. He said he had been tortured. He was told by American soldiers that he would be rendered to Jordan, where he would be further tortured. He was threatened with dogs, beaten, stripped naked, sexually harassed and abused, kept in isolation, and subjected to extreme temperatures. "Everything you can think of," Adel Zamel told the reporter. When he denied being linked to Bin Laden, he was locked in a small hot metal box without toilet facilities. At one point, he told his interrogator "'I am Osama Bin Laden please kill me,' I just wanted it to end."[62]

It is difficult to know why Adel Zamel was released in 2005. Others with far thinner dossiers were held much longer. It is unlikely the DoD accepted his denials. But DoD would well have known about the threats and the torture, and it may be that the USG wanted to avoid the risk of proceedings in US courts, where it could be revealed in graphic detail to US judges that torture had been used to extract information.

Adel Zamel Al Zamel lives quietly today with his family in Kuwait.

Nasser Najiri Al Amutairi

Nasser Najiri Al Amutairi was twenty-two when he left Kuwait for Afghanistan in late 1999. He was handed over in Afghanistan to the United States by the Northern Alliance in February 2002 and brought to Guantanamo Bay. He spent nearly three years there and was the first of the Kuwaiti detainees to be repatriated in January 2005.

Nasser's story is an unusual one for a Guantanamo detainee. He was accused of going to Afghanistan to fight on behalf of the Taliban, not Al Qaida. At the time, the Taliban controlled the Afghan government and were engaged in a civil war with the Northern Alliance, led by two violent warlords who were former enemies – Ahmad Shah Massoud, an anti-Taliban leader from the Panjshir Valley known as the Lion of Panjshir, and Abdul Rashid Dostum, who headed the Tajik-, Turkmen-, and Uzbek-dominated Jamiat-e-Islami. Nasser, as well as many others, viewed Massoud and Dostum as war criminals; they (as well as the Taliban) had indeed committed many atrocities.

The records of his hearing reported that Nasser said he did not wish to fight offensively or to support the Taliban. He defined himself not as a "jihadi," fighting actively against invaders, but as a "rabati," an Arabic term that denotes holding a defensive line in a war zone. He said that "rabat" meant waiting; that it was a kind of guard duty to mass on the border and create disincentives for fighting. He believed this was an honorable, religiously recognized function and that he would be a martyr if he was killed in this activity. The term derives from ribāṭ, an Arabic term that referred to guard duty at a frontier outpost in order to defend dar al-Islam, the house of Islam.[63] The one who performs ribāt is called a murabit. A murabit can come and go from the war zone as he pleases without obligation. Nasser viewed himself as effectively an Islamic peacekeeper.

Nasser displayed little knowledge or sophistication with respect to regional dynamics. He said he did not know that the United States was aligned with the Northern Alliance against the Taliban and said he would not have been a murabit on the lines facing the Northern Alliance had he known this. He knew that the United States had liberated his country and he would not have knowingly put himself in a situation that was adverse to the United States.[64]

Nasser was reported to have admitted that he had basic training on the Kalashnikov rifle and other small arms, but he never had occasion to fire his weapons or use his two grenades. He handed over his weapons to Dostum's troops in Northern Afghanistan. He indicated that he did so on the promise of safe passage out of the country, which did not happen. He was taken to the Qala-e-Jenghi prison, in Northern Afghanistan, where he was shot during an uprising of POWs on his second day there. He tried to leave but was handed over by Dostum to the United States and then sent to Guantanamo as a purported Taliban fighter. After his release, he said that the transcript of his CSRT hearing did not accurately report what he had said to the panel.[65]

The DoD challenged his story regarding rabat and claimed that he actively supported the Taliban.[66] It disputed his claim of neutrality toward the United States because he wrote a letter home from Guantanamo in December 2003, asking his family to pray for the destruction of America.[67] He had been in US custody at that time and tortured for nearly two years. Despite admissions of being on the battlefield and having weapons training, he was the first Kuwaiti released, presumably because of his limited role and intelligence value, although the United States never provided any rationale for why he was the first Kuwaiti to go home. Unlike most of the others, he had actually been on a battlefield, albeit in an obscure and certainly low-level role.

Upon his return, Nasser was held in custody in Kuwait and charged at the request of the United States with working for a foreign country, committing an act of aggression against a foreign country and training in the use of arms. Again, the United States provided no evidence. In June 2005, he was acquitted.[68] Again, the United States indicated anger at the absence of a conviction.[69] The Defense Intelligence Agency and the State Department produced cables stating that his acquittal was reversed on appeal and he was sentenced to five years at hard labor.[70] It is unclear whether he ever served that sentence.

5 TWELVE MEN

Abdullah Saleh Al Ajmi

Abdullah Saleh Al Ajmi's story is tragic. He was one of the first detainees brought to Guantanamo and also, inexplicably, one of the first released. He was twenty-three when he was captured and he died in a suicide bombing just before his 30th birthday.

Abdullah Saleh' precise activities in Afghanistan and Pakistan remain not fully known, as he was alleged to have gone AWOL from the Kuwaiti army and spending eight months fighting with the Taliban against the Northern Alliance.[71] He was also alleged to have confessed to being a jihadi whose goal was to kill as many Americans as possible.[72] He was not viewed as having been part of Al Qaida prior to his detention.[73]

At his ARB hearing, his non-lawyer military representative reported these purported confessions to the Board, after having held a single ten-minute meeting with Abdullah Saleh.[74] At the hearing, Abdullah Saleh contradicted his own representative. He said that virtually none of this was accurate and that he had been tortured into making false admissions.[75]

Fellow detainees confirmed that Abdullah Saleh had been badly tortured and that, in their view, he had been broken by Guantanamo.[76] His private lawyer, Tom Wilner from Shearman & Sterling, initially had a cooperative and friendly relationship with Abdullah Saleh. Abdullah Saleh referred to himself as the "Happy Detainee" and wrote to Wilner, "Mr. Tom, I would like to tell you that I'm fine and so are all my brothers. I thank you, Mr. Tom, and I send you my closing greetings." Yet some months later, he wrote Wilner a letter showing anger and hostility toward the advocate to whom he had recently showed such gratitude: "Thomas, I shall meet you tomorrow and hit you with a sharp, two-edged sword that will tear you to pieces, and you will be thrown to the hyenas to feed on, maul and bite you." The letter concluded, "To the vile, depraved Thomas, descendant of rotten apes and swine, I greet you with a kick, a spit, and a slap on your lying, rotten, ugly, and sullen face. I hope that this letter finds you burning in hell and receiving a sound beating from men who are to be counted." He signed his letter "fiercely and harshly."[77]

Wilner shared the view of Abdullah Saleh's fellow detainees that Abdullah Saleh's sanity had been destroyed during his time at Guantanamo. Wilner said, "I really think he was probably nothing when he went to Guantanamo. I don't think he was an enemy or anything, but I think Guantanamo made him crazy, turned him absolutely crazy." Wilner reported that Abdullah Saleh told him a story "where he was hung up by his wrists and they were hitting and hitting him, saying 'Are you Al Qaida or Taliban?' 'Are you Al Qaida or Taliban?' He said 'I'm neither. I'm neither,' and they kept hitting him." Finally, Abdullah Saleh said "'OK, I'm Taliban' and they stopped." Abdullah Saleh said to his lawyer, "That was better than saying Al Qaida, wasn't it?" But, of course, there were no right answers in these interrogations.[78]

Yet Abdullah Saleh was released to Kuwait in November 2005, one of the early group released; he was viewed as having low intelligence value and presenting only "medium risk." He was then tried in Kuwait at the request of the USG, but again the United States failed to provide evidence, and he was acquitted and released.[79] Senior USG officials claimed afterward they were disappointed that Kuwait had released him after the acquittal rather than continue to detain him or, in any event, that they expected he would move on with his life, get a job, and settle down.[80] According to a report prepared by the Defense Intelligence Agency: "He was apparently living a productive life in Kuwait prior to his traveling to Iraq to be a suicide bomber. It is unknown what motivated him to leave Kuwait and go to Iraq. His family members were reportedly shocked to hear he had conducted a suicide bombing."[81]

This was passing the buck, as his deteriorated mental condition was well known to his captors when they released him. Khaled Al Odah told me that Abdullah Saleh's behavior when he returned home was erratic, veering between being withdrawn and quiet, punctuated with outbursts of tremendous anger.[82] Other people who knew him also described him as unstable when he returned home.[83] Fellow detainees with whom I spoke were shocked that Abdullah Saleh was released given his condition.[84]

Khalid Al Odah told me that when Abdullah Saleh got home, he insisted that he wanted the Kuwaiti government to return his passport, but the Kuwaiti government was apprehensive about his leaving Kuwait in view of his mental condition. Abdullah Saleh repeatedly pressured his local Member of Parliament, who was also a fellow member of the Al Ajmi tribe, to get him his passport. The passport was returned. His family also introduced him to a young woman in the hope that getting married would help him settle down. She became pregnant with Abdullah Saleh's child.[85]

A little more than two years after his release from Guantanamo Bay, with his wife eight months pregnant, Abdullah Saleh drove a truck laden with 5 to 10,000 pounds of explosives onto an army base outside Mosul, Iraq.[86] The *Washington Post* reported that thirteen Iraqi soldiers were killed.[87] Forty-two people were wounded, and the explosion left a thirty-foot-wide crater in the ground. He was the only Kuwaiti to have been released who returned to violence. He also committed the single greatest act of terror of any former Guantanamo detainee.

Abdullah Saleh's Brief Life Story

Abdullah Saleh was one of twenty children from his father's two marriages. He had eleven brothers and eight sisters. His father was a machine technician with the Kuwaiti national oil company. The family lived in a modest two-story stucco house on a quiet side street in Almadi, south of Kuwait City. Unlike some other detainees, his family's means were quite limited, especially with twenty children to support.

When Iraq invaded Kuwait, Abdullah Saleh fled with his family to Saudi Arabia, where they lived for two years. On returning to Kuwait, Abdullah Saleh dropped out of school at the age of fourteen and spent most of the next few years hanging out with his friends. "He was a quiet, peaceful and fun-loving kid," his elder brother Ahmed recalled.[88] At the age of nineteen, looking for some direction in his life, he joined the Kuwaiti army and obtained basic weapons training. He was assigned to the Prince's Guard, stationed in Subhan near Kuwait International Airport. He attended Subhan's main mosque, which was rumored to have been a center for radicalism, although the Kuwait Ministry of Islamic Affairs monitors closely for extremism.

In January 2001, Abdullah Saleh took a leave of absence from the army to travel to Pakistan. It was rumored that he was motivated by an internet fatwa from a Saudi sheik that called for jihad against the Russians in Chechnya, although it is unclear why he would go to Pakistan to get to Chechnya. After two weeks in Pakistan, he returned to Kuwait.

Two months later, he left again for Pakistan. It is unknown whether he was permitted leave by the army or left without permission. In his Administrative Review Board hearing, Abdullah Saleh indicated that he wanted to take a four-month leave to do charity work and he believed that he had accrued sufficient leave and vacation time and could get retroactive approval when he returned. He was never charged with being AWOL upon his return to Kuwait.[89]

Abdullah Saleh was rumored to have followed a different fatwa on this second trip, for Muslims to fight against the Northern Alliance, which was battling the Taliban. He denied ever fighting or intending to go to Pakistan to fight. He claimed he went to Pakistan to do charity work and promulgate his religion.[90]

One of Abdullah Saleh's brothers said that Abdullah Saleh told him that he was going for jihad. His brother also said that he went to the Subhan mosque after Abdullah Saleh left, where people there said that they had set Abdullah Saleh on the right path after he had indicated his desire to fight against the Northern Alliance. Abdullah Saleh called his mother when he left, who shouted at him not to go.

After arriving in Islamabad, according to the DoD, he took a bus to Peshawar and then on to Afghanistan, ending up in Bagram, then the front line between the Taliban and the Northern Alliance. Abdullah Saleh was alleged to have been issued an AK-47, ammunition, and two grenades, and assigned to a defensive position against the Northern Alliance. The Taliban allegedly burned his passport, the investigative summary alleges, and he was told he would be killed if he tried to leave. In the months he spent there, according to the summary, Abdullah Saleh "fired his weapon only one time when he heard movement one night near his position."[91]

When the Northern Alliance advanced on Kabul in November 2001, Abdullah Saleh was said to have been dispatched east to Jalalabad, where Afghans seized his weapons, according to the DoD summary. He was reported to have walked toward the Tora Bora mountains and crossed into Pakistan after two weeks, where Pakistani security forces arrested him and handed him over to the Americans. The investigative summary concedes that Abdullah Saleh "never met anyone with Al Qaida."[92]

Abdullah Saleh was among the first wave of terrorism suspects to be sent to Guantanamo, arriving in mid-January 2002. He was kept outdoors at Camp X-Ray, besieged like all the others by insects, snakes, crabs, and rats. He told his lawyers afterward that he was frequently kept naked in his cage.

Abdullah Saleh was not allowed to meet with a lawyer until 2004. When he met Tom Wilner, who described him in the initial meeting as "polite and reserved," Abdullah Saleh expressed gratitude for the team's work on his behalf and he asked about his family. He described his mistreatment.

The guard who escorted Tom Wilner told him Abdullah Saleh was a "behavior issue." Abdullah Saleh appeared for his meeting with Wilner in orange shorts with fresh scabs on his knees as if he had been dragged on the pavement. He did not want to discuss what had happened but said that the guards "had defamed Islam." One of the other Kuwaiti detainees told Wilner that Abdullah Saleh's Quran and his blanket had been removed because of purported misbehavior.[93]

Abdullah Saleh described his ongoing treatment:

> Sometimes the guards turn the temperature so hot that you cannot wear a shirt. Sometimes they turn it so cold that is like the North Pole and they take your blanket away. At the beginning I was very badly beaten by U.S. soldiers and guards.... But the worst torture to me is that the guards make fun of my religion and dishonor the Quran.[94]

In a meeting two weeks later with Wilner, Abdullah Saleh told him that he and all his fellow detainees had been tortured at Guantanamo. His whole story to the DoD and the CSRT – that he had been on the front lines with the Taliban facing the Northern Alliance – was false and coerced through torture. "My whole story is made up," he said. "I didn't carry weapons. I didn't fight. I was not a member of the Taliban or Al Qaida." Abdullah Saleh said that he had told US interrogators at the detention center in Kandahar that he had fought with the Taliban because the guards "were beating the hell out of me." Abdullah Saleh explained, "I wanted it to stop," he said. "I told them what they wanted to hear."[95]

Wilner advised him to tell the truth to the Administrative Review Board, even if it meant contradicting earlier statements. Abdullah Saleh struck his counsel "as one of the least dangerous people at Gitmo. He just seemed like a kid who was lost."[96] Abdullah Al Saleh tried to tell his story against the backdrop of his own representative stating otherwise:

> *Assisting Military Officer*: In August of 2004, Al Ajmi wanted to make sure that when the case went in front of the tribunal, that the tribunal members know that he is now a jihadist, an enemy combatant and that he would kill as many Americans as he possible [sic] can.
> *Detainee*: That is impossible that I would say such a thing. How could I fight the Americans? They were with me in the military in Kuwait. I would've fought them in Kuwait, not here....[97]

Abdullah Saleh was not a cooperative prisoner. In 2004, he was praying and failed to obey a guard's order. He was IRFed. A team of six to eight armed soldiers walking shoulder to shoulder smashed into his cell, pinned him face down to the concrete floor, and then dragged him still face down, into solitary confinement. Abdullah Saleh had his arm broken during this IRFing.[98] By May 2005, Abdullah Saleh was in trouble again. In a scene reminiscent of the film *Life Is Beautiful*, he said that he grabbed a guard's microphone tied into the camp's public-address system. "This is General Al Ajmi and I'm in control now," he announced. "Everyone is going free."[99]

The GTMO security establishment was not amused. He was sent to an isolation cell. He lost access to books, to pen and paper and to his blanket. He told his lawyers that he was being forced to take medication. If he didn't swallow the pills, he'd be punished. "I feel like I'm falling off a cliff," he told a member of his legal team.[100] Abdullah Saleh became more combative. His lawyers saw him only behind a plexiglass screen. Guards told the lawyers that their client had developed a propensity for hurling his feces and urine, a "splasher" in the terminology of the GTMO guards.[101]

The United States broke Abdullah Saleh down, and then when they could not control him, it is a fair inference that it wanted to get rid of him. And it did. He became someone else's problem, so that the United States could then disingenuously claim surprise when he became a suicide bomber. The intelligence agencies did a lot of speculation after the fact. They tried to assess when he became "a hard-core jihadist."[102] Was he misled by preachers? Was it in Afghanistan that he was radicalized? Was it after he came home? Yet all the evidence points to a man destroyed psychologically by torture and his ordeal at Guantanamo. This was a theory that the United States would not accept.

In October 2005, the legal team finally came bearing good news – he was being released. Abdullah Saleh responded by cursing viciously at his attorney.[103] The decision to release Abdullah Saleh surprised everyone. The US military has never explained why Abdullah Saleh and four other Kuwaitis were freed, and why six others were still held, including two who were kept for more than an additional decade. On November 3, 2005, Abdullah Saleh and four other men were handed over to Kuwaiti security agents for the fourteen-hour flight home. Less than three years later, he committed a terrible crime and he was dead.

In interviews, former detainees condemn Abdullah Saleh's actions. They were tragic and wrong; they also hurt the prospects for freedom of every other detainee. But detainees who spoke about Abdullah Saleh believed he had not been a terrorist before he was sent to Guantanamo and that his treatment by Americans made him crazy. Abdullah Kamel Al Kandari and Abdulaziz Al Shammeri were imprisoned with Abdullah Saleh in Kohat prison in Pakistan before being transferred to US custody. He was normal then, they said, but Abdullah Kamel relates that "in Guantanamo he had been tortured too much and he said that [he would] get revenge ... in front of me he would tell [US forces] when I get out, I will make double bomb. I will kill you ... and they release him."[104] According to his lawyer, "he had gone crazy."[105]

In his suicide video, Abdullah Saleh described the Americans' desecration of the Quran and maltreatment of detainees. He said that detainees were beaten, given drugs, and used "for experiments." "The Americans delighted in insulting our prayer and Islam, and they insulted the Quran and threw it in dirty places," he said. He came to Guantanamo as a man with minimal or no experience in combat or any sort of leader, as having anything to do with Al Qaida, as having no apparent fixed sympathies or support for terrorism. He left a disturbed, angry, and vengeful person. His own captors failed to see it or chose to ignore it and appeared to try to push the problem down the road and make it someone else's. It ended in needless mass murder. Al Zamel, who shared a cell with Abdullah Saleh when they were repatriated to Kuwait and held while being investigated, said Abdullah Saleh was always plotting, for no reason, to attack the guards in the Kuwaiti jail. Al Zamel told me simply "Al Ajmi, he was like really nuts."[106]

Abdullah Saleh's suicide bombing was by no means the only incident of Guantanamo detainees being driven to attempt suicide. The DoD stopped recording suicide attempts in 2002 and instead reported "self-injurious behavior." Twenty-three detainees attempted a mass suicide in 2003.[107] In 2005, the US military revealed that in that year, there were 350 incidents of "self-harm." On June 10, 2006, the DoD announced that three prisoners had taken their own lives. Later reports criticized the government's reporting of the 2006 suicides; reporting based on interviews with Guantanamo guards stated that the DoD had initiated a cover-up, and some of these deaths were the result of death under torture. DoD has denied these allegations. Since June 2006, DoD has announced three additional detainee suicides at Guantanamo.[108]

The Consequences of Torture

Different individuals react differently to torture, abuse, and deprivation. Abdullah Saleh's deterioration was extreme. He continued to be uncooperative, which led to continued harsh treatment and solitary confinement. He was thus deprived of the companionship and support of his fellow detainees, support which so many detainees said was the only thing that kept them going. Wilner said, "Guantanamo took a kid – a kid who wasn't all that bad – and it turned him into a hostile, hardened individual."[109]

While his attitude toward personnel should not have had any impact on whether Abdullah Saleh's claims of innocence of terrorism were true or not, the military authorities seemed convinced that he was a terrorist, and they viewed his angry behavior as confirming their initial supposition. The "confessions" extracted through torture were accepted, and his testimony at the hearing that his previous statements were coerced was rejected.[110] The Administrative Review Board declared him to be an enemy combatant in late October 2004, but nevertheless recommended his transfer with continued detention elsewhere. They did not want to deal with the consequences of their actions.

Mohammed Al Daihani

Mohammed Al Daihani was also released in the group of five in November 2005, after spending more than three and a half years at Guantanamo. He was well educated, with an accounting degree from Kuwait University in 1989. He worked for the Finance Ministry from 1991 through 2001. Married with six children, he was thirty-six at the time of his capture. Mohammed was well known in Kuwait for his commitment to philanthropy, including his support of the Revival of Islamic Heritage Society and the Sanabel Charitable Committee. The Revival of Islamic Heritage Society executed contracts with donors for specific charitable projects and sent updates and photos of the projects. The Sanabel Charitable Committee, based in London, had been recommended to him by a member of the Committee. The Sanabel Charitable Committee was less formalized than Revival of Islamic Heritage, and Mohamed said he wanted to check that his donations were being properly used. He decided to visit the projects he supported he supported at the end of his annual summer vacation in 2001.[111]

Mohamed had never been to Afghanistan before seeking formal leave from the Finance Ministry for the visit. Mohammed flew to Karachi, was met by Sanabel representatives, and then flew to Quetta in northwestern Pakistan, crossing the border into Afghanistan on September 9, 2001. He was traveling on an official Kuwaiti passport, obtained through his position at the Ministry. He promptly came down with a serious gastrointestinal ailment in Kandahar and spent time in the hospital. By the time, he was released, 9/11 had occurred, and he called his family and told them he would try to get home as soon as possible. He requested that they ask the Ministry of Finance to extend his leave for another three weeks. Mohammed tried to get help from Sanabel, visited its Kabul office, and tried to escape across the Iran border but could not. He then went the other way and crossed into Pakistan in December 2001, after paying off some local tribal men.¹¹² Again, he was handed over to the Pakistan military, asked to be taken to his Embassy, was assured he would be, and then transferred to the custody of the United States. Mohammed is also quite sure he was sold for a bounty. He arrived at Guantanamo in May 2002, after more than four months in US custody in Afghanistan.

Mohammed was repeatedly asked during interrogations to explain what he was doing in Afghanistan. He readily admitted that he had contributed approximately $2,250 to the Revival of Islamic Heritage branch in Kuwait. He also contributed approximately $450 to the Sanabel Committee. When he was finally advised of the charges against him by the CSRT, he was stunned to learn that he was accused of being employed by the Revival of Islamic Heritage Society and that the Revival of Islamic Heritage Society in Afghanistan was listed as a terrorist organization. Sanabel was also listed as a terrorist organization; Sanabel was viewed by the government as a fundraising front for the Libyan Islamic Fighting Group, also listed as a terrorist organization.¹¹³

Mohamed was viewed by the USG as someone who could provide information on transactions of the Al Qaida network, as well as Al Qaida front NGOs and their plans for funding future terrorist organizations. He was assessed as a financial facilitator of terrorist activity, of high intelligence value and at high risk of taking actions against the United States.¹¹⁴

In preparation for the hearing, Mohammed submitted extensive documentation. Much of it was from family members in the usual format, discussing how much they missed him, needed his financial support, and describing how gentle and peaceful he was. These generalized statements were uniformly ignored by the DoD. But unlike others, Mohammed also sent letters from his Member of Parliament, as well as from co-workers and supervisors at the Kuwaiti Ministry of Finance.

Mohamed also submitted a Memorandum from the Legal Advisor for the Combatant Status Review Tribunals, who stated that "the facts of this case probe the outer limits of the definition of combatant."¹¹⁵ Yet the CSRT panel, despite the broad bureaucratic hint that the factual case was weak, classified him as an enemy combatant. An Administrative Review Board hearing held the next year made clear that the evidence against Mohammed was not only thin; it was fundamentally wrong.

First, the letters from his Member of Parliament and his employer particularized his long and extensive work doing charity for the poor in Kuwait. His Member of Parliament also attested that Mohammed consulted with him on solving social welfare problems and that Mohammed "has not any abnormal or backward ideas." Unless the United States wanted to assume that this Member of Parliament was either lying or in cahoots with terrorist activity, this was difficult evidence to ignore.

Mohammed could also document his activity in relief operations when there was flooding in Kuwait in 1997 and his numerous donations for relief around the world. He had donated to build a farm and support orphans in Indonesia, to dig wells in the Philippines, and to construct mosques in Indonesia, Benin, and the Philippines. He had the documentation to show that these were specific and targeted contributions through the Revival of Islamic Heritage Society. He responded to the summary of evidence by describing why it was wrong in every material respect:

> I know the Revival of Islamic Heritage Society; it is an official society from the Kuwaiti government. And it doesn't have any problems inside Kuwait or outside Kuwait. And more than a third of the Kuwaiti people donate to it. Its charity work is all over the world, even in America. But I donated to them. I did not work there. I donated. But I donated to it for some charity work. Maybe my last donation was at the end of the nineties, maybe '94. And this Revival of Islamic Heritage Society, donations to it are official, there's paperwork and documentation and it is watched by the Kuwaiti government. My last donation to it was about '94 to '95. But I am surprised that the accusation here is that I worked in it. I did not work in it. I am a government employee. I am also surprised that this society is considered a terrorist organization. Even though I remember that when I left Kuwait, I didn't hear anything about it being a terrorist organization or anything. To summarize I do not work there. And I donated to it a long time ago about 6 years before the events of September 11th. So if it was classified after September 11, I was in Afghanistan, so how can I be judged about something like that?[116]

Mohammed was accurate on all counts. The Revival of Islamic Heritage Society was an approved organization and licensed by Kuwait. Two branches outside Kuwait had been designated by the United States, but none of its operations in Kuwait was ever subject to sanctions or closure. And these two branches – in Pakistan and Afghanistan – were listed on January 9, 2002, when Mohammed was already in custody.

The situation with Sanabel was similar. Mohammed indicated that he made agreements for specific projects – building five wells in Afghanistan. He was not sent a formal agreement or updates, so he went to check that the projects were real and his money was being properly spent. He was told at the time that, although there were disturbances in the North, the cities and environs in Afghanistan were quiet and he would not be at risk for his personal safety.

Mohammed's understanding was that Sanabel was a charitable organization based in London, which was correct. He never had any information that Sanabel was a front for the Libyan Islamic Fighting Group – as the United States alleged, and he said he had never heard of it. (And the Libyan Islamic Fighting Group, for which Sanabel was allegedly a secret front, was not listed until December 17, 2004, in the United States and October 2005 in the UK.)[117] In any event, Sanabel has never been listed as linked to the Libyan Islamic Fighting Group.

Nevertheless, this philanthropic government accountant spent more than three and a half years subject to abuse based on allegations that were facially flawed. Mohammed afterward described his ordeal to the *New York Times* a year after his release. "Those blocks are designed so that you will not rest. There is metal everywhere. If anyone drops anything, you hear it. If anyone shouts or talks loudly, it disturbs everyone. If there is a problem at the other end of the block, you cannot possibly rest. After two or three weeks, you think you will lose your mind."[118]

Saad Al Azmi

Saad Al Azmi's story remains confused, and he has given contradictory accounts of what happened to him. He was twenty-two and unemployed when he left Kuwait to go to Afghanistan in 2001. He told the Combatant Status Review Tribunal that he was going to see his friend Adel Al Zamel, a fellow Kuwaiti and later a fellow detainee.[119] He stayed with Al Zamel for a brief time in Kabul and was able to get to Peshawar in Pakistan about a month after September 11, where he remained for about two months, before going to Karachi in December of 2001, again allegedly to meet up with Al Zamel. He was arrested by Pakistani intelligence authorities in Karachi and then handed over to the United States, which sent him back to Afghanistan, first to Kandahar and then to Bagram, where he was beaten and tortured. He arrived at Guantanamo in May 2002.

Saad was accused by the DoD of being an extremist, part of the "Takfir 7," the alleged extremist religious group in Kuwait. It is the same group that confronted a woman in Kuwait whom they viewed as behaving immodestly. Saad made clear in his CSRT hearing that there was no organized group called the Takfir 7; there were not even seven people involved in this incident. There were six; he denied there was any assault, and Saad was in any event acquitted of all charges.[120] These self-appointed morality police certainly behaved appallingly, but it was hardly an organized extremist group. DoD claimed in its Summary of Evidence that Saad was wanted in Kuwait at the time of his arrest in connection with the assault. He was not.

Saad was also alleged by the DoD as being part of Al Wafa, the Afghan charity, and part of Al Qaida. He was said to be with other Al Qaida members when he was arrested at a known Al Qaida safehouse in Karachi. An Al Qaida facilitator known as Riyadh the Facilitator was purported to be at the safe house where he was arrested. Saad's story that he had traveled to Germany and Switzerland to buy and then resell used cars was viewed as a common Al Qaida cover story and viewed as evidence of Al Qaida affiliation. The United States did not consider that this was a common way for people to make money traveling between Europe or the Gulf and South Asia, where used vehicles were in great demand because new vehicles were highly taxed.

Saad also had $6,000 in his possession, which the United States inferred he wanted to use for extremist activity. The United States viewed Saad as of high intelligence value and a high security risk.[121] The CSRT and the ARB said he should continue to be detained in 2004.[122] By November 2005, however, he was on his way home.

Saad had limited patience with the detention authorities. He explained to the CSRT he had never worked for Al Wafa. He said that he was in Karachi because that was where Adel Al Zamel was, whom he knew, and he did not know anyone else at the alleged safe house. He denied being trained at Al Farouq Training Camp, a well-known Al Qaida facility, as the USG alleged; and he denied being a member of Al Qaida.[123] After laying this out for the CSRT, he did not see any reason to cooperate further in repeating his story to the ARB, and he did not. When he was asked during his tribunal hearing whether he would take an oath to speak the truth, Saad replied: "If the court would prove me innocent, I am willing to swear." The tribunal would make no such promises and Saad declined to take the oath.[124]

Saad was one of many detainees whose cooperation with the various proceedings was limited or withheld. The hearings took place relatively close in time and largely overlapped in substance. The CSRTs and ARBs were believed by detainees to be designed to gain admissions from them that would be used to justify their continued detention. They also believed, correctly, that they were unlikely to result in releases.

At the ARB, while Saad declined to participate, his lawyers put a series of letters into the record from his parents, his siblings, and his Member of Parliament. Again, these materials did not address the specific charges or the specifics of his movements, his actions, or his beliefs; they spoke generally of his kindness, and generous nature, and his good reputation in Kuwait. His family wrote that he had relatives who were aged or dying. Also in this package, somewhat incongruously, were three copies of instructions to paint a certain office in Kuwait and the rent and insurance details for that office. The USG could not figure out why this material was included in the legal submission. Saad's military representative told the Administrative Review Board that it was unlikely that his lawyers would have submitted this material in error:

> A global law firm of the stature of Shearman Sterling represented by Mr. Koslowe a Harvard Law School graduate, seems pretty interesting to me that three copies of that would be submitted with the package. If you look closely it is page 21 of 31, there's nothing in here that is really a contract. There is no date on it. There's no reference to who is going to do the paint job and when it's going to be painted. It doesn't talk about the price of the paint job. It talks about how much the guy pays in rent, it's around $1,750 a month. It talks about how the insurance is going to expire in three months. What relevance that to do with a painter or painting company ... I can't imagine. Plus it is confusing too because it talks about painting the inside of office number six and painting the outside as well. This building has at least six offices and it's curious that they would ask him to paint, to specify paint the outside of the building and paint the inside of the building. The bottom line for me is it is not a contract; this maybe an attempt at some kind of communication with the Detainee
> Presiding Officer: OK
> Assisting Military Officer That it was submitted three times ... exact duplicates ... may be some significance to that.

It was a clerical mistake that these specifications for a random paint job were included in the filing, and the material was entirely extraneous. But the DoD found sinister overtones even in this innocuous administrative error.

The tribunal's three military officers decided that Saad was an enemy combatant who had been involved with an extremist group in Kuwait that supported Al Qaida and had worked for three months in Afghanistan for a group that purports to be a charity but is really a terrorist organization. It did not comment on the paint job.

After coming home, Saad sat for a long interview with a reporter from McClatchy News Service. Some of his story overlapped with what he had told the CSRT and the materials submitted on his behalf. Large parts did not. He told the McClatchy reporter that he'd never been to Afghanistan, yet he had told a panel of tribunal military officers at Guantanamo that he had traveled there for three weeks before returning to Peshawar in Pakistan in October 2001.

Saad also told McClatchy a detailed story about how he was arrested in his hotel room in Peshawar during a routine police check of guests' passports in August 2001. His visa had expired three days earlier. The police, he said, told him they'd have to take him for questioning. The police took him to the local jail and questioned him: "Why was he in Pakistan? Why had he traveled there before?"[125] "I told them I was a trader," Saad said. He said he suspected that their real interest was the money he'd brought with him. "After a few days, one of the police officers called me in from my cell and asked for a bribe," Saad reported. "I refused to pay it."

It is certainly possible that Saad was arrested in Peshawar in August 2001 and then released only to be rearrested in December or January in Karachi. It is certainly possible as well that Saad would have been solicited for a bribe and declined to pay it. But the Peshawar arrest was never mentioned by Saad in any proceeding prior to his release.

Saad also told McClatchy that he was sent by the police in Peshawar to a jail in Karachi, although he never mentioned a police transfer to the tribunal and indicated he had traveled to Karachi on his own after spending a month in Afghanistan and a month in Peshawar.[126] Saad told the McClatchy reporter that he was put in a cell in Karachi with about two dozen other men. He said they were taken out one-by-one to an interrogation room where two American men – one tall and thin, one short and stocky with glasses – sat behind a table. He said they introduced themselves as CIA officers. There is little doubt that he would have been interrogated after his arrest in Karachi, although it is unlikely that his interrogators would have introduced themselves as CIA officers or indeed introduced themselves at all. From their questions, Saad said, it was clear that they thought he was associated with Al Qaida. He pleaded with them to understand, he said, that he was just a businessman who'd made the mistake of not paying off a corrupt Pakistani cop.[127] But, again, at Guantanamo, he never told a tribunal about any shakedown by the Pakistani police when such a version of events would have been helpful to his case.

Saad told the reporter he spent about a month in the Karachi jail and was interrogated three or four more times. After that the US military flew him, shackled, and blindfolded, to a detention facility at Kandahar. After two weeks at Kandahar – during which American troops punched, kicked, and humiliated him, Saad said – he was flown to Bagram and kept there for a month and a half. The Americans transferred him back to Kandahar for about three more months before he was flown to Guantanamo, where he was held for about three and a half years.[128]

What was Saad's real story? Was it the one he told the USG or his family, or reporters afterward, or something else entirely? The USG found him to be a serious threat, a member of Al Qaida, affiliated with what it viewed as an Al Qaida front charity and found him at a Karachi guest house that it alleged was filled with senior Al Qaida officials. Yet he was one of the first to go back to Kuwait.

If the US believed the charges, then he was among the most culpable of the detainees, far more than other Kuwaitis who languished for years. If they did not, then their findings appear to be pretextual. The United States apparently made a decision that most of the men who had been around Al Wafa Charity were to be officially declared to be highly dangerous and Al Qaida-affiliated, yet should nevertheless go home very soon after these decisions were made. They would throw the ball into Kuwait's court.

Perhaps, the United States expected that Kuwait would follow the pattern of the Guantanamo hearings – convictions without evidence in the interest of accommodating a panicked ally. Kuwait's failure to throw people in jail solely because the United States said so caused significant friction between the two countries. It appears that these acquittals were factors in the detention for another decade of Fawzi Al Odah and Fayiz Al Kandari on charges that, even if true, were of lesser gravity than those of the five detainees released in 2005.

Fawzi Al Odah and Fayiz Al Kandari: Forever Prisoners?

By the end of 2006, all but four Kuwaitis had returned to Kuwait. In 2009, two more detainees, Khalid Al Mutairi and Fouad Al Rabiah, who had won their habeas proceedings (discussed in Chapter 7), were sent home. And then ... nothing.

Incoming President Obama had promised to close Guantanamo. Yet Obama also indicated there may be "forever prisoners," detainees who could not be charged and who would never be sent home. Fawzi Al Odah and Fayiz Al Kandari were still at Guantanamo. Were they to be forever prisoners? And if so, why?

Their stories were little different from their ten countrymen who had gone home. Because they remained so much longer than the others and because their histories were explored so much more deeply in their habeas corpus and Periodic Review Board (PRB) hearings (and I represented them before the PRB), the more detailed stories of their roads from Kuwait to Afghanistan to Guantanamo to ultimate release will be told in separate chapters. This chapter will present only a brief overview of their background, their initial capture, and the dossiers compiled against them by the DoD. Later chapters will discuss their habeas proceedings, which they lost, and their PRB hearings, which Fawzi won on his first time through the process, and which Fayiz lost the first time and won the second.

Fawzi Al Odah

Fawzi Al Odah's father was, of course, head of the Family Committee and had been vocal in making the case globally that all the detainees should be released. He was a regular protester in front of the US Embassy (second from left in photo below) (Figure 5.1).

Was Fawzi being held to indicate the United States' displeasure with the campaign by the Family Committee? Fawzi was also the lead plaintiff in two successful cases in the Supreme Court. Was the US retaliating for his advocacy? And he was oppositional at Guantanamo, a "splasher" and a leader of hunger strikes. Was that the reason that he continued to be held? He had lost his habeas case. Were all such detainees destined to be "forever prisoners?" Or was there something else that kept him incarcerated at Guantanamo Bay for nearly a decade more than his fellow Kuwaitis?

Fawzi's history was unremarkable for a Kuwaiti detainee, other than his long and positive connections with the United States. Born in 1977 in Kuwait City, Fawzi grew up in a close-knit, prosperous family. At the age of five, Fawzi traveled to the United States with his father as part of his father's pilot training. At the age of twelve, he traveled with his mother to visit his grandmother, who was being treated for cancer in Houston.

Fawzi graduated from high school and received a Bachelor's degree in Islamic Studies from the University of Kuwait in 1998. He worked for the Kuwaiti government in a number of positions with the Alms and Charities Agency, under the Ministry of Waqfs (religious endowments). He then went to work for a charitable NGO, Bayt Al Zakat, as a case worker for people in financial distress, and then as an Islamic studies teacher at the Farwaniyah School. He taught inmates at Kuwait Central Prison where, more than a decade later, he would spend a year at the rehabilitation facility on the prison grounds.[129]

Throughout this time, Fawzi lived at home with his parents and his four brothers and sisters. In August or early September 2001, he traveled to Afghanistan to distribute humanitarian aid and teach the Quran to young people. He brought approximately $5,500 in various currencies with him. These were savings from work that he intended to use as part of his

Figure 5.1 US Embassy Protest by Kuwait Family Committee Led by Khalid Al Odah.

charitable mission, which he expected to last for around two months. He traveled through Dubai to Karachi and then to Quetta where he crossed the border to Spin Boldak in Afghanistan. At a mosque in Spin Boldak, Fawzi met an Afghan who spoke Arabic named Abu Jarrah, who guided Fawzi to schools and needy families in the region. Fawzi began teaching in Spin Boldak and then went with Abu Jarrah to Kandahar, where he arrived on September 10, 2001. He rented a room and stayed for two weeks.

During his first CSRT reviews, in March 2006 and February 2007, he was designated as an enemy combatant, but the basis for his designation, while inaccurate in a number of its details, was relatively anodyne for a CSRT evaluation. The USG noted that he had traveled to Afghanistan before September 11, did charity work and religious teaching, tried to escape, and was captured along with others, some of whom were Al Qaida fighters, on the Pakistani border. According to the DoD, Fawzi went to a small camp outside Kandahar where he fired an AK-47 a few times but did not receive combat training. After September 11, Fawzi wanted to stay in a quiet place away from major cities, and he went to Logar Province, a rural river valley in Western Afghanistan.[130]

After the US bombing began, Fawzi tried to get out of Afghanistan and back to Kuwait. He went to Jalalabad and then joined a group of men heading for the Pakistani border. He was given a Kalashnikov, just as the others with whom he was trying to escape. After the group was targeted by US strikes, he split off with a smaller group of twelve men and spent five days in the mountains before crossing the Pakistan border, where he was brought to the same mosque and captured on December 18, 2001. He laid his Kalashnikov down as he surrendered to Pakistani border guards. He was transferred to US control on January 2, 2002, and arrived at Guantanamo around six weeks later, on February 13, 2002, where he was held initially at Camp X-Ray.

This first evaluation was probably the mildest of the Kuwaiti detainees. There was no apparent dispute that his objective was to do charitable work and he did it. He spent one day shooting a gun. He carried a weapon during his trek to the border; there was no evidence he used it and he handed it over.

Fawzi's January 2008 Detainee Assessment, however, was wholly different. Fawzi was now, after six years in custody, assessed as "High Risk" and of "High Intelligence Value." In this assessment, he was assessed to be a member of Al Qaida, and he is reported to have sworn bayat – a personal oath of loyalty – to Bin Laden. He was said to have been a member of a "London-based Al Qaida cell" in 1998. Seven other detainees, virtually all of them previously released, had been identified as part of this London Al Qaida cell. He was also identified as an "associate of UBL [Bin Laden] and Suleiman Abu Ghayth," purportedly by Kuwaiti security services. He was assessed to be "an extremist recruiter and courier and participated in hostilities against US and Coalition forces."

Rather than being a young man who once fired a weapon, he was instead assessed as having "attended militant training at Al Qaida and Lakshmi al Taiba (an extremist Pakistani organization) camps in Afghanistan and Pakistan" and was identified "as receiving suicide training." He was also said to have connections to extremist-affiliated NGOs and had received "coded communications from a transferred detainee." He was accused of having preached extremist religious views in Kuwaiti prisons and to have confirmed this to US authorities. It was claimed he had personally advised Bin Laden to escape US bombings in Jalalabad. The report said he was the last person to have spoken to Bin Laden by radio in the Tora Bora mountains.[131]

Fawzi was further identified as a close associate of an intended September 11 hijacker, Muhammad al-Qahtani. He was accused of having assisted in the distribution of jihadi videos in Kuwait urging men to fight in Bosnia and Chechnya. And while Fawzi had admitted that he had worked for a Kuwaiti charity in Kuwait, the United States put a more ominous construction on this charitable work: "Although not designated as a terrorist support entity, an intelligence assessment on the terrorist environment in Kosovo noted the Bayt Al Zakat [the Kuwaiti charity] fell under the umbrella of the Kuwaiti Joint Relief Committee (KJRC)." Trips Fawzi had taken with his family as a young teenager also took on a suspicious cast: "Detainee has an extensive history as a jihadist as evident in his presence with other mujahideen in Bosnia as a teenager."

All of this new inculpatory material was inaccurate with much of it bordering on ludicrous. He had never met or spoken to Osama Bin Laden let alone swore bayat. Again, it is not credible to think that a young Kuwaiti who had just arrived in Afghanistan for the first time a few weeks before would straightaway be giving advice of any sort to Bin Laden, let alone security advice.

Unlike at least two other released Kuwaiti detainees, Fawzi did not know Suleiman Al Ghaith, later the Al Qaida spokesman; their only connection was shared Kuwaiti nationality. He had never met al-Qahtani prior to Guantanamo, and the USG later conceded in any event that al-Qahtani was not a prospective hijacker and had nothing to do with September 11. Fawzi had preached in Kuwaiti prisons after he received his degree in 1998, but never called for anyone to fight in Bosnia. In any event, the Bosnian war was over by 1995. While Suleiman Abu Ghaith also preached in Kuwaiti prisons, there was no evidence that they overlapped in the same time period or at the same prison or ever met. There was no evidence from Kuwaiti security services making any allegations at all. The Kuwaiti security services evaluated Fawzi as not being a security threat.

As for Fawzi visiting Bosnia as a teenager, Fawzi's father, like many others from the Gulf, had long owned real estate in multiethnic Sarajevo (he still travels there regularly) and the family often vacationed there to escape the summer heat in Kuwait.[132] Fawzi did not receive suicide bomber training or any other training; he had fired a gun once. As for the purported London cell, whether there was a London-based cell or not, Fawzi had last been in London with his family on vacation when he was ten years old.

How did Fawzi go in less than a year from a young man who was assessed to have taken a brief leave to go to Afghanistan in 2001 to preach the Quran to someone assessed as a dangerous close colleague of Bin Laden, precocious terrorist operative, and potential suicide bomber? There are two keys to this inexplicable reversal in the Detainee Assessment. The most serious material against Fawzi and many others came from detainee informants.

As discussed earlier, there were a few specific detainees who appear in assessment after assessment as the source of information that is as damning as it is improbable. The jailhouse snitches and the US interrogators created terrorists and, from 2007 to 2008; they made one of Fawzi Al Odah. There can be little doubt that these informants did not randomly select certain detainees to implicate in terrorism. It seems reasonably likely that they were asked by US interrogators about certain detainees to obtain information from these reliably unreliable informants.

But why Fawzi? It is difficult to know for certain other than the fact that Fawzi was a noncompliant and uncooperative detainee. The Detainee Assessment stated: "Detainee has repeatedly refused to answer questions or talk to interrogators and has not revealed his training or associates in Afghanistan or his travel to Bosnia. Detainee has provided contradictory information or omitted key details of his extremist activities. While in detention, detainee has made statements that illustrate hostile intentions towards the US."[133]

It is difficult to reveal things that did not happen or to provide details about illusory activities. There is no doubt as well that Fawzi did feel a great deal of anger about being detained for six years and interrogated harshly about involvement in activities that were completely incredible from his perspective. And living under the uncertainty and brutality of his incarceration in Guantanamo certainly did not make him more compliant. The Detainee Assessment added:

> Detainee's overall behavior has been noncompliant and hostile to the guard force and staff. Detainee currently has 109 Reports of Disciplinary Infraction listed in DIMS with the most recent occurring on 13 December 2007, when he failed to give up his water bottle during afternoon meal trash pickup. Detainee has 13 Reports of Disciplinary Infraction for assault with the most recent occurring on 28 September 2007, when he initiated self-harm by scratching his lips causing his gums to bleed. Other incidents for which the detainee has been disciplined include inciting and participating in mass disturbances, failure to follow instructions and camp rules, damage to government property, provoking words and gestures, and possession of food and both weapon and non-weapon type contraband. On 24 July 2007, detainee was in possession of a razor hidden in his habeas mail. In 2006, detainee had a total of 12 Reports of Disciplinary Infraction and 63 so far in 2007.[134]

No, Fawzi was not a model prisoner. He was an angry prisoner. And attempts at self-harm did not distinguish him; as noted earlier, more than 350 incidents of detainee self-harm were recorded in one year alone. But being a disciplinary problem in 2006 and 2007 after five years of a Kafkaesque ordeal with no end in sight does not make someone a terrorist years before.

Fayiz Al Kandari

Fayiz Al Kandari, the last detainee to leave, was viewed by the USG as the Kuwaiti detainee most directly involved with Al Qaida. He and Fouad Al Rabiah were the only Kuwaiti detainees formally referred for trial by military commission. Charges against Fayiz were put forward in October 2008, with additional charges proffered in December 2008. He was charged with material assistance to terrorism and conspiracy. The charges permitted life in prison upon conviction or even death if he was convicted of acts in which people were killed. The military commission charges echoed earlier charges against Fayiz that arose in the CSRT and ARB proceedings. He was alleged to have provided support and resources to Al Qaida that included recruiting personnel to join the group, expert advice, assistance, and training. At various times, he was alleged to be a confidante of Osama Bin Laden, as well as his legal advisor, spiritual advisor, and close friend.[135] The charges were dropped without explanation in 2012, but Fayiz remained as an uncharged detainee and a prime candidate to become a "forever prisoner."

He was assessed "to have numerous connections to senior Al Qaida members and to have been an influential religious figure for Al Qaida fighters in Afghanistan. Detainee also provided ideological training to Al Qaida trainees at the al-Farouq Training Camp and the Islamic Institute in Kandahar."[136]

The government claimed he conspired directly to commit acts of terrorism with Bin Laden. He was also viewed as a leader of a Tabligh group in Kuwait, which the United States labelled a "Mujahideen Group." He was linked to the Al Wafa charity. These accusations spanned the entire spectrum of informant tips.

The DoD claimed that Fayiz had fought against the United States on the side of Al Qaida, during his single trip to Afghanistan from August 2001 to September 2001. He was suspected of having known about September 11 in advance. He was said to have produced and distributed audio tapes, videos, and flyers to recruit jihadis to fight in Afghanistan and to join Al Qaida. It was also recorded that he had been arrested and imprisoned in the UAE for advocating jihad. While in Afghanistan, the dossier stated, he was both a religious and military leader within Al Qaida and the Taliban: "The detainee frequently gave speeches to the recruits at the al Qaida training camps in Afghanistan, and to al Qaida and Taliban fighters in Afghanistan. The speeches were designed to encourage the students and the fighters in pursuing Jihad and to build their confidence and conviction in their mission."[137] As with other Kuwaiti detainees, Fayiz was assessed to have a close relationship to his fellow Kuwaiti and Al Qaida spokesman, Suleiman Abu Ghath.[138]

Fayiz was also believed to have "family ties" to an Al Qaida cell in Kuwait that had killed a US Marine; this was the 2002 Al Failakah island attack that had occurred after Fayiz was at Guantanamo.[139] He was said to have stayed in an Al Qaida guest house in Pakistan with other Al Qaida operatives. He was believed to have been taught at the Al Khaldun camp in Afghanistan to fire a Kalashnikov and to have received explosives training at the Al Farouq camp at a time when Osama Bin Laden was present. The US accused him of accompanying Bin Laden at Tora Bora at the time the bombing began.

After his arrest, Fayiz ran the familiar gauntlet from Bagram to Kandahar to Guantanamo, arriving in May 2002. Fayiz's Detainee Report noted that an unidentified foreign government service considered the detainee to be an extremist unlikely to respect either law or human life and a threat to the United States and its allies. That government took the view that Fayiz had the potential to be a high-level terrorist planner.[140]

As was the case with Fawzi, Fayiz was not a compliant prisoner:

> The detainee's overall behavior has been generally non-compliant. Assaults include spitting and throwing fluids on guards. A guard found a crude shank in the detainee's possession. Detainee has been a regular leader of prayer, and continually physically trains in his cell. He teaches martial arts on occasion to other detainees. The detainee has encouraged Muslims to cause problems for the guards at GTMO and conduct a strike. He also issued a Fatwa to not eat the chicken and meat at GTMO because Muslim law doesn't permit it. The detainee often complains about President Bush and the U.S. Government and stated that his "interrogator and her government are criminals."

Here again was a grab bag of allegations, mixing together weapons possession with the leading of prayers and breaking the boredom of detention by working out.

Who was this man whom the United States viewed as a "hardened terrorist," one of the worst of the worst who should be put on trial, potentially for his life? Taken at face value, these allegations were serious and concerning. But was Fayiz a very serious and high-level actor? The United States threw the book at him, but did the contents withstand scrutiny?

Fayiz was born in 1975 to a lower-middle-class family. His father supported a large family as a technician stringing wire for Kuwaiti telecom. Fayiz was the oldest brother. He completed high school and then tried a number of different courses of study before attending an Islamic college in the tiny UAE Emirate of Ras Al Khaimah. After receiving his degree in 1998, he served as a volunteer prayer leader at the Sabah Al Salam Mosque in Kuwait. While at college in the late 1990s, he traveled briefly to Pakistan and Afghanistan to teach young people to read the Quran. He did not go to Afghanistan again until August 2001, to do charity work in support of his cancer-stricken mother.

Upon arriving in Afghanistan, Fayiz spent a week in Kabul. He left after September 11 and taught Quran reading and memorization in a small village until the bombing began in October. He then sought to get out of Afghanistan traveling through Kabul, Jalalabad, and from there making his way, as had so many others, to the Pakistan border through the Tora Bora mountains.

Fayiz was in a village without television or internet in 2001. He said he learned about 9/11 and the bombings in October on the radio. While he was seeking to leave the country, he saw leaflets dropped from planes that said "Capture an Arab and get $5,000."[141] In the mountains, the bombing was intense. Flares lit up the night and bombs fell all around him. He saw men flying off the ground or pinned by falling boulders. He heard men say the shahidid (the profession of faith) with their last breath. He had a large stone fall on him, which pinned him to the ground and protected him "like a turtle's shell" from flying fragments. There were bodies everywhere and the entire landscape was covered with a gray chemical soot.[142]

Fayiz was captured on Eid al Fitr (December 16) in 2001 and taken to Bagram and then Kandahar. Fayiz said that when he was captured, he had a blue diary and his passport, which were taken by the American soldiers. The blue diary listed his movements and the people he saw. When he was questioned, he told the interrogator that all of the information was in the blue diary. He kept asking for the blue diary, and his interrogators said they knew nothing about it. He asked for it again at his CSRT and ARB proceedings. The diary was never produced or sent to Guantanamo; nor was the passport. He believed they were intentionally destroyed, so that he could not corroborate his story.[143]

Kandahar was worse than Bagram. Fayiz was held underground in what he believed was a CIA prison. He was kneed in the back, beaten with chains and shredded rubber hoses braided together, which he said was more painful than the chains. His head was covered. His ribs were broken and displaced from the beatings. He said it took six months for the wounds to heal.[144]

There is no doubt that Fayiz was a pious Muslim. He did lead prayers and taught the Quran in Kuwait. He was also part of the Kuwait branch of Tabligh, which encourages religious devotion and observance. The

Kuwait organization is government licensed and not on any blacklist. The United States also alleged he was a terrorist recruiter, but it never produced any evidence of recruitment videos that he made, which presumably would have been readily available.

When he went to Afghanistan in August 2001, Fayiz was twenty-five years old. His experience was as a prayer leader, not as a preacher or theological scholar. He had never met Osama Bin Laden, then or at any other time. Yet the DoD immediately elevated Fayiz to the status of religious, spiritual, legal, and military leader:

> Detainee was an influential shaykh amongst Al Qaida fighters, and has issued fatwas, he was referred to [by another] detainee as a scholar. YM-252 [the number of a detainee-informer] stated detainee was known as a senior cleric who could interpret the meaning of dreams and served as a consultant for UBL. YM-252 also reported detainee visited the al-Faruq camp two to three times a month and provided religious instruction, and provided instruction two or three nights a week at the Islamic Institute in Kandahar. Detainee frequently gave speeches to the recruits at the Al Qaida training camps in Afghanistan, and to the Al Qaida and Taliban fighters in Afghanistan designed to encourage their pursuit of jihad.[145]

YM-252 was Yasim Basardah, a Yemeni whom the *New York Times* reported as "unusually cooperative with interrogators"[146] and for which "interrogators were rewarding him with special treatment for his cooperation" despite the fact that "doubts arose among analysts and judges about the reliability of his information." The *Miami Herald* reported that Basardah's information was used in assessments for at least 131 detainees, including multiple accusations of "training at militant camps or taking part in the fighting in Afghanistan against the United States and its allies in late 2001."[147] Judge Kessler in the *Ali Ahmad* case found that Basardah had "shown himself to be an unreliable source whose statements have little evidentiary value."[148]

Apart from the government's own doubts about this serial informer, the notion that a newly minted Islamic college graduate and Quran reader would turn up in Afghanistan and immediately become a top official, a "shaykh," an issuer of fatwas, an advisor to Osama Bin Laden is as improbable as it is nonsensical. Similarly, the idea that he would be a legal advisor to senior Al Qaida leadership is equally so, as he had no expertise or specific training in law. Any person with training in the structure of Islamic extremist organizations would know that this is not the way it would ever work. These organizations are secretive and hierarchical and rely on trust and experience. Osama Bin Laden did not need and would not have accepted guidance from Fayiz Al Kandari; nor would Fayiz Al Kandari have had the temerity to believe himself remotely qualified to do so, let alone after a few weeks in Afghanistan.

We do not know which if any foreign intelligence service ever made allegations about Fayiz. Was it Kuwait? Kuwait supported his release. No evidence was ever produced to back up this allegation.

Fayiz is an intelligent man who had a keen sense of the absurdity of his situation and an unwillingness to remain passive. Fayiz was told by his guards that his lawyers were Jews so that he should not confide in them. This was repeated by multiple detainees. Fayiz smiled at them and said, "There are good people and bad people in every religion." They asked him whether he hated Osama Bin Laden. Fayiz told them that he disagreed with him. Fayiz made clear he thought killing innocent people was never justified, and that Bin Laden had "perverted Islam."[149]

"But did he hate him?" his interrogators insisted. Fayiz rejoined, "he has never done anything to me." And then unable to restrain himself he added, laughing, "George Bush, I hate him." His file duly recorded, "Expressed dislike for George Bush."[150] When his interrogators insisted that he met with two Al Qaida operatives in different parts of Afghanistan, Fayiz said they were hundreds of miles apart, "What am I Superman, I can fly? Can't you see this stuff is contradictory?" His interrogators were not interested in Fayiz's logic.

Fayiz told me the joke that was going around Guantanamo that expressed the approach of American interrogators:

> There are dangerous panthers in the village. A Frenchman, a Russian and an American are brought in to find the panthers. The Frenchman comes back with a dead panther. The Russian comes back with a dead panther. They cannot find the American. Finally, they see him behind a tree holding a little pussycat, beating the cat and shouting "Admit you're a panther, Admit you're a panther."

Fayiz laughed heartily and said, "That is Guantanamo."[151]

In addition to the Al Basardah allegations, twelve of the allegations came from Tariq Al Sawah, the Egyptian bombmaker, who provided 150 reports on fellow detainees[152] and whom a federal judge found to be inherently incredible.[153] Yet, Fayiz and many detainees lost years of their lives based on their fictitious accusations. Other allegations against Fayiz came from detainees who were tortured.

The assessment of Fawzi seemed to conflate strong religious belief with militant jihadism. He was assessed as being engaged in "religious indoctrination of Muslim extremists at the Imam Muhamad Bin Saud Institute in Dubai." This referred to his Islamic college, where he was a student, not a teacher; the college was in Ras Al Khaimah (an Emirate 120 kilometers from Dubai), not in Dubai; and the college itself was an authorized, regulated educational institution in the United Arab Emirates, where extremist activity was closely watched and suppressed by the ruling emirs. Nevertheless, his religiousness was held against him and equated with encouraging terrorism. An analyst noted: "Detainee will continue to use his religious background to seek a leadership position in the Islamic extremist community. Detainee will continue to recruit and mislead youth to follow a path of militant jihad which will place them in environments opposing US and Coalition forces."[154]

Fawzi resented the low-level, spiteful cruelty at Guantanamo. He would send letters and hear nothing for six, seven, or eight months. Then, a letter might come back to him from a family member. Except the letter would be completely redacted other than for the greeting and the signature. Only if there was bad news would it be included. He mentioned that Saad Al Azmi once received a letter that left unredacted only the news that his father was dead.[155]

Fayiz said he only received eight or nine letters in fourteen years. His family sent many, many more. Some prisoners were told they could not receive letters unless they confessed. And of course, there were never any family visits. Similarly, Fayiz related that medical care was withheld or delayed until a detainee gave interrogators what they wanted to hear.[156] When one Kuwaiti detainee was on hunger strike, he lost consciousness. Doctors were prohibited to treat him until he regained consciousness, while interrogators insisted he confess. Others on hunger strike were left alone in their own vomit or excrement. They were sometimes injected with drugs. The corpsmen would sometimes neglect to look for a vein and just inject into tissue. Fawzi protested being used "as an experimental subject."[157]

He spoke about the "psychological scientists" at Guantanamo who implemented a regime of alternating beatings, administration of psychotropic medications, constant sexual lures, Quran abuse and insults of Islam, extreme heat and cold, and being left in stress positions or in a fetal position in tiny containers for three days at a time. He was apparently referring to two psychologists, James Mitchell and Bruce Jensen, who designed a program of "enhanced interrogation," based upon Navy Seal training; their company was paid $81 million for regularizing the senseless torture of detainees who effectively had nothing to tell them.[158]

His interrogators told him, "You are Muslim but you are here. Allah did not help you; he is not with you. We overthrew a country that helps Muslims. God does not love you."[159]

Fayiz stopped cooperating with the interrogators. They asked the same questions; they tried to encourage him to inform on others. He spent a great deal of time in solitary confinement. In solitary, he had a cement platform with a thin ISO mat, a metal sink and toilet, and a fogged window so he could not see anything outside. He was constantly cold and hungry.[160]

Fayiz knew when there would be important visitors to the prison. The food improved and was more plentiful and the tone changed. Senior officers came through the cell block. He recalled a visit by Senator John McCain and other people from Congress in 2013. Prisoners cried out, "Torture. We are being tortured. You know what it is like. Help us." McCain said nothing and kept walking.[161]

I met Fayiz again in November 2021. "Here's my lawyer," he cried out when we met in the lobby of an office tower in Kuwait City. We hugged. He is sharp, funny, and emotional. There is much gray in his hair and beard now. He has married since he came home. He joked that when he first came home, Kuwaiti friends called him "Fayiz Mandela," and "Mohammed Gandhi Al Kandari." He had fought uncompromisingly for his freedom against great odds. He admitted he was angry about what happened to him. He does not forget. He said he felt pain for a long time, but he has learned from it and the pain is gone. He feels the experience now in a good way. He has given up his anger and says he now feels free.[162]

Fawzi feels no animus generally toward America or Americans. "A lot of Americans supported us." He said that he feels positive about humanity. "There are good and bad in all people and all places." He told me that "hatred will burn like fire." "Islam demands that you find the right way." He indicated that he has learned the most from his Guantanamo experience in the last two years when he has had time to reflect and consider what happened to him with the advantage of maturity. When he went to Guantanamo, he was like "food in the pot before it is seasoned." In retrospect, he says, it was a good experience.[163]

Fawzi says his life goal is to understand others and to understand other religions and traditions. He says that President Bush inadvertently put him on the "straight path" to finding peace, to bring peace to all, and to build bridges. When the wheels left the tarmac at Guantanamo, he felt that "everything bad will be gone." The torture, the pressure, the ordeals, all gone. "It was not 14 years, it was 14 minutes or seconds or moments." He felt liberated and calm.[164]

Fawzi works today at the Ministry of Public Works. He has an office-based job relating to road building. He has not left Kuwait and has no desire to do so. Fawzi is active on social media and has also made a thirteen-part video series on YouTube, talking about his time in Afghanistan and at Guantanamo as well as his beliefs.[165]

Fayiz indicated gratitude for the efforts of his country and the activity of the Emir, which he only learned of later. Before that, he had been told that his government was doing nothing and it made him bitter. He indicated he had later learned there were times when the release of Fayiz and Fawzi was the only request that the Emir would make when he met with the US president. He quoted the Emir, "I want my children."[166]

Fayiz noted that the working group from Kuwait visited frequently; he admitted he was not always pleasant toward them, but he said they often would bring food and supplies that were shared with the other detainees. Colonel Al Kandari (no relation), the head of Kuwaiti Intelligence, appears in silhouette in Fayiz's YouTube series and says that he told his American counterparts regarding Fayiz, "I will bring him by my hand and return him to his father."[167]

Fayiz felt he was racing against time to see his parents again. On the video calls, he saw his father was deteriorating. Fayiz had a vision at Guantanamo that his father would die soon. He was terrified that he would never see him again. His father would exclaim on the calls, "I want my son to bury me."[168] When Fayiz returned home in 2016, he was met by his father at the airport.

Their reunion was long and loving and emotional. It is difficult to watch the YouTube video of their meeting with dry eyes. But Abu Fayiz had cancer. He went to London for treatment while Fayiz was still at the Al Salam Rehabilitation Center. A few months later, Abu Fayiz died, and he was buried by his son.

6

The Final Four: Habeas Hearings for the Last Four Kuwaiti Detainees

The Kuwaiti detainees had filed their cases in May 2002, but the litigation up to the Supreme Court about whether there was any right to habeas corpus prevented substantive hearings from proceeding until after the court's 2008 ruling in *Boumediene/Al Odah*. By that time, eight of the twelve Kuwaiti detainees had gone home, and hearings for the four remaining Kuwaitis then occurred quickly over a four-month period from June to October 2009. A legal team from the law firm Pillsbury, led by David Cynamon, had replaced Tom Wilner and the Shearman team, and conducted all four hearings before Judge Colleen Kollar-Kotelly. Two petitions were granted and two denied in opinions issued between July 2009 and September 2010. The government did not appeal the two grants of habeas corpus, but promptly repatriated the two successful detainees. Two other petitions on largely similar facts were denied. This chapter discusses each of the four habeas cases and considers possible explanations for the different outcomes.

Khalid Al Mutairi

The US government filed a document called a Factual Return, setting out the factual basis for continued detention, on September 8, 2008. Pillsbury then filed a Traverse (the responsive document challenging the basis for detention) on March 30, 2009. There was extensive discovery and motions relating to what documents needed to be produced, whether certain information should be declassified, and the admissibility of particular evidence. The court held a two-day hearing on July 6–7, 2009, to present and argue about the meaning of the written evidence, but no live witness testimony was presented.

The court made clear that it would admit hearsay testimony, apply a preponderance of the evidence standard, and reject any presumption of accuracy and authenticity of evidence presented by the government.[1] The court would evaluate the evidence against the standard of whether the detainees "planned, authorized, committed, or aided the terrorist attacks that occurred on September 11, 2001," or harbored those responsible for those attacks.[2] In addition, the court would consider whether they could be detained as "part of" the Taliban, Al Qaida, or "associated military forces" that were engaged in hostilities against the United States or its coalition partners, including any person who has "committed a belligerent act in aid such enemy armed forces."[3] There was no issue of whether the Kuwaitis were involved with 9/11 or harbored the terrorists; the real question was whether they were somehow "part of" the Taliban or Al Qaida.

The court rejected the government's claim that it had the authority to detain individuals who only "substantially supported enemy forces" or who "directly supported hostilities" in aid of enemy forces but otherwise were not "part of" the Taliban, Al Qaida, or associated military forces.[4] It was unclear where the line between substantial or direct support of hostilities crossed over such that a person became "part of" the Taliban, Al Qaida, or associated military forces, a non-legal term that was never defined.

Khalid Al Mutairi submitted his own witness statement in the habeas proceeding. He stated that he took $15,000 in cash with him from Kuwait to Afghanistan because he planned to build a mosque. He entered Afghanistan after September 11. He asserted that he did not plan to stay long in Afghanistan, just long enough to make the donation and see that the mosque project got started. He left his return date open because he did not know how long this would take. He accounted for the cash that he brought.

After these few days in Afghanistan, where he made donations, he tried to cross into Pakistan, but the border was sealed, so he stayed with a friend for three weeks in a village near Kabul until late October. At some point before he left the Kabul area, he said his bag was stolen, which had most of his remaining funds and his passport. He then moved to another village because there was fighting around Kabul, and he stayed at a village near Khost with a friend of a friend for another month. He said he did not recall the name of the friend of the friend. Around the end of November, he paid a guide to take him across to the border to Pakistan, where he was captured and transferred to American custody.[5]

The thrust of the government's case in the habeas proceedings against Al Mutairi was that he "trained with and became part of" the Al Wafa charity, which the USG asserted was an "associated force of Al Qaida." But Al Wafa was only listed as an Al Qaida-linked charity in October 2001, after Al Mutairi had visited their offices and made his donation. Could he be held responsible for knowing the purposes of Al Wafa before the

US government did? The government also alleged that he "trained with and joined the forces of Al Qaida," without specifying any names, dates, or locations. It insisted he swore "bayat," the oath of allegiance to Al Qaida and Bin Laden.[6] Al Mutairi said he never swore such an oath and did not even arrive in Afghanistan until after 9/11.

Judge Kollar-Kotelly noted that some of the evidence in Al Mutairi's case had been "buried under the rubble of war," where the chain of custody or evidence was uncertain, and other evidence was based on "unfinished" intelligence. She recognized that a great many unsubstantiated rumors were put into initial reports. The court's reference to reports as unfinished suggested that, in her view, simply because something was found in an intelligence report did not make it worthy of judicial attention. Judge Kollar-Kotelly also referenced the multiple layers of hearsay, the reports of interrogations through translators, and the potential for error. She then pointed out the government's inexcusable mistake that cast grave doubt over its entire submission:

> In this case, for example, the Government believed for over three years that Al Mutairi manned an anti-aircraft weapon in Afghanistan based on a typographical error in an interrogation report. See Al Mutairi Classified Traverse at 27–28 (explaining that the Government's initial Factual Return filed on December 17, 2004, identified Al Mutairi as having manned an anti-aircraft weapon because an interrogation report mistakenly identified the individual as ISN 213 (AI Mutairi's identifier) instead of ISN [redacted], the individual who was accused of manning the weapon.[7]

In other words, an uncorrected numerical transposition led to the mistaken identity of Khalid as an Al Qaida fighter and his confinement for an additional five years.

Despite the government's argument that it should be the detainee's burden to show why he should not be detained, the judge put the burden of proof on the government.

> The Government bears the burden of proving by a preponderance of the evidence that Al Mutairi is lawfully detained. Accordingly, Al Mutairi need not prove his innocence. The Government must come forward with evidence demonstrating by a preponderance of the evidence that he is lawfully detained, and if the Government fails to meet this burden, the Court must grant his petition for habeas corpus.[8]

The court went through a detailed analysis of the evidence and, indeed, found significant parts of Khalid's evidence not to be fully credible.[9] The court credited the government's evidence that Khalid's route "was consistent with the route used by al Wafa to smuggle individuals into Afghanistan to engage in jihad." She also found that "his travel from Kabul to Khost was consistent (in time and place) with the route of Taliban and Al Qaida fighters fleeing toward the Tora Bora mountains along the Afghanistan-Pakistan border," and that "Al Mutairi's non-possession of his passport is consistent with an individual who has undergone Al Qaida's standard operating procedures that require trainees to surrender their passports prior to beginning their training." She analyzed his descriptions of his movements through Afghanistan and decided that there were material, temporal, and factual gaps, finding "Al Mutairi's described peregrinations within Afghanistan lack credibility." Because he was not apprehended until the end of December, there was a "missing month" that was not accounted for in his version of events. The court viewed the evidence as suggesting he stayed an extra month in Kabul and left in mid-November, which is when Kabul fell to the Northern Alliance.[10]

The government tried to argue that Al Mutairi was fighting with the Taliban against the Northern Alliance, and, on that basis, Al Mutairi could have been found to have been "part of the Taliban." The court agreed that evidence of fighting in the Afghan civil war against the Northern Alliance would be consistent with someone who had become "part of" the Taliban or Al Qaida. In addition, leaving Kabul when the Northern Alliance took over could, in the court's view, also be evidence of Taliban affiliation.[11]

The court also indicated that Al Mutairi had told different versions of what happened to his passport and how it was lost. Her opinion also pointed to other anomalies and inconsistencies in his story. Accordingly, the court held it "does not credit Al Mutairi's version of events that occurred while he was in Afghanistan."[12]

In other words, the court concluded that Khalid was probably lying about his activities and hiding what he was really doing. But that was not dispositive of Khalid's case. Judge Kollar-Kotelly concluded:

> Taking this evidence as a whole, the Government has at best shown that some of Al Mutairi's conduct is consistent with persons who may have become a part of al Wafa or Al Qaida, but there is nothing in the record beyond speculation that Al Mutairi did, in fact, train or otherwise become a part of one or more of those organizations, where he would have done so, and with which organization.[13]

The government also tried to point to the list of the detainees apprehended in Pakistan to suggest that they were all "captured Al Qaida fighters." The court, however, would not go that far. It found that if Al Mutairi gave his identification information to the person in Pakistan so that his family could be alerted, and if such information may have been transmitted at some point and found among Al Qaida personnel, this did not make Al Mutairi part of Al Qaida. Thus, an argument used by the government to label all seventy-eight men on that list as part of Al Qaida, and therefore enemy combatants, failed at the first hurdle in federal court. She found that it was not clear what the list was meant to record, when it was written, or how the information came to be on the list.[14]

With respect to Al Wafa, the court noted that there was evidence presented that it was both a charitable organization and a front for Al Qaida. The government did not introduce any evidence, however, to show that Al Mutairi knew or believed Al Wafa was anything other than a charity or that his contribution made him "part of" Al Qaida or an affiliated organization. Instead, the government argued that Al Mutairi had entered an Al Wafa training camp outside Kabul. But this was an unsupported assertion; there was no evidence of attendance at any camp or that Al Wafa even maintained such a camp. The government overreached, and the court would not accept that Al Mutairi was at a training camp when there was no evidence presented.[15]

The court made the important observation that "some of the statements in the interrogation reports proffered by the government lack credibility."[16] She proceeded to dissect with obvious anger much of evidence that the government chose to proffer to a federal court in the face of such clear unreliability. The compliant informers who had so delighted the eager interrogators would not receive the same unquestioned acceptance before a federal judge.

Judge Kollar-Kotelly also noted that the government had argued that Al Mutairi had fought with Bin Laden in Afghanistan in 1991 based on an item in his interrogation report. Not only was there no corroborating evidence that Al Mutairi ever was in or fought in Afghanistan in 1991, but she noted that the government was trying to argue that he was a fighter when he was sixteen years old.[17] This may have been credited by the Department of Defense, but not in this tribunal.

By pressing an inherently incredible version of events before a neutral fact finder, the government exposed its sloppiness in compiling evidence and in trying to suggest inferences that it should not have asked a federal judge to make. But that was not all. The government also presented as evidence Al Mutairi's statement made during another interrogation where he said, "I am Osama Bin Laden."[18]

The government introduced the statement to demonstrate that he was hostile to the United States, and therefore, this supported its argument that he was part of Al Qaida or the Taliban. Al Mutairi had said that, with all this legal process being so useless, he might as well be Osama bin Laden since he was never going to be freed from US custody. The government presented it as probative of terrorist involvement, but it was no longer the judge and jury in its own proceedings.

The government also alleged that Khalid had attended a meeting in Pakistan of Lashkar-e-Tayiba, an "affiliated organization" of Al Qaida, but again its only source was the statement of another detainee, who had no apparent basis for knowing who Al Mutairi was, when any such meeting may have occurred, or when Al Mutairi ever traveled to Pakistan.[19] Again, rather than buttress the government's case, it only called attention to the fact that interrogators would accept and include in reports information of dubious credibility to support continued detention and that it was now trying to ask a federal judge to act on the basis of the same poor quality information. Had the government relied only on Al Mutairi's travel route, his apprehension in Tora Bora, and his lack of a passport, it might have had a better chance of winning.

The theme that comes through the opinion repeatedly from Judge Kollar-Kotelly, a former federal prosecutor, is an expectation that the USG should not come to court trying to convince a US District Judge to accept submissions that lacked rigor or credibility and that she would demand plausible documentation and witnesses. She would not compromise her own independence of analysis or allow the government to carry its burden with such a shoddy effort, irrespective of what Al Mutairi had to say for himself. She put the government to its proof, and she found its efforts to be wanting.

Fouad Al Rabiah

Fouad's case was the second case heard by Judge Kollar-Kotelly in mid-2009. Al Rabiah's background was not in dispute. He was a fifty-year-old father of four with no military background other than two weeks of mandatory basic training with the Kuwaiti army, after which he was discharged with an injury. He was overweight, hypertensive, and had chronic pain in his neck and lower back.

As noted in Chapter 5, Al Rabiah had a long history of doing charity in conflict zones.[20] He traveled to Afghanistan in July 2001 and then decided to return in October to do fact-finding in an area of his charitable work, refugees, and medical infrastructure for their care. The government asserted he was not an aspiring aid worker at all but was a "devotee of Osama Bin Laden who ran to Bin Laden's side after September 11th." The government again put forward the argument accepted by the CSRT that he personally gave Bin Laden a suitcase full of cash at a gala dinner held with Al Qaida members in Afghanistan.

Judge Kollar-Kotelly found that Al Rabiah's story was well corroborated and credible and the government's was not.[21] In dealing with his background, and his reasons for traveling to Afghanistan, Judge Kollar-Kotelly was required to evaluate whether or not his ten-day visit in July 2001 was intended to identify areas where humanitarian aid might be delivered, and whether or not his return in October 2001 was "to complete a fact-finding mission related to Afghanistan's refugee problems and the country's non-existent medical infrastructure."

Concluding "[t]he evidence in the record strongly supports al-Rabiah's explanation," Judge Kollar-Kotelly noted that he had officially requested leave prior to his departure and quoted from two letters Fouad had sent to his family. In the first, dated October 18, 2001, the judge noted Fouad's communication with his family that "for ten days he assisted with the delivery of supplies to refugees and that he was able to take video 'reflecting the tragedy of the refugees,' but that he was unable to leave Afghanistan through Iran because the borders had been closed." As a result, Fouad "wrote in his letter that he and an unspecified number of other persons decided 'to drive four trucks to Pakistan making our way to Peshawar,'" and he also asked his brother to notify his boss at Kuwait Airlines that he was having difficulties returning to Kuwait on time.[22] He wanted to make sure that his supervisors were fully informed that he might be somewhat delayed in returning to his job as a senior manager at the national airline. Hardly the modus operandi of an Al Qaida terrorist.

Judge Kollar-Kotelly quoted from the second letter sent to his family, in which Fouad wrote that the Americans "thanks to God" are "good example[s] of humanitarian behavior." He added that he was "detained pending verification of [his] identity and personality" and that the "investigation and verification procedures may last for a long time due to the great number of detained Arabs and other persons," who had been fleeing the situation in Afghanistan, which "turned upside down between one day and night and every Arab citizen has become a suspect."[23]

Fouad again, having no motive to do so, was contemporaneously crediting the Americans, for whom he had affection and respect after his time living and studying in Florida. He knew it would take time, and he would be patient because he had confidence in American justice and rational behavior. He had reason to be sorely disappointed over the next seven years.

Judge Kollar-Kotelly also discounted the allegations regarding Fouad's supposed activities in Tora Bora, which were made by another prisoner who claimed that he "was told that al-Rabiah was in charge of supplies at Tora Bora." This tidbit from an informer was one of the principal charges made against him in the habeas proceedings.

The judge found that, with respect to the informer, again Tariq Al Sawah, who claimed to have been there, "although his allegations are filled with inconsistencies and implausibilities, the government continues to rely on him as an eyewitness."[24] She also noted that, although the informer witness had identified Al Rabiah as the man under discussion from his kunya, Abu Abdullah Al Kuwaiti, the government had conceded that another Abu Abdullah Al Kuwaiti, an actual Al Qaida operative named Hadi El-Enazi, was present in Tora Bora and also noted that even the interrogator had expressed doubt about Al Sawah's claim to have been an eyewitness at the time. Yet, the government continued to press forward with its case based on evidence that its own interrogator doubted. Although much of the ruling was and remains classified and redacted, the judge did note in the publicly released opinion that the report in the US dossier that Al Rabiah's oldest son was with him in Afghanistan was demonstrably wrong, given that Abdullah was only eleven in 2001.[25]

Judge Kollar-Kotelly also dismissed two other sets of allegations by the supposed eyewitness. "The Court has little difficulty concluding that [the informer's] allegations are not credible," and explained that, to reach this conclusion, she had also drawn on statements provided by Fouad's lawyers regarding Al Sawah, "based on, among other things, undisputed inconsistencies associated with his allegations against other detainees," and "his medical records, which obviously indicated mental health problems." "At a minimum," she added, "the Government would have had to corroborate [his] allegations with credible and reliable evidence, which it has not done." Until the habeas proceedings, the government had no need to corroborate anything or honestly evaluate witness credibility, holding men for years based on the most tenuous and facially incoherent tips from detainees like this one, who traded his integrity for hamburgers.

As for the purported gala dinner with Osama bin Laden and the suitcase full of money, Judge Kollar-Kotelly made clear that, in her court, there would be real evidence, not nonsense. "The only consistency with respect to [these] allegations is that they repeatedly change over time."[26] She singled out one claim that the feast had taken place in August 2001 (when Al Rabiah was in Kuwait). She also dismissed the allegation that Fouad had somehow, somewhere trained the 9/11 hijackers, presumably because he had a background in aviation. His background was in airline operations management, not in flying. The court noted, "it is undisputed... that Al Rabiah is 'not a pilot.'"

After rejecting the evidence of the testimony of a third supposed eyewitness because he had withdrawn his allegations, Judge Kollar-Kotelly then dismissed a fourth, even though it was "undisputed" that Fouad actually had contact with him in Afghanistan. Despite redactions, it appears that this informer made a statement that he had been told about Fouad having been seen with a gun. The judge made a point of discounting it because the supposed witness only "made this allegation while he was undergoing a cell relocation program at Guantánamo called the 'frequent flier program,' which prevented a detainee such as [redacted] from resting due to frequent cell movements."[27] She noted this was part of the "enhanced interrogation techniques" that US military regulations prohibited.

Finally, Judge Kollar-Kotelly addressed the torture issue directly. She drew the connection between the crazy stories told by unreliable eyewitnesses and the apparent corroboration by Fouad of these stories under interrogation. "It is very significant that al-Rabiah's interrogators apparently did not believe these [informer] allegations at the time they were made, and therefore sought to have al-Rabiah confess to them." The judge also noted that "al-Rabiah subsequently confided in interrogators [redacted] that he was being pressured to falsely confess to the allegations discussed above," and also that, although "al-Rabiah's interrogators ultimately extracted confessions from him," they "never believed his confessions based on the comments they included in their interrogation reports." She observed, "These are the confessions that the Government now asks the Court to accept as evidence in this case. From that point [the use of torture] forward, al-Rabiah confessed to the allegations that interrogators described to him." Despite the extensive redactions, Judge Kollar-Kotelly made a clear conclusion in the public opinion with respect to the use and impact of torture:

> Al-Rabiah's confessions all follow the same pattern: Interrogators first explain to al-Rabiah the "evidence" they have in their possession (and that, at the time, they likely believed to be true). Al-Rabiah then requests time to pray (or to think more about the evidence) before making a "full" confession. Finally, after a period of time, al-Rabiah provides a full confession to the evidence through elaborate and incredible explanations that the interrogators themselves do not believe. This pattern began with his confession that he met with Osama bin Laden, continued with his confession that he undertook a leadership role in Tora Bora, and repeated itself multiple other times with respect to "evidence" that the Government has not even attempted to rely on as reliable or credible.[28]

Through this Orwellian process, the United States sought to try him through a military commission with the possibility of execution and later to oppose his habeas petition. The judge explained:

> He made his confessions to reduce the abuse meted out by his interrogators "to obtain confessions that suited what [they] thought they knew or what they wanted [him] to say." He maintained his confessions over time because "the interrogators would continue to abuse me anytime I attempted to repudiate any of these false allegations."[29]

As she also noted:

> There is substantial evidence in the record supporting al-Rabiah's claims. The record is replete with examples of al-Rabiah's interrogators emphasizing a stark dichotomy –if he confessed to the allegations against him, his case would be turned over to [redacted] so that he could return to Kuwait; if he did not confess, he would not return to Kuwait, and his life would become increasingly miserable.[30]

Of course, whether he made a false confession or refused to confess, he was, in any event, not going home to Kuwait.

After making the point that the use of these methods was likely to "yield unreliable results, may damage subsequent collection efforts, and can induce the source to say what he thinks the interrogator wants to hear," Judge Kollar-Kotelly added, "Underscoring the impropriety of these techniques is the fact that [redacted], al-Rabiah's lead interrogator, was disciplined for making similar threats during the same period toward a Guantánamo detainee who was also one of the alleged eyewitnesses against al-Rabiah."[31]

Judge Kollar-Kotelly concluded:

> The Court agrees with the assessment of al-Rabiah's interrogators, as well as al-Rabiah's counsel in this case, that al-Rabiah's confessions are not credible. Even beyond the countless inconsistencies associated with his confessions that interrogators identified throughout his years of detention, the confessions are also entirely incredible. The evidence in the record reflects that, in 2001, al-Rabiah was a 43-year-old who was overweight, suffered from health problems, and had no known history of terrorist activities or links to terrorist activities. He had no military experience except for two weeks of compulsory basic training in Kuwait, after which he received a medical exemption. He had never traveled to Afghanistan prior to 2001. Given these facts, it defied logic that in October 2001, after completing a two-week leave form at Kuwait Airlines where he had worked for twenty years, al-Rabiah traveled to Tora Bora and began telling senior Al Qaida leaders how they should organize their supplies in a six square

mile mountain complex that he had never previously seen and that was occupied by people whom he had never met, while at the same time acting as a supply logistician and mediator of disputes that arose among various fighting factions.[32]

Her final holding:

> During the Merits Hearing, the Government expressly relied on "Occam's Razor," a scientific and philosophic rule suggesting that the simplest of competing explanations is preferred to the more complex ... The Government's simple explanation for the evidence in this case is that al-Rabiah made confessions that the Court should accept as true. The simple response is that the Court does not accept confessions that even the Government's own interrogators did not believe. The writ of habeas corpus shall issue.[33]

Here again, the court took the government to task for a case where the evidence was both weak and tainted; the inferences it sought were frequently absurd; the testimony of informants was often so embellished with improbable detail as to be laughable; and both the detainee and at least one informant had been tortured to extract purported confessions. The simplest way to draw a cover over this cruel, incompetent, disgraceful set of events was to send Fouad Al Rabiah home, which the government did shortly thereafter. Fouad returned to Kuwait in December 2009. Again, the Obama administration did so as a matter of executive discretion, not in deference to the court order, which it did not appeal.

When asked what he thought the United States should do about alleged terrorists, Fouad told me, "Take them to trial, let justice take its route. If a person is a terrorist, kills innocent people he should not be set free." But, he added, "I was kept there for eight years ... saying about me that I am the worst of the worst. Only when I went to court I was cleared."[34]

The habeas decision in Fouad's case made clear that the US executive would no longer have control over the process without judicial oversight and accountability. The government would need evidence that would be scrutinized rather than the ravings of desperate men looking to gain advantages as informants or words crammed into their mouths through torture.

Fouad had lost eight years of his life. His father had died, his brother had died, and his mother had a stroke and could not speak. Two uncles were gone. "I lost the childhood of my children," he said. His youngest child was six years old when he left, and nearly fifteen when he finally returned home.

"I lost so many things, but I know that I was right," he said. "I know that they were wrong."[35] He knew as well that Kuwaitis had a responsibility to help others. "We are well off in comparison to other countries....

We cannot see famine and natural disasters and do nothing."[36] Few men have given more to help others or suffered more for their compassion and sacrifice.

Fawzi Al Odah

It is unclear why the USG went after Fawzi Al Odah with a level of intensity and vitriol that it brought to few other detainees. As noted in Chapter 5, he was victorious in the Supreme Court twice. He was, to be sure, not a particularly cooperative or passive prisoner. He was a leader of the hunger strikes. None of this made him a terrorist or distinguished his biography from the vast run of Guantanamo detainees. Yet, the government put great effort into securing the denial of his habeas petition and it succeeded.

In Fawzi's case, Judge Kollar-Kotelly reproduced verbatim the same rulings on evidence, burden of proof, presumptions, and standard of detention as she did in the Al Mutairi and Al Rabiah habeas cases, but she took a very different view of the evidence. She divided the evidence into three categories: Fawzi's trip from Kuwait to Afghanistan in August 2001; his subsequent travels and activities until his capture with an AK-47 near the Tora Bora mountains; and, after noting that these two categories of evidence were enough for the government to meet its burden, she also discussed a third category of evidence that Fawzi admitted to visiting a camp in Kandahar which was more likely than not Al Farouq, Al Qaida's primary training camp.[37]

Fawzi had never been to Afghanistan before August 2001. It was undisputed that he took three weeks of leave from work and intended to spend two weeks teaching poor people in Afghanistan. He traveled through Dubai, which the court indicated "raises immediate questions." He initially said he remained there for some days and "as much as a week," but the court emphasized there were records that showed he arrived on August 13 and bought a one-way ticket to Karachi for the next day.[38]

The court found that because it was only the second foreign trip he would have taken by himself, it was unlikely that he had forgotten how long he had been there, despite the fact that eight years had elapsed between the trip and the hearing.[39] The court spends a fair amount of time in considering and rejecting counsel's point that there is nothing odd about going to Afghanistan through Dubai, stating, "Nowhere in the record did Al Odah ever explain that he bought a one way ticket to

Dubai because he believed it was the most direct route to Afghanistan" and made a finding that "Al Odah has not offered any credible explanation based on the evidence in the record that would explain his trip to Dubai en route to Afghanistan."[40]

Yet, curiously, there was no evidence to suggest any improper or nefarious purpose in going through Dubai, which, as any Gulf resident would know, is a key transit point to the subcontinent, with far more flights to Pakistan than would go direct from Kuwait. It is curious as well, given that the many detainees who went through Iran were also suspected of taking the preferred Al Qaida route. It is not clear what would have been the most innocent-appearing route from Kuwait to Pakistan or Afghanistan. And Judge Kollar-Kotelly in other cases, as well as other judges in habeas cases, did not find the purchase of a one-way ticket unusual, as it was difficult to know for certain when projects would be completed. In reviewing Judge Kollar-Kotelly's decision on appeal, the D.C. Circuit also seemed to find it significant that Fawzi paid cash for his ticket, again not an unusual thing to have done at that time in the region, especially as tickets to the subcontinent were quite cheap and people in the Gulf use cash far more than, perhaps, US federal judges. Even today, a one-way ticket from Dubai to Karachi can be purchased for around $100.[41]

Here, the court seemed to be taking issue with points of detail that seem largely irrelevant to Al Odah's purpose for going to Afghanistan or that people with knowledge of the region would have found worthy of note. While in previous cases, Judge Kollar-Kotelly largely ignored what she viewed as non-credible explanations about how detainees were spending their time after September 11 and the US invasion – the missing weeks or month – she was now focusing on why a Kuwaiti admittedly on his way to Afghanistan would stop in Dubai and why he would say that he stayed a few days longer than he did.

The court found that once he arrived in Karachi, Fawzi's route created further suspicion as to his purpose – a flight to Quetta, a car to the border, and then to Spin Boldak, just over the border, where he tried to find a place to do charitable teaching. The government contended that Al Odah's purpose in making the trip was to join the Taliban in its fight against the Northern Alliance.[42] The Spin Boldak portion of Afghanistan, however, is in the southernmost part of Afghanistan near the Pakistan border, which was under firm Taliban control. The battle between the Northern Alliance and the Taliban was in the north, hundreds of miles away; it was only after the bombing began that the Northern Alliance began to move south toward where Fawzi had been.

In Spin Boldak, Fawzi said he met with a man whom the court found he had admitted was a Taliban official. Fawzi said this official took him around the countryside to teach at several schools in the area. The government argued, and the court found, that this contention was not credible because Fawzi could not provide the specific names of students he taught, the specific names of the schools at which he taught, or the specific names of his fellow teachers. The court also found that meeting with this Taliban official was proof of Taliban affiliation.[43]

Of course, at the time, there could have been no suggestion that September 11 would occur, and all officials in that area would have had Taliban association, as it was the de facto government of most of Afghanistan, including Spin Boldak. If he wanted to teach at a school, the Taliban would have been in charge. Nor was the United States at war with the Taliban or involved in the battle between the Taliban and the Northern Alliance before September 11.

After some period of time, this official took Fawzi to a camp for a day. While at this camp, Fawzi admitted that he engaged in brief target shooting with a Kalashnikov AK-47 rifle. Fawzi then traveled to Kandahar, also a southern town controlled by the Taliban and far from combat with the Northern Alliance.

Fawzi admitted that he was in Kandahar on the day of the September 11 terrorist attacks. After September 11, on the recommendation of this same official to get out of big cities like Kandahar, he rented a car and drove from Kandahar to rural Logar Province, also south of Kabul and near the Pakistan border. He said he made this trip to try to stay safe and try to find a way out of Afghanistan.

The government pointed out that if Fawzi felt unsafe, he could have left Afghanistan more quickly by retracing the route by which he arrived. Of course, that assumed a knowledge of logistics and geography of a huge country where he had recently arrived (and where he did not speak any local language). Poor route planning or sense of geography should not equate with terrorism, but this was considered further proof that he was hiding terrorist involvement.

While in Logar Province, Fawzi sought out someone recommended by his initial guide, and he stayed with that person at his home for a month, where he left his video camera, passport, and other documents. Once the US bombing started, Fawzi moved again, traveling to Jalalabad in southwest Afghanistan, where he stayed for a number of days. At some point during this stay, he was given a Kalashnikov AK-47 rifle. Fawzi then left Jalalabad and, on foot, headed through the White Mountains in the Tora Bora region. Fawzi carried his AK-47 and had it in his possession when he reached the border sometime between mid-November and mid-December 2001.[44]

Fawzi asserted in his habeas statement that the camp he visited had young people there, was not a terrorist camp and that it was common to learn how to fire a weapon as virtually everyone in Afghanistan had one and needed to know how to use it; that his route in Afghanistan was suggested to him by people who knew the terrain; and they told him that this was the best way to avoid danger and find a way out of a war zone. He did not explain why he had overstayed the initial two to three weeks for which he sought leave.

In many respects, Fawzi's story was not dissimilar to those of Khalid Al Mutairi and Fouad Al Rabiah and, indeed, in certain respects, less inculpatory. Unlike his two fellow Kuwaitis, Fawzi left to go to Afghanistan *before* September 11, when the prospect of a future US attack in Afghanistan would not have been within contemplation. He took a similar route through Afghanistan as the others, staying in villages and then through Jalalabad and Tora Bora. Like many others, he did not have his passport or other travel documents with him. He could not account for a "missing month" in his chronology. He had a history of previous charitable work. He did not go to Al Wafa.[45]

Yet the judge focused on certain parts of the story which, taken together, in the court's view, yielded a different outcome than the previous two habeas petitions. First, as discussed earlier, the court focused on his stop in Dubai, but the court did not try to articulate why a stop in Dubai would be probative; it might have been useful for Fawzi or his legal team to have provided a brief discussion of Gulf transportation logistics, but they could not have known how large that issue would loom. Second, the court focused on his inability to name specific villages, schools, teachers, or students, finding that failure not credible even given that eight years had elapsed, he had never been to this area, and he was in small villages where he did not speak the local language. Afghanistan has thirty-four provinces, each one of which has more than a thousand villages. Fawzi did recall being in larger towns such as Spin Boldak, Kandahar, and Jalalabad. The court also did not consider that Fawzi had spent the last eight years isolated and abused, rather than trying to reconstruct in detail his brief time in Afghanistan.

The court put strong weight on the fact that Fawzi spent one day learning how to fire an AK-47 at a camp. Although one day of learning how to fire a gun at the time may not have been unusual, the court put that together with evidence that the date of his visit was September 11, 2001, and it concluded that this camp was likely to be Al Farouq, which was an Al Qaida camp in the same general location and that the trainer had a name similar to the trainer at Al Farouq. In addition, there was evidence that Al Farouq had disbanded the day after September 11, which was Fawzi's departure date. On this basis, the court found it more likely than not that Fawzi had attended Al Farouq, which was a devastating finding given the close association of Al Farouq with Al Qaida. The court also found that Fawzi's travel "pattern" was consistent with many fighters, although the judge knew that it was also a familiar travel pattern of many who were not fighters.[46]

The court found it highly suspicious that Fawzi did not simply leave Afghanistan immediately after September 11, by the shortest route, through Spin Boldak back to Quetta, rather than moving on to Logar Province and then to Tora Bora. His pattern of staying at houses and his surrendering of his passport, the court held, were consistent with Al Qaida and Taliban operating procedures. The court stated that this pattern "reflects that Al Odah made a conscious choice to ally himself with the Taliban instead of extricating himself from the country." Based on this evidence, the court made its finding "more likely than not that Al Odah became 'part of' the Taliban's forces."[47] The court ignored purported identification of Fawzi by detainee-informers, finding that it did not need to consider that evidence because it had already found that the government had presented adequate factual information to meet its burden. Fawzi Al Odah would spend five more years in Guantanamo.

Why did this case come out so differently? To be sure, there were certain factual differences with Khalid Al Mutairi and Fouad Al Rabiah's cases, including most importantly the day of training at a camp, which the court inferred was the notorious Al Farouq camp, and his apprehension with an AK-47. His stay in Dubai and his routing were not remarkable. There are only so many routes into and out of Afghanistan, and Fawzi was no expert. That he stayed for longer than two to three weeks was also not explained, but again not remarkable; the others had gaps in their chronologies. There was also an admission that he sought out a Taliban official when he arrived in Afghanistan, but this was in August of 2001, when the Taliban controlled the great majority of Afghan territory.

The suggestion that Fawzi went to Afghanistan for purposes of jihad is dubious in that, in August 2001, while there may have been civil conflict between the Taliban and the Northern Alliance, this was not a jihad between Muslims and non-Muslims: It was a civil war among different regional and tribal groups, all of whom were Muslim. Nor was there any indication or evidence that Fawzi had any knowledge or views with respect to that conflict. And unlike other released detainees, he never got near any battlefield. Yet, the Authorization for Use of Military Force (AUMF) defined as grounds for detention becoming "part of the Taliban." While there was no evidence that Fawzi even became "part of the Taliban" in any formal sense, or indeed that the Taliban ever accepted non-Afghans to be "part of" it, the court compressed its analysis in time and space and made this finding, which was dispositive of Fawzi's petition.

One important difference between the different outcomes was that the government's presentation of its case against Fawzi was not as troubling as in the cases of Al Mutairi and Al Rabiah. Its evidentiary submission did not put forward outlandish evidence or theories. There were no suggestions of Fawzi fighting with Osama Bin Laden as a sophomore in high school or presenting Bin Laden with sacks of money or immediately becoming Bin Laden's spiritual mentor. There were no suggestions of bringing an eleven-year-old child to fight. Fawzi's case was not surrounded by the stench of torture, although he had certainly been abused. There was no evidence of record that either the witnesses against him (which the court held it had ignored) or Fawzi had been in the "frequent flyer program" or that there were threats of death or forced rendition. Perhaps the best explanation for this result, however, was that the law was changing and becoming far less favorable to detainees. The D.C. Circuit wanted lower courts to follow much tougher rules. While nominally the USG had to prove its case rather than use the detainee's interrogations against him, Fawzi's petition was denied largely on the basis of his own words. As discussed in Chapter 4, after Fawzi's hearing and before the court's decision, the D.C. Circuit decided a number of cases that cast doubt on the judge's earlier approach on the burden of proof and evidentiary standards.[48] After the earlier hearings, the D.C. Circuit ordered lower courts to take the detainees' confessions and interrogations into account. The government could now meet its burden by challenging the statements of detainees.

The D.C. Circuit also had recently decided that federal judges needed to apply a "mosaic theory" to the evidence.[49] It directed that the district courts should not "weigh each piece of evidence in isolation, but consider all of the evidence taken as a whole."[50] This method of judging evidence, although sounding intuitive, differs from the ordinary process of assessing evidence. Normally, when a piece of evidence lacks reliability, it is not admitted. With the mosaic analysis, courts can deny habeas petitions solely on evidence where no individual item is individually probative, but if the government can throw enough questionable evidence at the court, it may form a "mosaic" that sticks.

Fawzi's habeas case may have been slightly different from the earlier Kuwaiti detainees, but the legal environment for habeas was changing, and the results across the board reflected a new and more stringent approach to habeas petitioners.

Fayiz Al Kandari

Fayiz Al Kandari was the last of the Kuwaiti detainees to have his habeas merits hearing and the last detainee to have an opinion in his case issued. After extensive litigation regarding evidentiary issues, the court held a five-day merits hearing from October 19 to 23, 2009. The opinion was issued eleven months later, in September 2010.[51] By this point, courts were becoming even more hostile to detainee petitioners.

Here again with Fayiz, there were similarities to the cases of Khalid Al Mutairi and Fouad Al Rabiah, but the court was laser-focused on the differences, with particular emphasis on contradictions in Fayiz's own statements and the court's view that his version of events at the hearing was not credible in light of his earlier admissions. The court rejected Fayiz's assertions regarding the generalized inaccuracy of translations and interrogation reports, indicating that it would hear arguments only as to specific errors regarding particular documents; this was a virtually impossible standard to meet as it would require comparing translations and summaries of interrogations to find specific mistakes or mischaracterizations when the interrogations had taken place up to seven years earlier. Here again, as with Fawzi, the court indicated that it did not need to consider the USG's additional and questionable evidence from informers, which it found to be "in equipoise," but could rely solely on Al Kandari's own statements and admissions against interest to find against him. Importantly, Judge Kollar-Kotelly noted:

> The Court emphasizes that Al Kandari has not argued in these habeas proceedings that any of his statements were the product of abuse or coercion. While Al Kandari makes a general claim in his declaration that he was subjected to abusive and coercive interrogation tactics by the United States, he does not claim that he ever made any statements that were the product of such alleged abuse and coercion. Similarly, while Al Kandari makes a general claim in his declaration that his interrogators "tried to make me confess to things I did not do, and to say things about other people I did not know," he does not claim that such alleged efforts were successful – i.e., that he in fact made false statements as a result of these alleged interrogation tactics. Indeed, neither Al Kandari in his declaration nor his

counsel at the Merits Hearing claimed that Al Kandari has ever made false or inaccurate statements because of the Government's alleged abuse and/or use of coercive interrogation tactics. Moreover, when specifically asked by this Court during the Merits Hearing if Al Kandari was advancing a claim of abuse in this case, Al Kandari's counsel explicitly acknowledged that Al Kandari's generalized claims of abuse are "not relevant to what the Court has to decide." Accordingly, there is no claim in this case that, as a result of coercion, Al Kandari made statements to interrogators that he knew to be false, such that his statements, although accurately reported, are unreliable.[52]

The tactical decision not to press the torture issue allowed the court to review all of his various statements and not to grapple with coerced confessions as it had in earlier cases. The judge did not consider whether there was some cumulative impact of years of abuse and whether it affected the overall reliability of his statements. It is unclear why that decision was made, especially given the role it played in the first two hearings.

The court considered Fayiz's activities as falling into three principal chronological phases. According to his narrative of events, Fayiz stated that he went to Pakistan in June 2001 and met with a respected Sheikh. He left Pakistan in or around August of 2001 for Afghanistan, traveling first to Kandahar before going to Kabul. As with Fouad Al Rabiah, upon his arrival in Kabul, Fayiz also went to the local office of Al Wafa. He stated that he went to Al Wafa because it was "[o]ne of the principal charitable organizations in Afghanistan at that time," and, again, similar to Al Rabiah, he "never had any reason to suspect" that Al Wafa was involved with Al Qaida.

At Al Wafa, Fayiz asked about doing charitable work and was directed to a village an hour outside of Kabul, arriving in early September 2001. While there, Fayiz worked on a charity project digging a well for the community. He stayed in this village through September 11, and remained until the bombing began in early October. He stated that he decided to try to leave the village and get out of Afghanistan; he went back to Kabul and the Al Wafa office, which was closed. A taxi driver told him he should go to Jalalabad and offered to drive him there for a large sum of money; the fleeing Gulf Arabs were almost always charged high rates to get to the border.

The fighting around Jalalabad was intense, and Arabs were being rounded up by police and militias. After a few days at the house of a Saudi whom he met, Fayiz joined with a small group of Arabs who were trying to flee the fighting through the Tora Bora mountains, where, like so many others, he was captured and handed over to US custody.[53]

Judge Kollar-Kotelly took issue with this version of events on matters large and small. She noted that Fayiz had given conflicting statements about to whom he spoke at Al Wafa, first saying it was an unidentified worker because the director was not there, at another time indicating that he spoke to someone whom he believed was the director, and a third time to an unidentified man with a beard who was neither Saudi nor Kuwaiti. This seemed like nitpicking about a brief meeting eight years before, which only resulted in him being directed to a village to dig a well. But in the new legal environment, the court was now drilling down on coherence, consistency, and detailed recollection of facts.[54]

The judge also pointed to minor inconsistencies about Fayiz's decision to travel to Pakistan, as he said in one interrogation that he went to Pakistan to look up a Sheikh whose name he could not recall and with whom he had communicated in the past. Later, however, he said that he had been invited by the Sheikh, whose name he did know, Sheikh Arrahmani, to study at the Sheikh's madrassa. Fayiz also told interrogators that he had first heard about Al Wafa from Sheikh Arrahmani, but when later asked who had first told him about Al Wafa, stated only that he "used to hear about it." At various times, he also said he went to Al Wafa to make a donation and to ask where he could do charitable projects.[55] None of these inconsistencies seem very meaningful on minor points. They could also suggest that in early interrogations, where there was little hope of a positive outcome, Fayiz did not want to be particularly forthcoming with information. But they were now viewed as evidence of lying.

Judge Kollar-Kotelly also pointed out that Fayiz told one interrogator that he traveled south right after the bombing began before heading to Jalalabad but later stated that he left directly for Jalalabad. She also found that, like the others, there were holes of events in the chronology, in Fayiz's case, two "missing months." Now the missing months were significant.

Fayiz also provided conflicting statements as to whether he had ever met a distant cousin, Anas Al Kandari, who had organized the bombing at the US Marine facility on Failakah Island in Kuwait in 2002 (after Fayiz was at Guantanamo), stating to interrogators that he met him during his brief visit to Al Wafa and other times saying he had not.[56]

Of greater relevance, Fayiz made the same statement that Fouad Al Rabiah made and which Judge Kollar-Kotelly accepted in that case – that he "never had any reason to suspect" that Al Wafa was associated with Al Qaida. Unlike Al Rabiah, however, Fayiz acknowledged that he was aware that Suleiman Abu Ghaith was present at the Al Wafa office in Kabul during his visit, although he maintains that he did not see or speak with him at that time. He also acknowledged that he knew Suleiman Abu

Ghaith became the Al Qaida spokesman after 9/11, but did not know that at the time. This also figured significantly in the court's opinion.[57]

The court also focused on the fact that Fayiz admitted that he had been given a weapon when in Tora Bora, taught how to use it, and spent time with certain men whom he knew were affiliated with Al Qaida.[58] The court found it not credible that an unknown noncombatant totally unaffiliated with the fighters would be given a weapon and allowed to wander freely in the Tora Bora area in close proximity to known Al Qaida operatives during a time that the battle of Tora Bora was raging. She drew the inference that the weapon was given to him by Al Qaida.

Judge Kollar-Kotelly analyzed Fayiz's statements critically to question his credibility, but her prime concern was his proximity to known Al Qaida figures and her view that they would not have armed him and allowed him to be present if they did not believe him to be supportive of their cause, even if he was not an active fighter. But that conclusion depended on her prior conclusion that it was Al Qaida that gave him the weapon, by no means the only reasonable inference and unsupported by any evidence.

Judge Kollar-Kotelly restated in Fayiz's case the same formulation that she had laid out in the earlier cases – that the government should be put to its proof and that a detainee should not lose his case because his version of events was not credible. But Fayiz's concessions about whom he knew and was with at the time were too close for her comfort. The court noted:

> While Al Kandari does not bear the burden of proving his innocence, the Court's finding that his version of events is not worthy of belief is itself of some probative value. Recent D.C. Circuit precedent counsels that the provision by a detainee of an implausible explanation for his activities in Afghanistan is a relevant consideration in these habeas proceedings given the "well-settled principle that false exculpatory statements are evidence often strong evidence of guilt."[59]

Her initial view that it is not the detainee's burden and that detention could not rest on the detainee's statements was no longer her approach in evaluating evidence. She was also now willing to look at generalized patterns put forward by the government without reference to specific corroboration of guilt of the individual detainee. She did not acknowledge that many young men trying to flee Afghanistan through the mountains to Pakistan under American bombing suggested mass flight from danger; instead, she now viewed the consistency of the stories as evidence of Al Qaida counter-interrogation training. This too was a new approach she had derived from recent D.C. Circuit precedent.[60]

She concluded:

> [It] is inconceivable that Al Qaida, the Taliban, or their associated enemy forces, would willingly arm Al Kandari with a Kalashnikov rifle and take the time to train him on its proper use, unless Al Kandari himself was part of these organizations. While there is no direct evidence in the record that Al Kandari personally used this weapon against the United States or its Coalition partners, such evidence is not required. Importantly, by Al Kandari's own admission, he was aware that the individuals he chose to associate with while in Tora Bora were members of and were associated with Al Qaida and/or the Taliban. Though his motives for coming to Afghanistan and his activities prior to the Battle of Tora Bora cannot be conclusively determined on the present record, at a minimum it is clear that Al Kandari knew by the time of his stay in Tora Bora that it was more likely than not that he was joining forces with and lending support to Al Qaida and/or the Taliban. This is all the Government need prove.[61]

Judge Kollar-Kotelly moved quickly past the government's other evidence. The informer statements about Fayiz's key role and closeness to Bin Laden would not withstand scrutiny, and so she relied on Fayiz's own words instead. Rather than penalize the government for its improbable assertions as she had in her first two decisions, she simply ignored them.[62]

The court had adopted a different, unacknowledged approach to the evidence. The circumstances leading to why there were inconsistencies among Fayiz's many interrogations were not explored. The government's submission of nonsensical allegations about Fayiz's role was ignored. The court did not explore the specifics of the general representations of abuse. Fayiz had a gun, and he met Al Qaida people when he and hundreds of others were trying to escape. That was enough. Fayiz Al Kandari would spend another six years at Guantanamo.

7

The US Government Re-engages

Ten of the twelve men had now been released. Eight had been sent home without going through the habeas process at all. Two had gone through full habeas hearings and won; the Obama administration quickly sent them back to Kuwait. But Fawzi Al Odah and Fayiz Al Kandari had gone through their habeas hearings and lost. Their appeals were quickly and summarily rejected. Were they to be forever prisoners? What else could be done?

There had been no communication between the government and the lawyers for Fawzi and Fayiz for more than two years. Ambassador Daniel Fried, the senior State Department official chiefly responsible for Guantanamo, said he would not speak to any lawyers for detainees. With respect to Fawzi and Fayiz, there was a stalemate. At last, in 2011, there was a glimmer of hope.

Marcia Newell, the Core Group member based in Washington, approached then-Secretary of State Hillary Clinton at a social event in mid-2011 and said with a smile, "You and I are on opposing sides of an issue."[1] Newell said that she represented the Kuwaiti detainees, and so she presumed that they could not discuss the matter but hoped maybe they could at some point. Secretary of State Clinton told Newell that she should call Dan Fried.[2]

There were no promises of anything, but at least there was a US government official now willing to talk, assuming that the Secretary of State would remember her reply to Newell's gambit, meant what she said, and would tell Ambassador Fried. Newell wanted to do her homework, understanding what role Fried played, whom he knew and trusted within the bureaucracy, and how he would approach the matter. She learned that Fried was the right person to talk to at State; the Secretary of State or her immediate deputies would not get involved in specific discussions about individual prisoners. They required "plausible deniability" if such matters became public or created a diplomatic or political firestorm. Low-level officials would not have the influence to move decision-makers. Guantanamo was Fried's principal assignment, and he had the trust of both career officials and the Secretary as a thorough and savvy senior foreign service officer.

The Core Team also wanted to find out from people who knew Fried whether he was a hawk or dove on Guantanamo – would he be opposed to discussing repatriation of detainees whose habeas petitions had been denied or was he looking to find ways to try to move out those who were not "high-value detainees?" Did he want to shrink the number of presumptive "forever prisoners," or was he comfortable with the apparent new status quo of only releasing those who had won their habeas cases? Did he have credibility with officials at other agencies, who were generally much more hard-line and tended to view the State Department as soft?

Although Ambassador Fried had been supervising Guantanamo since President Obama took office, he had not had any contact with the Core Team. A casual remark at a cocktail party was a thin reed on which to base a strategy and would not necessarily lead to anything. A cold call to Fried would also not be likely to be effective.

The Core Team followed the traditional Washington way of setting up an informal line of communication: finding a mutual friend or contact to make an introduction with the instruction that, whatever the outcome, the friend could communicate that the person seeking the meeting was serious, authorized, and discreet. It would not end up in the newspapers. Who knew whom, and who might make an introduction of Newell to Fried?

The Core Team did its due diligence. Fried had a reputation within the Department for being thoughtful and intellectual. He liked to mentor younger people, and he liked to background journalists on complex foreign policy issues, as long as he was not quoted. He was viewed as open-minded.

Newell learned, importantly, that Fried was also well respected by colleagues within the defense and intelligence establishments. He was not viewed as just another State Department bleeding heart. He could bring agencies together and mitigate in-fighting. Journalists viewed him as an informed and reliable source who provided useful information without crossing any lines.

Through a friend of a friend, Newell was introduced to Rob Watters of the Madison Group. Watters was a well-known, bluff K Street lobbyist. He had good connections at State and Defense, but did not know Fried directly. Watters in turn put her in touch with Chris Cooper, who worked with Madison. Cooper worked his contacts at the Communications Office at State. Cooper was pessimistic, as his contacts told him that Fried was quite negative about the release of detainees who had lost habeas cases. Fortunately, Fried's public statements became more positive as time went on through 2011. Cooper was able to set up a first meeting between

Newell and Fried, with Cooper also joining. Fried reiterated that he did not talk to lawyers, but Newell and Cooper were not lawyers, so it would be okay to meet.

The meeting took place not at the State Department, but at a coffee shop in downtown Washington in May 2012. It appears that he did not want this to be an official, minuted meeting, with Newell's presence in the building registered. Over a cacophony of bean grinders and espresso makers, Newell suggested to Fried that an intergovernmental working group be formed of US and Kuwaiti officials from a variety of areas within their governments to discuss Guantanamo, as well as to visit with Fayez and Fawzi. Newell wanted to explore solutions that would create a framework for ongoing dialogue. She emphasized that Kuwait wanted a forward-looking approach that would honestly consider and try to address security risks and concerns. An interagency working group with both governments would create a structure for continuing discussions.[3]

Fried was well prepared. He said he had been considering for some time a "parole-like" approach. The Obama administration had said it wanted to turn away from the backward-looking national security or criminal law paradigms and try to repatriate men who could safely be released without fear of future violence. Fried had pressed for the Executive Order that had been issued a few months before creating a Periodic Review Board, but the National Security Council had not moved forward in creating the infrastructure that would make it an operational entity. Fried said he had been in contact with the Department of Defense, and he was reasonably confident that if the two agencies could reach consensus, the rest would fall into place. The Periodic Review Board could be set up to play this forward-looking, parole-type role.[4]

"Do you really think you can do that?" Newell responded, laying on the charm. "That's what I do," Fried replied, and he took it on as a priority mission. Shortly thereafter, Fried invited Newell to a meeting with Jeh Johnson, then General Counsel to the Department of Defense (and later Secretary of Homeland Security). Johnson was receptive, and he delegated Paul Lewis, a senior aide, to be the point person at the Pentagon. Lewis was about to be appointed the Department of Defense's Special Envoy on Guantanamo, and this was his principal responsibility. Ray Mabus, the Secretary of the Navy, was also eager to assist and to move prisoners out of naval custody. Things were beginning to move.[5]

There were no guarantees, but if the various agencies were open to talking, there was some possibility of forward momentum for Fawzi and Fayiz. Fried began to move the idea actively through various government channels. He knew the bureaucracy and how to work it. The Kuwaiti government was already on board. The Inter-Agency Working Group was constituted and became a mechanism to get the two governments speaking to each other again.

This initial meeting led to subsequent larger meetings in 2012, with Ambassador Fried, the veteran Kuwaiti Ambassador to the United States, H. H. Salem Abdullah Al Jaber Al Sabah, and ARH, whom the Emir had appointed as Ambassador Plenipotentiary for this issue. Although ARH was a private lawyer representing the Family Committee, the Emir wanted to signal that he had his trust. It gave ARH a unique ability to have productive discussions with everyone without locking in either government to any particular position.

Those back-channel communications laid the groundwork for a comprehensive negotiation based on candid communication of each government's requirements and red lines. The Kuwaitis also sought to have ARH participate in the regular visits to Guantanamo by Kuwaiti officials, but Fried was averse to the idea of having a private lawyer, even one given special status by the Emir, travel to the prison and meet with detainees as well as Guantanamo personnel. But ARH nevertheless quickly made himself a trusted interlocutor and problem solver.

In some of the later negotiations, the US government asked ARH to reach out to the Kuwaiti government to allow a non-Kuwaiti national captured in Iraq as a member of Daesh/ISIS to be resettled in Kuwait. This ISIS member was a Badoon, a stateless person from the region but without Kuwaiti citizenship. This was a surprising request as the United States would not return two long-detained non-terrorist Kuwaiti nationals to Kuwait because of alleged security risks, while at the same time asking for Kuwait to take a non-Kuwaiti admitted ISIS member. The United States did not press the point, but dialogue continued to create a process that focused on addressing security threats or dangers posed in the future rather than rehashing the uncertain, often unreliable, and fragmentary evidence of what had occurred on the Afghan–Pakistan frontier more than a decade before.

This forward focus led to the full implementation and activation of the Periodic Review Board (PRB or Board), which was an entity representing six key units of the US government – the Departments of State, Defense, Justice, Homeland Security, the Director of National Intelligence, and the Joint Chiefs of Staff – to review the cases of detainees who remained and determine whether they could be safely released.[6] Over the course of months, Fried worked with numerous stakeholders within the government to put meat on the bones of the Periodic Review Board process. Fried worked through his contacts to identify people in other agencies who were knowledgeable and reasonable. The Board was to conduct periodic hearings of those still considered enemy combatants. It needed to make decisions by consensus; in practice, unanimity would be required to release a detainee. The PRB's remit specifically directed the Board to focus on the assessment of whether a detainee posed a continuing significant security threat to the United States.[7] Fawzi and Fayiz's habeas defeats would not necessarily make them forever prisoners.

While it was clear that the Obama administration did not intend the PRBs to be yet another kangaroo court, the composition of the board was not promising. The Department of Defense and the Director of National Intelligence had real institutional investment in taking a hard line. They had approved and overseen torture. DoD had been the decision-making authority in the CSRTs and ARBs, which overwhelmingly found in favor of continued detention. DoD had been indoctrinating the detention teams at Guantanamo for years that they were guarding the "worst of the worst," men who supported attacks on the Pentagon and the World Trade Center.

Of course, Rumsfeld and Cheney were gone, and the Obama Defense Department had different values and priorities. But it retained its core mission, and the professional infrastructure remained largely intact, including J. Alan Liotta, a DoD lawyer who was appointed to be the DoD representative to the Board. Liotta was a hard-liner who had been appointed as head of detainee affairs in February 2006 under then-Secretary Rumsfeld. In February 2007, Liotta had been appointed deputy to Deputy Assistant Secretary Cully Stimson, the Defense Department official who had gave a radio interview urging corporate America to stop hiring law firms that defended Guantanamo detainees.[8] Liotta replaced Stimson when Stimson resigned under fire for expressing those views publicly; no doubt such views were still common within the department.[9] Liotta had been threatened with contempt when he was asked to appear before the House Foreign Affairs Committee in 2009 to explain why the Department of Defense had allowed interrogators from foreign nations to interrogate the Guantanamo captives while simultaneously forbidding visits from Members of Congress. Liotta's unconvincing explanation was that the Geneva Conventions obliged captors to protect captives from "public curiosity."[10]

This was nonsense, as the detainees were never given a choice as to whether they wanted to meet with either foreign interrogators or Members of Congress. Members of Congress who traveled to Guantanamo were likely to be less threatening to detainees than Chinese or Jordanian interrogators. Nor were Members of Congress "the public," and the Geneva Conventions were designed to prevent prisoners of war from being displayed in public places, which Guantanamo was not. Finally, it was ironic that Liotta would invoke the protections of the Geneva Conventions when the Bush administration, in which he had served, had held that they did not apply.

If Liotta was a no vote and the decision was not unanimous, the decision would then go up the principals – the Secretaries of Defense and State and Homeland Security, the Director of National Intelligence, the Attorney General, and the Chairman of the Joint Chiefs. The defense and intelligence political leadership were unlikely to overrule career staff to clear a Guantanamo detainee for release.

The inclusion of the Joint Chiefs meant that the chain of military command had an additional vote, and while the uniformed military may have had a somewhat different perspective from the civilians at the Pentagon, their servicemen had been implicated in some of the worst abuses both in Afghanistan and at Guantanamo. Would these representatives clear men for release and implicitly agree that they were not the "worst of the worst?"

The Department of Homeland Security, created in the wake of September 11, had a similar institutional mission directed toward fighting terrorism. The Department of Justice had been defending scores of habeas cases and had taken an extremely hard line in these proceedings.[11] While the Department of State was institutionally less invested in what had come before, it only had one vote. It would likely have difficulty getting hard-liners to change their views.

Nevertheless, this was a new administration headed by a new president who had renounced torture and who had pledged to close Guantanamo. It wanted to find some acceptable way to reduce numbers through repatriation to countries willing to work with the US government, although the task was complicated by Congressional legislation that prohibited any detainee from being brought to the United States.[12] It was difficult to convince third countries to accept detainees when the United States would not.

The Core Team needed to find a way to include Fawzi and Fayiz within the group that could effectively navigate the new process. It had to make the best of the tribunal that had been appointed and to formulate a strategy that put these last two men on the right side of the dangerous/non-dangerous line.

Now that there was a new process, it also became critical to build trust between the two governments and to give the US confidence that Kuwait would be a partner in ensuring that, if the final two detainees were released, Kuwait would provide the necessary support and security infrastructure so that there would be no material risk of a repeat of the rapid release of detainees without supervision or the Al Ajmi suicide bombing tragedy. The United States wanted the detainees to be held for some period of time in Kuwait under verifiable supervision and did not much care about whether there was a basis under Kuwaiti law.

The Kuwaitis wanted to provide security infrastructure, but it had to be consistent with Kuwaiti law, which did not permit indefinite detention without trial. The United States was distrustful and vague and viewed the Kuwaiti law argument as an excuse for inaction; the Kuwaiti team viewed the United States as unwilling to agree to practical solutions and dismissive of Kuwaiti sovereignty and legal process. The days and weeks of captivity dragged on as the governments remained stalemated.

ARH and the Core Team were eventually able to open a regular channel of communication with both the US government and the Kuwaiti government. ARH used his knowledge of both political and legal cultures to fit those needs within the necessary frameworks in both countries. But how could Kuwait agree to further custody without due process under Kuwaiti law?

Finally, ARH had his eureka legal insight. A Kuwaiti statute allowed a parent to request the assistance of the Kuwaiti government to commit a child who needed inpatient medical or psychiatric care. If there was a basis for such inpatient treatment, the Kuwaiti government would agree with the parents, evaluate the child, and provide appropriate care. This was not a criminal proceeding or arbitrary detention. It was a protective measure for the benefit of the child. There was no restriction on the age of the child that could be subject to the statute. This would allow Fawzi and Fayiz to come home, see their families, and receive the treatment and help that they likely needed after so many years at Guantanamo. This was not imprisonment, which Kuwait would not do without trial and conviction based on evidence under Kuwaiti law. To be sure, if Fawzi and Fayiz were held as children in need of care, their freedom of movement would be reduced, but a rehabilitation center could be readied that would have good facilities and services. And most of all, Fawzi and Fayiz could see their families.

How would the families feel about this? Would Fayiz and Fawzi's parents agree? How long would they agree to accept commitment to the rehabilitation center? More importantly, would Fayiz and Fawzi agree? While they technically could be sent to the rehabilitation center on their parents' application and without their consent, it would be untenable if they did not agree. The US government would also require that Fawzi and Fayiz agree not to challenge their commitment to a rehabilitation facility in court when they returned to Kuwait.

ARH believed that it would be far better for the detainees to be in Kuwait, where they could be visited by family members until they were ready for release and reintegration into Kuwaiti society. Rehabilitation in Kuwait was a solution that everyone should be able to accept. But would they?

Through patient negotiation, a dialogue was undertaken between the US government and the Core Team to design rehabilitation facilities that would be both secure and therapeutic. Newell had long experience in project management, and she suggested the development of "punch lists" to understand the United States' minimum requirements for security and Kuwait's maximum capacities for a rehabilitation program acceptable under Kuwaiti law and embraced by the families and the returning detainees. This involved top medical and psychological personnel, benchmarking with other rehabilitation facilities, religious counseling, and physical rehabilitation in an atmosphere that also permitted extensive family involvement.

Once the dialogue became tripartite and cooperative, it gained momentum. Ambassador Fried had moved on from the Guantanamo brief, but his astute and effective role within the US government laid a strong foundation for the next stage. By 2013, there was a process in place that could potentially result in the release of Fawzi and Fayiz.

The Core Team needed a new lawyer to negotiate the new process, who would be able to present the very different type of advocacy that was required to convince a skeptical panel that these men posed no security threats and that the Kuwaiti government would maintain its commitments. They also needed a lawyer with knowledge of the region and the culture, who could work with the families and with Fayiz and Fawzi, who, after years in limbo, were angry at their treatment and skeptical that any initiative proposed by the US government would lead to a different result than all of the other proceedings. Fawzi and Fayiz wanted representatives who would pound the table and demand apologies and compensation. They wanted to make a public record of their ill treatment. They wanted to fight and push back against the evidence of past wrongdoing – to make clear that they had been wrongly held. But if they were to be effective witnesses in their own case for repatriation, they needed to understand and embrace the process, trust their lawyers, and devote time and care to removing the carapace of rage and despair. Recriminations would do nothing to achieve the overarching goal to get them home.

The legal team needed to avoid detailed engagement on the purported bases for their initial detention. It needed to deal with the fact that Fayiz and Fawzi were viewed as leaders in various acts of rebellion or opposition to the detention, including hunger strikes, and refusals to cooperate in various aspects of the detention regime. As in many institutions, in predicting future dangerousness, the detaining authority often viewed passivity by inmates as a sign of reform and active opposition as a sign of continued commitment to aggressive action. Fawzi and Fayiz had not been passive.

Fawzi and Fayiz needed a legal team that understood that this new proceeding was not an adversarial proceeding in the normal sense. The goal was to persuade, to humanize these detainees, and to work with them, so that they could maintain their own sense of self-respect yet still project an image of stability and calm for the future.

The Core Team identified me, who also, not coincidentally, is the author of this book. My law firm, Lewis Baach, was a litigation firm in Washington that had been working since early 2002 on a pro bono basis for Guantanamo detainees. The firm was an early member of the group known as the Guantanamo Bay Bar Association, volunteer lawyers that cooperated and coordinated on strategy in advocating for detainees. Lewis was also the Chair of Reprieve US, which represented numerous detainees and ran the Life After Guantanamo working to ease the adjustment of resettled detainees.

As a small firm with a long commitment to human rights, the partnership had little hesitation in taking on these cases; Guantanamo Bay was, in their view, the defining moral and legal challenge of this generation of lawyers. It raised fundamental questions about the rule of law in a time of stress. It squarely placed at the center of American legal culture the issue of whether indefinite detention without trial would be allowed in the United States under the Constitution. It posed the question of whether torture was part of the American legal process.

Lewis Baach were not "cause lawyers." The firm represented banks and hedge funds and foreign governments and international liquidators in asset recovery matters. The firm advised lawyers on professional and ethical issues. There were no table pounders or TV lawyers. The firm could focus carefully on the objective of getting Fawzi and Fayiz home and how best to achieve it. In 2013, my firm and I joined the team for the last and most difficult lap. I had known Marcia Newell for years and had great respect for what the Core Team had been able to accomplish through patient, strategic litigation and negotiation. William Brown and ARH were lawyers' lawyers who wanted a quiet, swift end to the ordeal of the Kuwaitis.

Michael Williams, Fried's deputy, who took over on an interim basis after Fried moved on within the State Department, agreed with Newell on a detailed punch list of what was required and the critical path to get there. When Newell probed what the punch list should specifically contain, Williams told her, "Go watch 'The Wire,'" which was a gritty, profane cable television series about drug dealers and police in Baltimore. What did Guantanamo have to do with violent drug crime in West Baltimore?

The show is framed by omnipresent and intrusive surveillance and wiretapping. The drug dealers use burner phones and other evasive actions to avoid detection. The police need to find countermeasures to ensure security and try to prevent violence. The punch list would need to provide specific measures to ensure that these detainees would be comprehensively surveilled and supervised and not simply released back into Kuwaiti society after leaving rehabilitation.

Michael Williams soon took a different position within the government, and President Obama appointed Cliff Sloan as the first Special Envoy to Close Guantanamo. The team would need to negotiate with yet another new official. But the position had been elevated, and Sloan had direct access to both the President and Secretary of State John Kerry. He had a stellar resume and a sterling career, having spent time as a Deputy Solicitor General as well as a clerk for Justice Stevens (who had written a number of the major Guantanamo decisions for the Supreme Court). Quite coincidentally, he was an old friend of mine and our family. While that would not affect the process or the outcome, it allowed for an ease of communication and exchange of views so that we could discuss clearly what each side needed to solve this unique problem.

Sloan was blunt: There was no trust at the moment on the part of the United States with respect to Kuwait keeping promises about security. The State Department was still smarting from the quick releases. It had lost credibility with other agencies because State rightly or wrongly had expected longer detention. He was not interested in what had been agreed or not agreed between the governments, or what was or was not feasible under Kuwaiti law, or whether the United States had or had not provided evidence. The other agencies were angry, and this made his job more difficult.

Kuwait would have to demonstrate its commitments and show the infrastructure in place to ensure Kuwait's pledges would be implemented.

He also indicated that the United States viewed Kuwait as not as proactive as it should be with respect to terror finance generally. It was not just Fayiz and Fawzi; Kuwait needed to show cooperation and measurable progress to plug what the United States viewed as Kuwaiti holes in the global terrorist infrastructure.

The United States had certain red lines. It would accept the rehabilitation matrix but needed a process that would ensure the required inpatient treatment of returned detainees for a period of at least one year. To be sure, these men would receive PRB hearings on the individual merits of their specific cases, but Kuwait's ability to provide security guarantees would be critical to a positive outcome.

The Core Team decided to propose that the year be divided into two halves. The first six months would be on an inpatient basis, with family allowed to visit freely. The second six months would allow Fawzi and Fayiz to leave during the day as long as they were back in the evenings and attended scheduled sessions with care professionals. They would surrender their passports and not leave Kuwait for an agreed period of time.

After extensive discussions back and forth involving Sloan and his deputies, as well as Newell and me, and between Sloan and the other "stakeholders," there was finally agreement, provided that the US government was able on request to obtain from Kuwait information and documentation of compliance with the agreed conditions. The Core Team also prepared, in conjunction with Dr. Adel Al Zayed, the head of the rehabilitation center, a detailed rehabilitation manual that would be the reference work for what was agreed and the standard to measure compliance.

Fawzi and Fayiz's parents agreed readily to the rehabilitation center option. While they would not have their children back in their homes as quickly as hoped, their boys would be back in their country. They could see them, hug them, and plan the future with them. Their sons would not die at Guantanamo.

The next step was to gain the clients' agreement to our strategy. It was certainly possible that they would not agree to further unwarranted impingement on their liberty after all this time. They might not agree to be treated as presumptive extremists who needed to be "deprogrammed" or rehabilitated. They might refuse to commit another year of their lives to anything less than total freedom.

It was clear that the Periodic Review Board hearings would require a great deal of preparation with the detainees. But it was also clear that the hearings would focus a great deal on providing enforceable security guarantees and assurances. The support of the Kuwaiti authorities and the bona fides of the residential rehabilitation center would be as important as the testimony of Fawzi and Fayiz themselves. The optics within the United States, with a hostile Congress and certain dug-in elements of the defense and intelligence establishment, were a critical additional dimension of the multidimensional chess game about to begin.

8

The First Periodic Review Board

Lewis Baach was retained formally to represent Fawzi Al Odah in March 2013. The Family Committee also wanted Fayiz Al Kandari to consolidate his representation with Lewis Baach and implement a new, more cooperative strategy, but Fayiz elected to stay with his trusted, but much more aggressive lawyer, who had by then retired from the military. We had just one client, but a lot of work to do and not much time to do it.

I had never been to Guantanamo. I had been working on Guantanamo-related matters for more than a decade but had never been required to visit the base. My civil case regarding torture involved the British detainees; I had seen them in London, as Tony Blair had prevailed upon George Bush for their release. I had also litigated the force-feeding cases, which required expert doctor visits to gather evidence from detainees about their treatment and health. Many of my colleagues in the "Guantanamo Bay Bar Association" had been to Guantanamo dozens of times, spending months there. They made clear how difficult the US government made it to have constructive access to the clients.

"Everything at Guantanamo is hard," my friend Clive Stafford Smith, then head of Reprieve, told me. There were usually two flights per week through Fort Lauderdale and a flight through Jacksonville Naval Station. Jacksonville was for habeas visits only, but not permitted for PRBs. For PRBs, one needed to go through Fort Lauderdale. What if your client had both a habeas and a PRB? You had to choose and say which proceeding was the sole purpose of the trip, leading to more time, more cost, and more trips. Flights were frequently cancelled or subject to long delays.

Although Cuba was only ninety miles away from South Florida at its closest point, the flights to GTMO took nearly three hours; the Fort Lauderdale plane for the PRB teams was an old turboprop, and it could not fly over Cuban airspace. Instead, the flight went over water until it had just about reached Haiti and then made a wide turn to approach the landing strip on the leeward side of the bay on the far eastern edge of Cuba.

In order to be admitted, it was necessary to have a security clearance and a valid invitation. A security clearance generally took months, and invitations often arrived at the last minute or too late for a scheduled visit.

If papers were not in order in some small way, boarding was denied, and if someone had been allowed to board the flight in Florida and then discovered not to have the right credentials, they were not allowed onto the base and would be sent out on the next flight, sometimes bumping someone already booked on that flight and leaving that passenger stuck on the island for up to a week. I was bumped once from a return flight to Florida by an arriving passenger whose passport had expired, but had been allowed on the flight; the invalid passport was not caught until she arrived in Guantanamo. She had to go back on the same plane. I was forced to provide a not insignificant financial incentive to another passenger to avoid staying five extra days and missing my wife's birthday. Nearly all the flights were full, and lawyers were at the bottom of the priority list. Despite the rickety old planes, tickets were expensive.

Cell phones did not work at Guantanamo; old-style telephone cards were available to be used at pay phones. Lawyers were generally housed in Bachelors' Officers Quarters on the leeward side of the base, but the detention facility was on the windward side, requiring a bus ride to the pier, an early morning ferry, and then another bus to the detention facility. The chow hall was open until 6:30 p.m.; if you were late returning to the leeward side from a client visit, dinner came from vending machines. You could also grab dinner at the windward side McDonalds or Subway and get the last ferry back.

The detention facility was a city within a city. It was ringed by reinforced, blast-proof concrete and razor wire. A giant sign at the gate was emblazoned, without irony, with the Joint Detention Force logo and motto, "Honor Bound to Defend Freedom," in huge letters. After passing through the gate, counsel would go through a security checkpoint and then into a makeshift sally port that housed the guards. You would enter; the door would be locked behind you; and you would show credentials and be searched. Everything that was brought into the sally port was examined. Detainees would often look forward to receiving food or gifts from home or clothing or supplies that the lawyers would pick up at the Naval Exchange. The rules that governed what could or could not be brought into the detainee meetings changed virtually every visit. Small DVD players would be allowed in; detainees would all request them; but by the next visit, DVD players were no longer allowed in, so the lawyers would bring back a bunch of unusable DVD players and confront very disappointed clients. Sometimes hot food would be allowed in; sometimes snacks only; sometimes nothing at all. Some detainees would decline the visit when they learned they would not be getting anything from home or something they had urgently requested on the last visit like a pair of sandals or shampoo. Or the client would cancel the next day's visit. The lawyer–detainee relationships were tenuous in any event, given the absence of results and clear timelines. The guards promoting the narrative that the lawyers were Jewish spies did not help.

Most importantly, Guantanamo detention authorities insisted that every detainee have a complete body search, including body cavities, before being shackled hand and foot and put in the barred van to be taken to the meeting area with the lawyers. Not surprisingly, many detainees hated the breach of privacy and the discomfort of being stripped and having probes shoved in their anuses and under their testicles before meeting with their lawyers. Such intrusive searches, on top of everything else, were more than many wanted to endure a second time each day, as they were required to go back to their cell areas for lunch and go through the same process in the afternoon. Legal visits were difficult enough without that added humiliation, and we all understood that there were days in which detainees were not mentally prepared to work with us, either during the afternoon session or even at all, especially as many of them had been seeing lawyers for years with no apparent result.

Meetings were held in two trailers, each of which had a barred cell on one side and a small table on the other side with two plastic chairs and a large hook in the floor to which the client was shackled with a carabiner. There was a camera in the room for continuous surveillance; we were told that the cameras recorded video only, although over time there were a number of incidents that made clear that there was sound recording capability as well. We operated on the assumption that whatever we said could be overheard.

No legal pads were permitted. All notes were taken on loose sheets of paper that were then handed over to the security teams to be reviewed for classified material. This generally took some weeks. The notes were sent from Guantanamo to the secure facility in Crystal City, Virginia, and ultimately, the declassified portion of the notes would be released to the lawyer. I did not envy the classification team the review of dozens of pages of my handwriting, although they found plenty to black out. So much of the preparation relied on memory of what was said because the notes from visits close in time to a hearing rarely made it back before the hearing date. Notes were taken with the soft plastic inside of a Bic pen, as the hard outer plastic casing was viewed as a potential weapon.

There was grumbling about all the difficulties that Guantanamo imposed, but it was far better than what our clients were experiencing. And we could leave. There was generally good esprit de corps and sharing of information among the lawyers. Cheap wine and beer could be purchased at the Naval Exchange, and the days' events were often discussed over drinks in plastic cups in the evening. Other lawyers fortified themselves for the long, hot evenings with bottles of rum from the Naval Exchange (from Puerto Rico, not from over the fence in Cuba).

Our first hurdle to seeing our client was getting a security clearance, both to be permitted to visit Guantanamo and to have access to classified material about the client. The forms were long and detailed. They required that every foreign visit that I had made for the last seven years be documented, as well as a listing of all foreigners with whom I had met in that time. I was an international litigator. I had 167 foreign trips recorded in my passport for which I was required to account in detail. The government also asked for lists of friends, relatives, and neighbors, nearly all of whom were duly asked whether I had ever mentioned to them any particular interest in violently overthrowing the US government.

I rushed the form to the relevant authorities in April 2013; the clearance came through nearly ten months later. During that time, I could not review any classified material or see my client. But there were plenty of other things to do.

Another Habeas Challenge

At the time that we were retained, we were focused on the PRB process, as there were no available remedies in court. In early 2013, however, President Obama, during his State of the Union, announced the withdrawal of all troops from Afghanistan, with half of all troops to leave that month and the remainder withdrawn by the end of 2014. The president's rhetoric was unambiguous: "By the end of 2014, our war in Afghanistan will be over."[1]

Given that the standard under the post-September 11 Authorization for Use of Military Force was that the United States could detain individuals only until "active hostilities" between the United States and opposing forces in Afghanistan had ceased, and the president had now declared a date certain for the cessation of hostilities and had started to draw down troops, there was a strong argument under the Law of War that all detainees were required to be released no later than the end of 2014. Renewed habeas petitions could be filed to seek a declaration that the detention authority would cease at that time.

There was always the risk that the executive would argue that the president's statements were rhetorical and prospective and that there could be "active hostilities" even after the war was over. We had some hope that the Obama administration would not play such semantic games or argue that the Global War on Terror was everywhere and forever so that the withdrawal from Afghanistan was irrelevant. Nevertheless, this was an opening to bring new habeas proceedings, which, even if not successful, could create pressure on the government to implement a PRB process that would avoid requiring complex and novel questions regarding the Law of War and the scope of executive authority to be submitted again to the federal courts.

A new habeas proceeding would at least put their cases back on the government's agenda. President Obama's statements were clear, and it would be difficult for the president to say that was not what he really meant or for lower officers in the chain of command to contradict their Commander-in-Chief. Nor would it be easy for the government to tell a court that it could say one thing for public consumption and something quite different in court. In addition, it could force the government to give up its studied ambiguity on what the Global War on Terror was, where it was, what criteria would determine whether it continued, and how to know when it was over.

The Third Geneva Convention requires that "prisoners of war shall be released and repatriated without delay after the cessation of active hostilities." What was the definition of "active hostilities," short of a formal declaration of the end of the war, which had never been formally declared in the first place?[2] There was guidance in the Third Geneva Convention and official commentaries that made clear that a formal peace treaty was not required. A ceasefire, even a tacit ceasefire, might be sufficient, even if military operations continue. And "without delay" indicated that the process needed to be put into motion quickly.

Without combat troops in the country, the United States, it could be argued, was no longer fighting the war in Afghanistan that had been the basis for the AUMF. It had been nearly a decade since Justice O'Connor had written in the *Hamdi* case that the right to detain during wartime lasted only until the war was over, and the courts were leery of extending that right indefinitely. "If the practical circumstances of a given conflict are entirely unlike those of the conflicts that informed the development of war, that understanding might unravel."[3] Had it by now unraveled?

It had been nine years since Justice Kennedy had written in *Rasul/ Al Odah*, "Perhaps, where detainees are taken from a zone of hostilities, detention without proceedings or trial would be justified by military necessity for a matter of weeks, but as the period of detention stretches from months to years, the case for continued detention to meet military exigencies become weaker."[4] Could there really be a valid military necessity for continuing to keep Fawzi Al Odah in Guantanamo?

We were not naïve about the likelihood that a federal court would take the bold step of using the president's statements as a formal declaration of the cessation of hostilities if the government said otherwise. If the War on Terror was everywhere and forever, the withdrawal of troops in Afghanistan might not equate to the cessation of active hostilities in that new kind of war. We also knew that, despite some broad statements of general principle by the Supreme Court, after more than eleven years, not one detainee had been released through direct court order.

We were also concerned that a court might hold that the end of 2014, the date when President Obama said the war would be over, had not yet arrived, and at the time of filing hostilities were still ongoing. Anything could happen; policies changed all the time for political reasons, security reasons, or a host of other reasons. Courts generally do not decide the legal consequences of hypothetical future actions. The court could hold that the dispute was not ripe for decision.

At the same time, given the clear statements that had been made and the commencement of drawdowns, this was not a vague declaration of future expectation. Superpowers could not pull out overnight after twelve years of combat. Chaos would result, as would be demonstrated tragically in Afghanistan in 2021. And if we had to wait until the last soldier left Afghanistan, proceedings could not even begin until 2015, and Fawzi would have lost another two years.

Our most significant concern was not that we would lose but that it would lead the government to dig in its heels on repatriation in retaliation. It might be seen by the US Working Group as inconsistent with good faith in ongoing negotiations. It was also possible that the PRB would be delayed until the principal legal questions were determined in the new habeas proceedings. But now that the Core Team was talking to the State Department, we could ask and try to obtain some guidance.

From our discussions, it became clear that the focus of the State Department was on facilitating and expediting the PRB process; the habeas proceeding would be on a separate track within the Justice Department. We could litigate both the new habeas petition and the PRB without jeopardizing Fawzi's release. On September 18, 2013, before anything had happened with respect to Fawzi's PRB (and before we had even received security clearances), we filed a new habeas petition, asking for Fawzi's immediate release and repatriation upon cessation of hostilities – no later than December 31, 2014, as declared by the president. Any continued detention after that would serve only a punitive purpose and not a prophylactic one, which was not permitted under the AUMF and the Geneva Conventions.

Any hopes that the Obama administration would take a more nuanced view of the War on Terror or executive power were quickly dashed. The government argued that it was speculative that it would fail to transfer Fawzi promptly when hostilities have ceased. The government also submitted affidavits from senior military officials that made clear that the president's statements were not declaring the end of hostilities. They were merely aspirational, they argued. Effectively, the cessation of hostilities would occur when the Department of Defense said so. Thankfully, by the time the judge issued her opinion rejecting our arguments and denying the petition in August 2014, Fawzi had already been cleared by the PRB. Whether the existence of a habeas proceeding may have had some impact on the PRB result cannot be known, but the existence of an additional avenue of potential relief, in our view, was useful to keep Fawzi's case visible and legally significant.

Fawzi Al Odah received his notification in February 2014 that he would have a full PRB hearing. Shortly thereafter, security clearances came through for the Lewis Baach legal team. We went immediately to the secure facility in Crystal City to review Fawzi's classified material, including health and disciplinary records. Without referencing any classified material here (Fawzi told me everything about his behavioral record in any event), I quickly became aware that we would have issues about Fawzi's conduct at Guantanamo. He was a leader of resistance to many of the arbitrary rules at Guantanamo and to his indefinite captivity without charge. He had been a leader of the hunger strike. He had been force-fed for long periods of time. He had repeatedly sought privacy for such things as going to the toilet or taking a shower and tried to block the windows into his cell with towels or paper. Fawzi had thrown bodily fluids at guards. And there were innumerable smaller, technical infractions, and such infractions had increased with the length of his captivity. We would not be able to argue that his model behavior as a detainee was an indicator that he would not be dangerous in the future.

With four months until the hearing, there was a huge amount to do. We knew from Marcia Newell's and my dialogue with the State Department, and from ARH as a member of the Interagency Working Group, that our task would have at least four distinct and critical components.

First, even before meeting him, we knew that Fawzi was angry and cynical about his detention and doubtful that yet another hearing process would provide a meaningful opportunity for release. We were his third set of lawyers, and the previous two had won certain battles but lost the war; he was still stuck at Guantanamo. Why should this new bunch be any different? If Fawzi was going to be a forever prisoner anyway, why should he humiliate himself before yet another group of American captors who, he might well presume, had no intention of releasing him?

A first critical task was to build trust and to convince him that we had good reason to believe that the PRB process was different. This was not going to be easy. While certain early PRB petitions had been granted, no one had yet gone home. We were reading political and bureaucratic tea leaves. While we thought it was worth his time and effort and, most of all, his commitment to diligent preparation, why should he agree with our assessment? Fawzi's family was an important part of that effort to convince him. But they saw him only rarely in video calls that were monitored. Trust in the attorney–client relationship was also necessary. So, the first challenge was to connect directly with Fawzi himself.

Second, Fawzi needed to know that although the process might focus less on 2001, it would be rigorous in ascertaining whether or not Fawzi himself would pose a security threat in the future if he were released. In other words, had he matured, was he remorseful about the past? This was somewhat difficult and delicate. Of course, Fawzi was more mature; he was thirteen years older than when he left home. He had suffered torture and abuse. But his disciplinary record was problematic. We would need to neutralize that record before the Board to convince it that his oppositional conduct should not be taken as a predictor of future risk.

And for what was Fawzi to be remorseful? He had maintained, through pressure and struggle and torture for all these years, that he had done nothing wrong and he had never been charged with any crime. A PRB, like almost all tribunals making what was in effect a sentencing decision, would look toward expressions of regret and remorse as an indicator of maturity and responsibility. Did Fawzi need to express remorse? Would he? For what? How could he convince the Board that he had learned from his experience without admitting to something he had not done? He could not and would not do that, and, indeed, there was always some risk that any admissions about previous conduct would just be used as a basis for further detention.

On the assumption that Fawzi could be convinced to participate, the next challenge was to work with him to shape his presentation so that the Board had confidence that here was a man that they could look in the eye (virtually, from Crystal City to a conference room in Guantanamo) and feel comfortable that he was not a terrorist threat; that he was not angry; and that he was not hiding any buried resentments or antagonisms that could cause a problem later. The presentation needed to be factually honest, but the emotional tone in engaging with the Board was critical.

Third, full acceptance of both the rigor and the benefits of the rehabilitation process by both Fawzi and the United States was necessary. Would Fawzi agree to another year without his freedom, even in Kuwait with access to his family? Would the United States accept that the agreement of Khalid Al Odah under Kuwaiti law, and Fawzi's promise not to challenge Khalid's decision to commit Fawzi to the rehabilitation center, would be honored once he was home? Other detainees who had not been committed by their parents had been to the rehabilitation center but left in a matter of days. Would this new process provide confidence to the government that the same thing would not happen again?

Fourth, the Board needed to be convinced whatever they believed about Fawzi's future dangerousness – which everyone recognized was difficult to predict with confidence – that the Kuwaiti government would present and implement a comprehensive security plan that would monitor, detect, and prevent any reasonable prospect of Fawzi engaging in extremist conduct. The US government needed to know that Fawzi was being thoroughly monitored; that he would not leave the country; and that he would not participate in extremist fundraising or other activities. Kuwaiti commitments to security and counterterrorism would be as much on trial as Fawzi Al Odah.

Meeting in Guantanamo

We made our first visit to Guantanamo from February 24 to 27, 2014. We landed on the airstrip on the leeward side and cleared security through an empty airplane hangar. An old school bus carried us up the hill to the Bachelor's Officer's Quarters (BOQ). We passed row upon row of empty open-air shelters with toilet and shower facilities, enough to hold thousands of people. These were built in anticipation of some possible exodus of refugees from Haiti or Cuba or some other troubled region within rafting distance of Guantanamo. These had stood empty for more than twenty years.

These shelters were what President Trump proposed in early 2025 to be used to house up to 30,000 migrants while their cases for asylum were being adjudicated. The facilities were hopelessly dilapidated and could not house 3,000 people, let alone 30,000, and none of them adequately. As of October 2025, 710 migrants have been shuttled through the base; they were mainly held in Camp 6, which had been used for detainees.

Continuing past the shelters, we passed a large chow hall, a firehouse, a small grocery store, and a busted-up basketball court. We reached the BOQ at the top of the hill with a view of the sea below. The BOQ is a wide cinder block building with a check-in and a pub-entertainment room housing a huge television, usually tuned to sports, a pool table, and vending machines. The staff, like most of the staff on the base, are Philippine nationals, whom the US government is allowed to hire at less than the US minimum wage; they were paid around $3 per hour.

The rooms were spare but spacious, laid out in two wings on opposite sides of open-air cinder block corridors that run at a perpendicular from the main building. It was oppressively humid outside despite the desert-like vegetation. The rooms themselves are air-conditioned to meat-locker level. Earlier generation televisions fuzzily broadcast Armed Forces Television and a few random US local network affiliates, which broadcast local news and weather from Detroit, which was forecasting snow. Most mornings, we would leave our rooms and see crabs scuttling along the cement outdoor corridor or a giant lizard blinking in the sunlight. Feral cats, left behind from prior deployments, roam the base.

As Carol Rosenberg wrote in the *New York Times*, "Guantanamo is a large naval base, which has the trappings of small-town America and the amenities of a college campus, and functions like a cross between a gated community and a police state."[5] There is a school and a restaurant with karaoke and a huge Naval Exchange on the windward side. The Cooper Field complex has five astroturf fields and a 400 meter track. A parched area with sand pits and low, brown grass is a nine-hole golf course. There are housing nodes, depending on rank and marital status, that vary between college dorms and Southern California-style split-level suburban houses. There are bowling alleys and movie nights and small boats for rent. Guantanamo has its own radio station, staffed by service people, with the motto "Rockin' in Fidel's Backyard." They sell T-shirts (Figure 8.1). This is where soldiers and visitors live. Then there are the Joint Detention Force prison facilities.

The detention zone is a base within a base, staffed by a large detachment of soldiers working around-the-clock shifts, guarding an ever-dwindling number of prisoners. Here, there is no sense of small-town America or a college campus. Guards with machine guns patrol the perimeter.

Figure 8.1 Radio GTMO.

Turreted, armored jeeps with large protruding guns patrol outside the multiple layers of razor wire that form an outer perimeter. It is shrouded from view by tarpaulins, so the detainees never see the sea. There are naval vessels stationed off the coast to watch for detainees who might escape, where they would confront sharks swimming off the coast. None has ever made it even through the first layer of security.

My colleague, Kate Toomey, and I were up early and took the first ferry to the windward side. It is about a twenty-minute journey, pleasantly breezy before the day's heat. We catch a bus from the windward side dock and meet the officers assigned as Fawzi's Personal Representatives to the PRB. One officer for Fawzi's case was an Air Force Major who had recently been transferred from a group that had been guarding nuclear missiles in the Mountain West. The second officer was an older reservist who had been called up repeatedly since 2001. This was "better duty than Iraq or Afghanistan, believe me," the second officer said, referring to earlier deployments. They prefer not to be named.

None of the military officers viewed this as an assignment that would help their careers. We had seen in transcripts of earlier hearings that military representatives did not have the interests of the detainee in mind. Some had spoken against their detainees. These military representatives for the PRB were not lawyers, and it was unclear at first if they would be advocates or adversaries. The military representatives would be in the room when we spoke to Fawzi and they would be in the room when the PRB hearings were held. This would not be a normal attorney–client meeting. We were concerned that if we tried to exclude them, they would be unsupportive of Fawzi's release, and if we included them, they might reveal privileged material or make comments at the hearing that could be harmful. We knew that we really had no choice but to work together and, as they would be the only people in the hearing room who actually worked for the United States, we needed to convince them as well that Fawzi was a good and safe person who should be released.

Our lead military officer made clear that he had no preconceptions about Fawzi or anyone else; that he had been assigned a mission; and that he would carry out that mission to the best of his abilities. He would assist us and Fawzi and work to put forward the best presentation that was possible, consistent with the facts. He kept his word. As did all the military representatives working on PRBs.

Our first stop before going to see Fawzi was the Office of the Military Representative, a low-slung bungalow on the windward side, where we would meet the other military representatives and review classified material on the secure system there. We could also review pleadings and our notes. It allowed us to have the substance of the material in our heads for the interviews because we could not show Fawzi any classified material or refer to such material specifically. We were also able to access the PRB Secretariat website, which was a public site that often-contained questions that recent panels had put to other detainees. This gave us at least some data points on a potential roadmap for our hearing. At the very least, Fawzi needed to be prepared for every question that had previously been asked that we could access.

Our military representatives had a car that they could use, and after the first visit, they would kindly come down to the ferry pier and give us a head start on the day. After a winding drive, we arrived at the perimeter of the detention facility of the prison within the island fortress. The detention facility also had its own separate command and mission statement (Figure 8.2). Despite the documented record of abuse on an industrial scale, its mission statement proclaimed its responsibility for the "safe, humane, legal care and custody of law of armed conflict detainees."

We had arrived. We needed to be friendly, professional, and helpful to our client in any way that we could. One of those ways was to let the authorities know that we would be cooperative and respectful and would hope for reciprocity. A number of detainee lawyers had treated the military personnel with indifference; some were confrontational. It certainly did not help their clients.

Figure 8.2 Joint Task Force Guantanamo.

The security check took time. We went through metal detectors and were thoroughly searched. The same protocol governed our departure with a turnover of the day's meeting notes to the security team before being permitted back into the sally port. Some of what we brought for our clients was removed from our bags, including food treats from home. It made no sense to argue with the guards on duty. They had their orders, and we would need to deal with any issues later and in writing.

We left the sally port and went up the stairs to the makeshift trailers to meet Fawzi. Fawzi had been brought earlier by truck and was locked into the half of the trailer that was a cell. He was shackled hand and foot with a connecting chain, and the guards unlocked the cell and brought him the few feet to the other half of the cell. They attached him by his leg shackles to a hook built into the floor. I asked whether that was necessary and was told it was regulation. I asked about releasing his hand shackles. After a nervous glance between the guards, they took the hand shackles off, so he could shake hands and more easily make notes with the inside of his Bic pen.

My first impression of Fawzi was how young he appeared. He had come to Guantanamo at age twenty-four and was now thirty-seven. He had some gray in his hair and beard. But he had been on hunger strike for years, and he was extremely slight. His weight had dropped as low as 108 pounds (51 kg.); he might have weighed 120 pounds when we first met (56 kg.). His jumpsuit was way too big. He indicated that the hunger strike had long-term effects on his health, especially his digestion, and he was not able to eat many foods or in any significant amounts. I sent regards from his family, whom I had spoken to before my visit, which drew a first smile. But he was not especially engaged. It was clear to me he had few expectations and he was there because his father had asked him to be. We were just another bunch of lawyers. There were also two military officers in uniform in this cramped half of the trailer. He was told they were on his side, but he had little reason to believe this was true.

Fawzi made clear that he was innocent; he would never say otherwise because he would not lie; and he did not believe in any process set up by the US government. I told him that I had no secret insights but that I had been watching events at Guantanamo for more than a decade; that Obama may not be perfect, but he was certainly not George W. Bush with respect to Guantanamo or terrorism or torture; and that Obama also needed to find a way to clear out Guantanamo and keep his campaign pledge. That did not mean any specific detainee would be cleared, but the goal appeared to be to grant clearances unless there was a good reason not to. This was a major refocusing. Yes, Obama had talked about forever prisoners, but it was not inevitable that Fawzi would be one. He had a loving family, a supportive government, and whatever the US government may have believed about him, we did not think they viewed him as among the worst. The real challenge was finding a way to convince the PRB that it was safe to release him, without also insisting that everything the US government had done to this point was all a terrible, indefensible injustice, even if it was.

We also spent a good part of our first day talking about life at Guantanamo. Fawzi said he was a pious Muslim, but he was not any sort of religious leader. To the contrary, as time had gone on, many detainees had become far more outwardly pious and began to question the piety of others. Fawzi had been questioned by fellow detainees for wearing shorts on very hot days. Fawzi knew what constituted proper religious practice, and he was not going to make his incarceration even more uncomfortable because of self-appointed scholars who kept trying to impose new restrictions that were not required.

Fawzi was often questioned by other detainees whenever he was reading a book that was not a religious book. He loved John Grisham; indeed, I had brought him a copy of Grisham's latest, *Sycamore Row*, which Grisham had inscribed and signed for Fawzi. Grisham had been a supporter of Reprieve's work on Guantanamo for years and a friend of Clive Stafford Smith; he was happy to cheer up a detainee who was a fan. The authorities would not let me give it to him; I was told the book was viewed by the soldiers who review reading material as too negative and skeptical about justice being done. Even without his inscribed Grisham novel, Fawzi read widely; he had taught himself good English through his reading and watching American television shows that were permitted (they could not watch news) while he was living communally in Camp 6. Because of his disciplinary infractions, however, he spent a good deal of time living in isolation in Camp 5.

Fawzi made clear to us that he had spent many years being extremely bitter and angry. He admitted he was frustrated and miserable when he arrived. Some guards treated him professionally and respectfully; others did not and seemed to take satisfaction in making all of the detainees miserable, writing them up, calling in the Immediate Reaction Force to extract them violently from their cells when an order was not followed immediately. Immediate Reaction Forces were used extensively during hunger strikes or to take detainees to medical visits when detainees did not want them. I had seen the IRFings and heard the screaming on the hunger strike videos.

Fawzi indicated that he became so frustrated and angry that he felt he no longer had a stable sense of his identity and that he "was losing who he was." He had been a calm and happy person before he arrived. He no longer was. He felt that he was finally starting to approach a place where he had been able to regain some feelings of peace. There was a spark of optimism that we hoped we could work with.

I asked him directly about "splashing" of feces and urine on guards, as those records would certainly be before the PRB, and it would strike bureaucrats sitting outside Washington as pretty extreme. Fawzi was a bit sheepish, but admitted this behavior, reiterating that he was expressing his anger and resentment when he was mistreated. He conceded that this was a wrong way to do so. He said he did things "that were not of his character," and he had stopped doing these things. I suggested to him that the direction of his behavioral issues would be important and that he should keep that in mind as we moved toward his hearing.

By the end of the first visit, Fawzi was beginning to think about his future and to express a measure of reflection, embarrassment, and even remorse about some of his behavior at Guantanamo. He conceded that he had no animosity toward Americans as a people and did not blame them for his detention. He made clear that he grew up in a home where America was lionized not attacked. He told me that he was not an extremist; we joked about the fact that the Americans thought he was overly religious and many detainees thought he was not religious enough. He did not believe that there was any "conflict of civilizations"; it was a political nightmare started by a small group, Al Qaida, to which he had no affiliation or knowledge outside the news. The response by the United States to the 9/11 attacks had ensnared many innocent people, he said, including himself.

I knew from speaking to Khalid and the Core Team that Fawzi was extremely close to his family. He was the oldest brother, and he had been a friend, a mentor, and a delightful and funny big brother to his five younger siblings. He said he was particularly close to his sister Dalal, who was nearest to him in age. Many were children when he left; now, some of them were married with children of their own. Fawzi was a self-declared Mama's boy and worried about his mother's ailments as she aged. While Fawzi may have been too young to marry at twenty-four when he left Kuwait, he was now thirty-seven, old by Kuwaiti standards for marriage. He had missed so many years when he too should have been getting married and starting a family. His mother wanted to find him a bride. He was eager that she do so. His love and concern for this large and loving family were genuine, and they would be a rock for his rehabilitation and reintegration when he returned.

We knew our next stop needed to be a visit to Kuwait to complete the other critical half of the presentation to the PRB. Not only was it imperative to work hard on documenting the rehabilitation program and the security arrangements with Kuwaiti government officials, we also needed to get to know the family in depth, so that we could present this family to the PRB as people who had suffered much, who dearly loved Fawzi and, most important, who would never allow him to get into any difficulties again. We could not just put in the same bland letters in English that spoke in general of Fawzi being kind or funny or peaceful when they last were with him thirteen years before. We needed to convince the board to receive videos of the family into evidence, which we viewed as most effectively conveying our case to the Board. Videos had not been submitted in any of the many previous proceedings.

Meeting the Al Odahs

The Lewis Baach team traveled to Kuwait shortly after arriving back from Guantanamo, where we met up with the Core Team. Our job was to paint an authentic picture of Fawzi as a son, a big brother, an uncle, a mentor but, even more important, to come to show that the Al Odahs could and would provide for and protect Fawzi upon his return. We needed to visit Fawzi's house, see his room, present his family members as real people living in a real place, who were trying to get on with their lives while trying to make sense of what it is like to lose a first son, an eldest brother, for thirteen years. They were trying to maintain hope and keep a family together under terrible strain and grief. They needed to show that their love would be warm, but tough; he would not slip through the cracks. We wanted to do as much of the hearing as we could in English so that there would not be the barrier of translation between Fawzi and his family and the Board, including the videos.

The Al Odah home was spacious and comfortable, attractively but not lavishly decorated. Although Kuwait is an observant and relatively conservative country, unlike other places in the Gulf, we were welcomed to meet with both male and female members of the family. The Al Odah women wear the traditional abaya and headscarf. They are all highly educated, speak English, and interacted comfortably with our team. Family members were most concerned about Suad, Fawzi's mother, who suffers the most from Fawzi's absence and is frequently in tears about her son. The rest of the family members were not certain that she would be able to get through an interview or complete a video. A loving and emotional mother, she would and did do everything possible for her son, including the making of a heartbreakingly effective video.

Mama's Boy

Suad spoke with warmth about Fawzi as a young man and his loving commitment to his entire family. A highly educated woman who is a graduate of Kuwait University, Suad spent many years as a teacher of geography at the leading girls' high school in Kuwait City. She had retired by the time we met in 2014. She had been married to Khalid at that point for nearly forty years and had lived with him in the United States during his training with the US Air Force. She spoke some English but was more comfortable in Arabic; the quotations below are taken from the English transcript.

Fawzi is her oldest; oldest children, especially boys, hold a special place in Kuwaiti society. She told us "I love all my children, of course, but have always been especially close to Fawzi, my first-born child. I believe that I know him as well as anyone on earth." He set a standard for his siblings with his kind treatment, his gentle play, his strong academic record, and his low-key piety. She was proud that he also graduated from Kuwait University, the leading academic institution in the country, and was pleased that he wanted to help people and had trained as a social worker before becoming a teacher of religion and morality at a government school operated by the Ministry of Islamic Affairs. She also recounted that when her mother, Fawzi's grandmother, was ill with cancer and being treated at M.D. Anderson Cancer Center in Houston, Fawzi, then a teenager, accompanied his mother to spend weeks there, lifting his grandmother's spirits and monitoring her care.

Suad has four other children, two girls and two boys. Her oldest daughter, Dalal, teaches statistics at Kuwait University. She is married with two children. Her next child is a boy, Suleiman, who is a businessman and accountant, also married with a child. The next daughter, Fatima teaches early childhood education, and Suad's youngest, Ahmed was a Lieutenant in the Kuwaiti military. All five of her children have university educations. Fawzi had never met any of his nieces and nephews but has seen them on periodic Red Cross video calls, where he was playful and tried to make them laugh in the strange environment of a seeing on a screen an uncle they had never met imprisoned halfway around the world.

Suad was worried when Fawzi left for Afghanistan in August 2001 because it was a dangerous part of the world. Of course, no one had any idea that September 11 would occur and transform a few weeks of anxiety about a volunteer trip to a conflict zone into an ordeal involving indefinite detention by the United States. For many weeks, Suad did not know where he was or even whether he was alive. She learned eventually that he was alive but in prison. She thought he would be sent to the Kuwaiti Embassy and then sent home and did not learn he had been sent to Guantanamo until February 2002, when a Kuwaiti friend of Khalid's called and said she had seen his name on a list of prisoners. For the next twelve years, she suffered with insomnia and cried herself to sleep. As she told us this, Suad wept and wept.

Suad was pleased that she could at least see Fawzi on the video calls that had been organized by the Red Cross beginning in 2009, but the pain of his distance and her inability to touch or hug or kiss her son caused her pain as well. I told Suad that I would be seeing him again very soon and I would hug him for his mother. She at last smiled through her tears.

Suad was concerned about her son's health, the digestive issues arising from the hunger strikes, and how gaunt and fragile he appeared. She said that he tried to be cheerful and reassure them that he was all right. He remained very interested in the family's lives and activities. He seemed genuinely delighted that his kid brothers and sisters were happy and making their way in their lives and careers. But Suad knows her son and knew from the calls that he was very concerned about his mother's great sadness and anxiety and the uncertainty of not knowing when, if ever, she would be able to welcome him home. She shared Fawzi's concern that he was already thirty-seven, which was old to get married in Kuwait. Suad wanted Fawzi to have the joy of family. Mothers or sisters in Kuwait identify potential marriage partners who will be compatible. But this was a difficult process because of Fawzi's age, because no one knew when Fawzi would come home, and because Kuwaiti families might be reluctant to have their daughter marry a man who had spent all those years in such a horrendous environment.

Would Fawzi be able to function? Would he be psychologically strong? Would he be able to work? Would he be able to form attachments to a wife and ultimately children? Suad was confident that he would, but she knew her son; others might not see him as marriage material given his ordeal.

Suad's message on video to the PRB concluded:

> Life brings both joys and suffering. I am grateful to have five healthy and loving children. [My] country ... was invaded and looted by Saddam Hussein. My husband fought with the US military to liberate my country, and we have since lived a quiet and prosperous life. But for the past twelve years my first born has been taken from me. I hope in my old age to be blessed with the joy of having my eldest son at home with me and my family, where we can take good care of him, and I ask for his swift return.

We were hopeful that anyone on that board with just a bit of empathy would see the strength of that bond of love between mother and child and that Suad would give Fawzi perfect care and ensure, with maternal ferocity, that he would not get far from her sight, let alone present any sort of security risk.

Abu Fawzi

We also spent time with Khalid Al Odah, who organized our various meetings, and also made a video for the Board. Khalid had the easy charm and can-do confidence of an ex-military officer. He is a proud father and grandfather. Among his grandchildren are three boys, from three of his children, all named after their grandfather; he loves to spend time with Little Khalid, the son of his son Suleiman, who lives with Khalid and Suad in the Al Odah home, and Littler Khalid, the son of Dalal, and now Littlest Khalid, the son of Ahmed. The girls, who live with their husbands' families in the Kuwaiti way, visit three or four times weekly. Ahmed, Khalid's youngest son, had just been promoted to first lieutenant in the Kuwaiti army when we visited. Ahmed lived with his wife and son in a new wing in Khalid's house.

Khalid Al Odah retired in 1986 as a Colonel in the Kuwaiti Air Force before beginning a very successful career in business in Kuwait. He had trained as a pilot at Webb Air Force Base in Big Spring, Texas, a military town that trained innumerable pilots beginning during World War II until it shut down in the late 1970s. He remembered his time in Texas as "the best time of my life."[6] He loved the freedom and openness of America, where he found it easy to make friends. After growing up in a small and closely-knit society where networks were somewhat closed, he was delighted by the welcome he received, despite being a foreigner. He recalled being greeted with food by neighbors as he moved into his apartment. He proudly told me he obtained his wings from the US Air Force, after training on Cessna T-57 and Northrop T-38 jets.

Khalid spent three and a half years in Texas. During his leaves, he traveled widely throughout the States. He laughed about "getting his kicks on Route 66" and receiving quite a few speeding tickets along the way. After returning to Kuwait and continuing his military career, he was sent to France, learning to fly Mirage aircraft for about five months. He flew the Mirages back to Kuwait, where he was part of the first interception fleet.

The great inflection point for Khalid, as for most Kuwaitis, was the First Gulf War. Khalid spent the war in Kuwait and fought alongside American forces to liberate his country. He tried to find a safe place outside Kuwait for his wife and five children, who ranged from his oldest, Fawzi, who was then thirteen, to Ahmed, who was one year old. Suad refused to take the family out of the country. She told him, "If you stay, we will stay." They all remained throughout the war.

Despite being retired at that point, Khalid was an experienced military officer and became one of the leaders of the Kuwait Resistance Forces under the command of General Khaled Boodai, who served as the eyes and ears of the Americans, working with Air Force General Charles Horner. Khalid had four or five resistance cells under his command. He had one of the few satellite phones in Kuwait that he used both to guide targeting against Iraqi positions and to call family members of resistance fighters outside the country. Khalid recalled with pride that more than a decade later, General Horner told the *Los Angeles Times* that without the help of the Kuwait Resistance Forces, "The liberation of the people of Kuwait would have been more costly to the coalition forces and the people of Kuwait." Khalid still kept the yellowed clipping which he showed me with pride.

Following the victory in the Gulf War and liberation of Kuwait, Khalid attended the celebrations for American troops, bringing along Fawzi. Fawzi climbed onto the Abrams tanks and hugged and shook the hands of American soldiers coming out of the turrets. It was a joyous and lasting moment for Fawzi and Khalid and the Al Odah family.

As a man who owed his successful military career and his ability to live as a free man in a free country to the United States, Khalid spoke with great sincerity when he told me, "My family and I will remain forever grateful to the American Government and people for their liberation of our country." This was a view strongly shared by nearly everyone we met in Kuwait. While no doubt there were extremists in the region and indeed in Kuwait, those who lived through the invasion and were facing the prospect of lives as vassals of the brutal Saddam Hussein found the thought of taking up arms against their liberators beyond comprehension. This made Khalid's discovery that Fawzi had been taken prisoner even more inexplicable. "I knew that my son was not a terrorist or an enemy of the United States."[7]

In early 2002, Khalid learned that his son was alive. Fawzi wrote a short letter that Khalid received through the International Committee of the Red Cross, saying that he was in the custody of the American military and that he would prove his innocence and be home soon. Khalid was confident that he would shortly get his son back. "I also knew that the United States is a country that obeys the rule of law and that Fawzi would be able to get a fair court hearing in which he would have a chance to answer and defend any charges against him."[8]

His belief that American due process would sort out the truth and return his son faded as year after year passed. Yet, Khalid remained active and tried to maintain a positive outlook. He was proud that his son was a lead plaintiff in two of the cases that went to the Supreme Court, which established the right of detainees to challenge their detention in an American judicial forum. When two Kuwaitis were released in 2004, he thought that the family's nightmare would soon be over. When he was told by Fawzi's lawyer after the Supreme Court decision that Fawzi had won, Khalid replied, "This is what I love about the United States. Even if sometimes the Government does something wrong, the courts are there to uphold the law and protect the people." It was a sadder and wiser Khalid that I met nearly a decade later to prepare for the PRB hearing. He and Fayiz's father were regular peaceful protesters at the US Embassy in Kuwait City, calling for the release of their sons.

Khalid did not know exactly why all of the other detainees, other than his son and Fayiz Al Kandari, had been released, most of them long before. Many of Khalid's friends told him that because of his role on the Committee and Fawzi's role as lead plaintiff, he and Fawzi would both be punished with Fawzi's continued detention. Khalid did not want to believe this, but it certainly stuck in his mind. "I do not know the reasons for Fawzi's continued imprisonment, but our family has never given up on his return to Kuwait and never will."[9]

Khalid and the family were committed to doing whatever they could to facilitate Fawzi's release. When asked for his permission to request that Fawzi be committed to the Rehabilitation Center for a period of at least a year (including six months as a full-time inpatient), he agreed with alacrity. He told the PRB that, of course, after all that time, "Fawzi will need professional help, including extensive medical and psychological rehabilitation and counseling to equip him with the skills to once again become a productive and well-adjusted member of Kuwaiti society." He quickly made the written request to the Kuwait Attorney General for Fawzi to be committed to the center for as long as was necessary in the judgment of Kuwaiti mental health professionals, spiritual advisers, and security officials to ensure that Fawzi was ready to reintegrate and posed no danger to himself or others. He looked forward to the prospect that Fawzi "is on Kuwaiti soil. And we're going to visit him. We will see him. We can embrace him. We can see him."

Khalid had visited the Al Salam Rehabilitation Center with a delegation of both Kuwaiti and American officials to inspect the facility when it opened. He told the PRB by video how effective it appeared to him; how much he wanted Fawzi to receive help; and how impressed the American officials were when they visited. After not having his son at home for thirteen years, he was ready and willing to impose further restrictions on Fawzi's freedom as long as he could have his son in his home country, where he could see him. Fawzi could later live at his family home until he married or even afterward, providing emotional and material support. Khalid had already engaged in the familiar Kuwaiti custom of adding on a wing to his house for two of his sons. There was room for another wing. Today, Fawzi lives with his wife and three children in that wing.

Khalid told me that he routinely speaks with youth groups about faith and how Islam is a religion of peace and tolerance. Fawzi was raised in that tradition, and the family had always had friends of all nationalities and religions. Khalid also worked with returned Guantanamo detainees to ensure that they renounce violence and radicalism. He understands that, despite best efforts, he cannot ensure that everyone heeds his message.

Although "I do not believe that Fawzi would be susceptible to such [extremist] views," Khalid was going to be sure to limit Fawzi's peer group and encourage him to put his life as a detainee behind him as much as possible. Through periodic calls and letters, Khalid, a caring and observant father, saw the change in his son. When I asked him about the difference between Fawzi at twenty-four and at thirty-seven, he answers,

> It's a lot of years, you know Eric, about 12 to 13 years spent there and he was very young at that time and now he is a very mature man. You can see that from the way he behaves, the way he talks, the way he thinks. When we talk to him, he doesn't want to talk about anything except to enjoy the time with us at this hour. This is a mature thing from Fawzi. He is looking forward in a very mature way to get back home.[10]

After our talk, Khalid took us on a tour of the house. We went up to Fawzi's room, which was as he had left it in 2001. Khalid talked about how close Fawzi was to his mother and how much she had suffered. He tried to talk less about his own feelings; Khalid's identity for the past thirty-seven years to all who knew him had been "Abu Fawzi," father of Fawzi. But for more than a third of those years, his oldest son had been gone.

Khalid's eyes misted over, as he felt the years of loss and allowed himself the hope of seeing his son. He had spent more than a decade fighting for his son and the other detainees. He had mentored the young men who had come home. When his son comes back "I want to rest. I want to stay home. I will look after my son and my family."[11]

I asked Khalid whether he wanted to tell the PRB about his plans for Fawzi and his family. He looked directly into the camera:

> My son deserves to go back home, and I have a very blessed family, very caring family, very loveable family. And they will embrace Fawzi when he comes back. They will look after him very carefully and they will keep an eye on him all the time. They will help him to integrate him into the society and with the family. So please, consider this and get my son back home.[12]

Brother and Sisterhood

Fawzi's sister, Dalal, is a dynamo. Four years younger than her brother, she is also a graduate of Kuwait University, in statistics and mathematics; she teaches three sections of statistics at the University and does the exam grading for two more sections. Dalal was twenty when Fawzi was taken prisoner. They were the two oldest children and had been very close to each other, as well as mentoring their younger siblings. She and her children always participated in the video calls with Fawzi.

Fawzi's mother and Dalal were in charge of finding a possible wife for Fawzi. She said that on every call, he tells them both, with a laugh, to "look for a good woman." Dalal said that they found a lovely woman whom they thought would be a great match, but after a year of waiting with no sign of when Fawzi would return to Kuwait, she became tired of waiting and married someone else. Dalal has a large circle of friends, but she was nearly thirty-four when we met, and virtually all of her peer group is married.

Dalal was hopeful that Fawzi would return soon. She accepted the rehabilitation center. She made clear that everyone would be visiting all the time, not just Fawzi's parents, five siblings, in-laws, nieces, and nephews but a large group of aunts, uncles, cousins, and their grandmother. "Not just the small family. Also, the big family." When I suggested it would be very crowded at the rehabilitation center, she agreed with a laugh.

It was unmistakable from our visit that the Al Odah family would provide a nurturing and watchful environment. We were eager to show these loving, hopeful people on video to the PRB. In our view, they could not help but fall for the Al Odahs. But as will be seen, this was easier said than done.

Rehabilitation and Security

While the home environment would be important, we were also aware that the Board would be at least as interested in the rehabilitation center and the security infrastructure.

Khalid arranged for us to tour the rehabilitation facility and to make certain that the "punch list" of items the United States wanted were in place and could be shown on video. One blazing hot morning, Marcia Newell and the Lewis Baach team arrived at Kuwait Central Prison. The Al Salam facility was in a repurposed hospital wing of the prison. We met the warden and waited in the main building. The walls were covered with posters declaring "Death to Drug Dealers." Children had visited the prison and had made elaborate dioramas that were on display. In one, a drug dealer had been arrested and put in a cell; another showed his trial before three judges; and a third featured a doll-sized drug dealer with a dark hood over his head and a noose around his neck on the gallows (Figure 8.3). Moments later, we boarded a shuttle bus for the drive to the hospital block and passed the real gallows, sitting under a metal canopy for shade. Kuwait has the death penalty, but it was not often used; after a five-year hiatus, however, there have been twelve people executed since 2022.

Dr. Adel Al Zayed met us at the prison hospital and took us upstairs to the Al Salam Rehabilitation Center for a tour that we captured on video. Guards sat outside a thick steel door, which they opened for us. The door slammed shut with a loud clang, cutting us off from the rest of the hospital, a convincing sound effect. Dr. Adel was briskly friendly and spoke perfect English. He was not only the Director of the Rehabilitation Center but also in charge of Mental Health and Alcohol and Drug Rehabilitation Services at the main public hospital in Kuwait, as well as the head of the department of psychiatry. He was a qualified psychiatrist in a country that had relatively limited experience with modern psychiatry.

Dr. Adel did his medical degree at Kuwait University and then left to do his residency in psychiatry at the University of Edinburgh in Scotland.

Figure 8.3   Kuwait prison: doll. Photo by author, May 2014.

He became a Member of the Royal College of Psychiatrists and returned to Kuwait, where he was appointed a consultant in psychiatry and then a senior consultant. He supervised two junior psychologists. Their workload was significant, as drug and alcohol addiction are serious problems throughout the Gulf, including in Kuwait. Narcotics move through the region, often through Iran, and although Kuwait is nominally dry, alcohol comes in through smuggling networks, often brought in by foreign diplomatic pouch.

Dr. Adel had founded the Rehabilitation Center, designing it from scratch as an interdisciplinary program. He worked closely with a respected Islamic scholar, Dr. Khaled Al Oteibi, who was professor of Islamic Studies at Kuwait University. When I noted it seemed unusual to have a psychiatrist working in tandem with a senior religious scholar, Dr. Adel laughed. He said that a critical part of the program is to make certain that patients are not extremists or, if they are, that they are rehabilitated to a more moderate and peaceful way of life.

"We make certain they do not have wrong thoughts." Dr. Adel told me. I teased him, "Dr. Adel, you are a British-trained psychiatrist; I thought in modern psychiatry, there is no such thing as 'wrong thoughts.'" "In Kuwait," he said with a smile, "there are wrong thoughts."

We continued our tour. He described how he and his team did the research and evaluation for establishing the center. He made clear that there was great interest and support throughout the government, including from the Emir. He and his team were sent to Saudi Arabia to see how the rehabilitation program was designed there and what services were provided. The Saudi program famously had extensive athletic facilities and a swimming pool, but that was Saudi style. Kuwait was different.

When Dr. Adel and his team returned from Saudi Arabia, they prepared an extensive report, recounting their discussions with Saudi officials of the challenges and issues that returning detainees had faced and how they were addressed. Dr. Adel and his team provided their candid views of what appeared to be more or less effective. In his view, luxury was less important than active engagement and dialogue with key professionals on a regular basis and interaction with family.

Dr. Adel's team was also sent to Egypt, which had a program that was not dealing with detainees but had extensive experience with religious radicals. Through on-site visits and their own research, the Al Salam team developed what they viewed as best practices, given the unique challenges of dealing with men who had been through the long Guantanamo ordeal. He told me that the Kuwaiti government guaranteed full support in providing resources and would accord full deference to their clinical judgment.

The facilities were far from posh, with a small exercise room with free weights and a basic exercise bicycle, a library, conference space, a small kitchen with a microwave, and spare bedrooms. There was a fenced, secure outdoor space. Dr. Adel thought that having the facility in a wing of the prison hospital made clear that patients were not at a country club; they were not being punished, but their environment was secure, and they were being monitored at all times with their freedom of movement limited.

Dr. Adel had visited Guantanamo four times and had met Fawzi to do psychiatric evaluations twice before. His predecessor, Dr. Al Shati, had been on the first trip by Kuwaiti officials in 2008 and also had met the Kuwaitis who were then still there, including Fawzi. They were asked to assess the mental state of the detainees who might be coming home. There was great concern about men decompensating at Guantanamo; they were aware of the Al Ajmi tragedy. Long-term incarceration without trial, potentially for life, was unfamiliar and dangerous ground from a mental health perspective.

Dr. Adel met Fawzi, first in October 2013 and then in March 2014. He was joined at those meetings by Dr. Al Oteibi, the Islamic Studies scholar and preacher, and Colonel Al Kandari, the head of Counterterrorism for the Kuwaiti Intelligence Services. Each of them had their own perspectives and issues, but it fell to Dr. Adel to evaluate Fawzi's mental state, to decide whether he was ready for release, whether he could be helped therapeutically, and to figure out what the critical mental health issues might be given his long detention under conditions of fear, hostility, and uncertainty. Dr. Adel said that in Kuwait any prisoner who has been detained for more than five years was required to go through a rehabilitation process before release given the inevitable impact on mental health; Fawzi had been detained for more than twelve years.

Dr. Adel had some initial concerns because when Dr. Al Shati had evaluated Fawzi in 2008, he expressed the view at the time that Fawzi "was not ready to cooperate, and he's stubborn." Dr. Adel was pleased that the man he met in 2013 and 2014 was, in his clinical judgment, quite different from the one described by Dr. Al Shati.

> I think that Fawzi had matured so much to have this totally complete shift from Dr. Al Shati in his assessment, and how he changed through his period of time. Fawzi at this point was very much aware of what was needed to be done. He was keen to look into his future, think about his marriage, work, getting back to Kuwait, being integrated again into society and with his family.[13]

Dr. Adel was not sugarcoating the situation. He observed that there was more difficult work ahead. Fawzi had issues with anger management, which "is expected after a long time in prison." Fawzi had made progress, but he admitted he needed to do more. Fawzi was also aware of his own impulsivity, how he quickly reacted, or overreacted to what he felt was an affront to his dignity or personal autonomy in a way that was counterproductive to his own best interests in a prison environment. Dr. Adel said that Fawzi was accepting of the rehabilitation program, indeed acknowledging that he needed it and could benefit from it, despite the further restrictions on his freedom. Dr. Adel thought that Fawzi had grown much more introspective and accepting of the need to address his issues to make a successful readjustment.

We asked Dr. Adel how his experience with Fawzi compared with his long experience with extremist patients over the course of his practice. He indicated that those who harbor extreme views tend to be defensive, denying, and uncooperative. They did not accept guidance or treatment or engage honestly on these issues. Fawzi, in his view, had come a great distance to open himself to honest dialogue and therapy.

Dr. Adel's clinical judgment was positive. He knew that there were no guarantees or certainties about what a patient might have in his mind or how he might behave in the future. "We have much hope that Fawzi will benefit from the rehabilitation services. But you know, being a scientist, I cannot give you confirmation that it's going to be definitely successful because we still need to assess Fawzi in more detail when he's back and carry out a good battery of assessment to his capacity."

Dr. Adel made clear that there would be no social promotion through the rehabilitation program. Each of the professionals would meet and compile a monthly report on Fawzi's progress. "If we felt at any stage, it was not successful, we will see how we can make it successful to reevaluate the process, whether the problem comes from the rehabilitation services or is coming from the detainee himself." But if there were problems, they would be reported, and unless the professionals unanimously agreed that he was ready to progress to leaving during the day or going home, he would stay where he was. "It's the responsibility of the psychiatrist to preserve the safety of the patient and the safety of the community," he added.[14]

We talked about Fawzi's family support structure. When they last met, Dr. Adel said that his family asked him to take one of Fawzi's T-shirts back to Kuwait. Fawzi became emotional and insisted he would only give them the T-shirt that he was wearing when he got home and could give it to his mom. He also talked about his gratitude toward his father for his endless efforts to secure his release.

I asked Dr. Adel whether he had any final thoughts that he might wish to convey to the PRB. He said that he intended to maintain contact with Fawzi even after he left the center to be sure that he is doing well. He indicated that other detainees had approached him for help when they found themselves in difficult situations. Fawzi too agreed that he needed help. Dr. Adel thought that embracing the fragile reality of his situation was the most promising indicator that he was ready to come home.

Although the tripartite team of psychiatrist, imam, and security official was unusual, we thought it would be useful to speak to all of them so that we could get a sense of how the various pieces would work together. We paid a visit to Dr. Al Oteibi. He is something of a celebrity in Kuwait, as his Friday sermons are often televised and circulated widely on the internet. He is an expert on Islamic law and practice, with a doctorate from the Islamic University in Medina, where he spent thirteen years teaching. He is a member of the Assembly of Muslim Jurists of North America, answering issues and questions that arise from members of the Muslim community in the United States and Canada. He was also head of the Sharia Department of the Kuwait Charities House, a government-established organization. He is a respected, charismatic scholar and preacher, but his demeanor was relaxed, open, and friendly.

Dr. Al Oteibi's role at the Al Salam Rehabilitation Center was to provide religious counseling and guidance and "if necessary to correct any misconceptions that the detainees may have about Islamic doctrines and principles, and in particular to ensure that the detainees properly understand and adhere to Islamic prohibitions against violence and extremism." He had worked with many young men "whose religious views have been distorted in an extremist direction." He had found good success in working with young people "at the university, in the prison, and in daily life, in a calm deliberative way to reorient them to a correct view." He found that, as a trained and well-known scholar, he was able to communicate openly and that patient dialogue was far more effective in bringing young people with extremist views back to a proper understanding of their religion than more punitive or aggressive approaches. He had been appointed by the Ministry of Information to work on more effective communication with a dialogical approach to religious doctrine.[15]

Dr. Al Oteibi, a member of the Inter-Agency Working Group, also submitted a statement to the PRB in which he recalled his visits with Fawzi at Guantanamo. He made clear that he had candid and trusting discussions with Fawzi and that Fawzi's religious views were neither extremist nor supportive of violence. Dr. Al Oteibi had spent much of his career with men whose twisted views of Islam, promulgated by those using Islam as a means to their ends, had led them to violence. He was clear. Dr. Al Oteibi was experienced with extremists and, in his view, Fawzi was no extremist.

Colonel Abdullah Mohammed Yousef Al Kandari is the Director of Counterterrorism for the Kuwait State Security Service. His training is in military intelligence. His concerns were neither medical nor spiritual. He was a security man – austere, tough, and formal. He had dealt with terrorists. He had put many people in Kuwait Central Prison. He worked closely with intelligence officials throughout the region and with the US intelligence services. He well understood that the region and the world contained real threats, and it was his job to prevent terrorist incidents. He was not a man who would take chances on predicting the future or whose approach would lead to giving people the benefit of the doubt. But he submitted a sworn statement that was remarkable in the clarity of his views:

> As an intelligence official, I cannot speak with 100% certainty concerning whether a detainee will engage in extremist activities. Nevertheless, I have extensive experience in dealing with extremists and based on my meetings with Fawzi Al Odah, it is my best judgment that there is no material risk that Fawzi Al Odah will engage in terrorist activity, but we will of course remain vigilant to prevent such activity in any event.[16]

We wanted to show the PRB that the process that had been established was ironclad at every step. We met with the Chief Prosecutor of the Kuwaiti Department of Public Prosecution. It was his official role to order Fawzi's commitment to the Al Salah Rehabilitation Center under the Kuwaiti statute. We brought him the required medical evaluation of Dr. Adel, the request of Khaled Al Odah for rehabilitation for Fawzi, and a signed undertaking from Fawzi that he would comply with all terms of his commitment to the rehabilitation center and that he would take no steps to challenge that commitment legally.

The Chief Prosecutor submitted a statement to the PRB outlining the requirements of the process, stating that the necessary formal documents had been submitted and that there could be no valid way to prevent or challenge that process from going forward under Kuwaiti law. To similar effect, we submitted the statement of the Superintendent of the Kuwaiti Central Prison, describing the security arrangements at the prison generally and at the Al Salam Center.

We were also fortunate to have the cooperation of senior members of the Kuwaiti Royal Family, including Sheikh Mohamed Khaled Al Sabah, the Deputy Prime Minister and Minister of the Interior of Kuwait, and Sheikh Mohammed Sabah Al Sabah, the former Foreign Minister. Sheikh Mohamed Khaled submitted a letter to the PRB, noting that he had spoken on multiple occasions with both Presidents Bush and Obama and that he had stressed on each occasion that "the return of our sons under mutually agreeable and appropriate security measures" was "of the utmost priority to the Government and people of Kuwait."[17] He repeated to the PRB his "personal commitment" to implement its diplomatic agreement with the United States in its domestic law and that Fawzi "will be reintegrated with his family and Kuwaiti society humanely and in full compliance with the conditions that our governments have agreed upon to ensure the security interests of both nations."[18] He specifically referenced participation in a full rehabilitation program at Al Salam Rehabilitation Center as well as post-discharge security controls, monitoring and reporting requirements.

Sheikh Mohamed Sabah provided details regarding specific nonclassified security measures to be implemented with respect to Fawzi's repatriation, including the filing of monthly reports, using a template supplied by the US Department of State, requiring extensive information regarding Fawzi's status, employment, contacts, and activities, including financial transactions. He noted that these measures could not be challenged and that Fawzi had signed an undertaking binding under Kuwaiti law to comply in all respects. Fawzi had agreed to surrender his passport and GCC identity card and was prohibited from leaving the country without prior permission from State Security for an initial period of three years subject to renewal based on consultation between the two governments. He was also subject to a three-year regime of daily curfews from dusk until dawn, and his religious attendance would be monitored as well.

ARH also submitted an overview statement, describing his long and warm relationship with the Al Odah family including Fawzi. He discussed the founding of the Committee with Khalid and the quest for due process. He aptly termed this legal effort "in the finest tradition of seeking civil and human rights through established systems of justice."[19] ARH described his involvement as legal advisor to the Committee; his regular meetings with the Emir, the Prime Minister, and the Foreign Minister; and the design of the rehabilitation program and the security checks. He laid out the history of the Inter-Agency Working Group and his ultimately obtaining agreement to his attendance as Minister Plenipotentiary. He summarized his activity in communicating to each of the two governments the expectations, requirements, and limitations of the other. He also made clear his personal commitment to oversee full compliance with the agreed conditions.

Countdown to the Periodic Review Board Hearing

Our team left Kuwait in May 2014, with less than a month to prepare for the hearing scheduled for June 4. We had multiple videos and more than a dozen witness statements. The Board would see a loving, committed family, willing to comply with any and all conditions to bring their son home. They would see that the medical, psychological, and religious establishments were comfortable with Fawzi and had constructed a detailed infrastructure that met the requirements that the United States had specified. The security services believed that Fawzi would not pose a threat, but they were not relying on trust; they had comprehensive surveillance and registration requirements in place. The most senior officials of the Kuwaiti government, up to the level of the Emir, were engaged and putting their integrity and the future of the bilateral relationship on the line to secure this repatriation. All that remained was the challenge of preparing the key player, Fawzi himself, to communicate to the Board that he was the kind of person who could give the Board confidence that he could be safely released.

We were confident that Fawzi was exactly the kind of person who should be released. He was focused on a productive and safe future. He wanted to marry. He wanted to live with his family. He wanted to work. He had lost thirteen years of his life and was not looking to lose any more.

But the US government was not releasing anyone on the basis that it had made an unconscionable mistake in detaining him. Fawzi had been found to be an enemy combatant through multiple hearings in multiple proceedings. He had lost his habeas proceeding before a federal judge, who found that he had been associated with Al Qaida and the Taliban (and who had granted two other petitions). Fawzi was not going to reverse those findings in the PRB. But at the same time, we knew he was never going to admit to having done something that he did not do or that his detention was justified. He needed to show he was not angry; he was not filled with a sense of outrage at the injustice that had been done to him. He needed to show that the United States had taught him some useful life lessons. How could we thread this needle?

On one level, this was not difficult. Fawzi was positive by nature. But he could get very angry very quickly. He had been subject to countless and senseless indignities year after year. His disciplinary record was long. If the questioning took a certain turn, things could deteriorate in a hurry. We needed to prepare for the hearing both in terms of anticipating specific questions and in creating an emotional environment that would be positive.

I told Fawzi that, while I understood his long ordeal and his strong feelings, on the day of the hearing he needed to be what I jokingly called a "Zen Muslim," a man of piety but deeply peaceful and calm. He should try to give his testimony and answer questions in English and only use the interpreter if he needed help either in understanding the questions or with the right word in English for an answer.

There was extensive information available regarding the questions that PRB panels had asked other detainees, many of which were repeated from hearing to hearing, and some of which were quite clueless and indeed insulting to pious Muslims. We needed to review those questions, discuss accurate, factual responses, and not tell the Board that some of their questions were stupid. If anyone had to tussle with the Board, and ideally no one would, I would be the fighter. Not Fawzi.

Fawzi also had to work on his own statement for the PRB, which needed to be accurate and to be delivered as a great statesman might deliver a critical speech. It was to be natural, candid – but also the performance of a lifetime, as in many respects his future life was indeed on the line.

Over and over, we reviewed the expected questions that had been asked of other detainees:

> How do you feel about America and Americans?
> Can you define and describe your views regarding jihad and takfir?
> What do you think about the death of Osama Bin Laden?
> If you were approached when you went back to Kuwait and asked to support Al Qaida in the Arabian Peninsula [Al Qaida in its original form had splintered and morphed by 2014], or another terrorist or extremist group, what would you say?
> If one of those groups threatened your family to get you to join or to support AQAP or a terrorist group, what would you say?

And there was the frequently asked question, which was not only ridiculous but to Muslims blasphemous. Muslims are taught that Mohammed was the last prophet, and Allah would not make revelations thereafter. Yet many detainees were asked:

> If Allah spoke to you and commanded you to join or to support AQAP or an extremist group, what would you do?

We agreed that I would point out the doctrinal impossibility implicit in the question and quickly move on.

We also reviewed more practical questions about Fawzi's family, his activities in 2001, his views as to his obligations as a Muslim when Afghanistan was attacked, and his knowledge and involvement with certain groups. He would also be asked about the rehabilitation process and how he would interact with others whom he might meet, in the rehabilitation center or otherwise, who expressed extremist views.

We also knew that the United States somehow had become convinced that another detainee, Zamel Al Zamel, was Fawzi's cousin and that they were somehow indirectly in touch.[20] It was clear that although Al Zamel had been released years before, the United States was more worried about Al Zamel's views than Fawzi's and was concerned that he would somehow radicalize Fawzi if Fawzi were released to Kuwait. Al Zamel was not related in any way to Fawzi; Fawzi had only known him years before as a fellow detainee. This was more bad information that remained untested but may have led to years of additional detention.

Finally, we spent time on the key questions: How was Fawzi different now? What had he learned? What mistakes had he made and how would he do things differently? Here again, Fawzi's genuine maturation and reflectiveness led us to a narrative that was factually accurate, that showed the insight he had gained, and, implicitly, the judgment and peace of mind that he had lacked thirteen years earlier.

He admitted that he was miserable and frustrated when he arrived and that he showed great anger and aggressiveness in response to being treated as "the worst of the worst." He met hostility with hostility. He made clear that some years ago, after all the Kuwaitis had been released other than he and Fayiz, and he had to contemplate the prospect of being a forever prisoner, he realized he was losing himself. In Kuwait, he had been mellow and relaxed; at Guantanamo, he was constantly agitated. In Kuwait, he had been happy; at Guantanamo, he had become deeply depressed. He committed himself to reclaiming himself through self-reflection and faith. He was focused on his family and his future. He knew that he could not just resume his life as it had been before. He wanted to be a private person, without politics or ideology. If he knew in 2001 what he knew now about the world and its geopolitical dangers, he would have had the judgment and maturity not to have put himself in harm's way in a zone of conflict.

Finally, it was June 4, 2014, the date of the hearing. Guantanamo was even hotter and stickier than usual. Our hearing was in Camp 7. Camp 7 was a separate series of trailers set up for meetings and hearings behind fields of razor wire. Fawzi had never been there, but I had done a walk-through of the facilities the day before. I was not allowed to have any of my legal colleagues attend the hearing with me; the team was to be Fawzi, one military representative, and I. Two television screens had been set up in our room. One was linked to the PRB hearing room in suburban Washington. Another screen was linked to officials who would watch the unclassified portions of the hearing from Washington, as well as to military officers sitting next door to us in Guantanamo.

We had wanted to show the PRB the videos we had made in Kuwait, but we had been informed a few days earlier that the Board members had declined to watch them during the hearing; instead, we were told they promised they would watch them afterward. As a matter of effective advocacy, we were troubled that they would not allow our case to be presented in a logical and compelling way, but the PRB was going to do it as it chose. We made a motion for the videos to be presented, but it was denied. We would frequently refer to the videos and hope that they would be "must-watch TV" for the PRB members.

Fawzi arrived shortly before the time for the hearing began with a group of six guards. He was, as usual, shackled at the wrists and ankles, and a waist chain linked the shackles together. We hugged, and he smiled and whispered in my ear, "Zen Muslim. I am a Zen Muslim." The guards then attached his leg shackles to the hook in the floor. He would be chained to the floor throughout the hearing.

I gave my opening statement, which had gone through many, many drafts with the Core Team, but I knew it was relatively unimportant.

I would review the evidence, but that would not change. My main contribution would be to ensure the panel that the security and rehabilitation guarantees were ironclad. I wanted to deal with some of the difficult facts that the Board would be aware of in any event and try to put them in context. It was far better to anticipate and interpret those facts than to ignore them or have them raised for the first time with aggressive questioning of Fawzi. I told them:

> Fawzi is a man of dignity who has been living under very difficult and uncertain circumstances for a very long time. Adjustment to prison life has not always been smooth for him. There have been times in earlier years when he has been upset and angry, has shouted or acted out, when he threw food and more. He participated in the hunger strike. Fawzi is the educated son of a middle-class family – he was not raised to adapt to being a prisoner and did not always do well in that difficult role. Through his own choices and because of his own wish to stop being angry and to reclaim his personality and self-control, he has become much calmer over the years. His disciplinary record reflects that fact. Importantly, however, we are not here to consider whether Fawzi was good at being a passive prisoner; we are here to consider what he will be like as a citizen looking forward.

I also took some risk by dealing with the allegations against him, thinking that they would be asking about them in any event and that it would be better coming from me rather than Fawzi:

> Fawzi is not and has never been a terrorist. Things have been said about him over the years that are nonsense: people who have proven themselves time and again to be unreliable have said that he was part of terrorist groups in places where he has never been. We are not here to discuss what happened long ago, but this Board should be aware that these accusations are simply incorrect. Some of these I will need to address in the classified portion of this proceeding. As I mentioned, the unclassified summary incorrectly identifies Mr. Al Zamel as Fawzi's cousin.
>
> What else is wrong? The unclassified summary references assertions that he belonged to an Al Qaida cell in London. It references these, even though it expressly indicates a lack of confidence in such statements. But it does not state the key fact contradicting this allegation – Fawzi has never been to London other than once as a child.

Also critical were the views of Fawzi's military representative. The lead representative would be sitting on the other side of Fawzi. We had spent many hours together working on the hearing and with Fawzi. There was trust in the group. Both officers were deeply committed to being accurate and producing the team's best work. The statement of the Major confirmed his confidence that he and his military colleague believed in Fawzi and his future, and they did not view him as presenting a security risk. The only man in the room in uniform was supporting Fawzi to his superior officers and other senior officials in the bureaucracy.

In the end, however, Fawzi needed to win – or lose – his own freedom through the presentation of his statement and his reply to questions. To use a baseball metaphor that Khalid Al Odah would have known well, Fawzi hit it out of the park. His English was perfect; the translator said not a word. Fawzi was relaxed; he was natural. He engaged with the panel. He knew his statement so well that he spoke it with his head up, making eye contact with the panel through the video camera. He was reflective and spoke with visible emotion and affection: "For these long years, I have been inspired by the love and loyalty of my family."

He knew that going home was not simple: "I have been here in Guantanamo Bay in detention since I was 24 years old. I have changed and the world has changed during these years. Reintegration into my home, my family and my community will require hard work and professional attention and assistance."

Fawzi spoke of his family's and his own personal gratitude to the United States. "My father and my family have always felt immense gratitude to the United States for liberating us from Saddam Hussein and the Iraqi invaders." He spoke with pride and amusement about his mother and sisters' unceasing efforts to identify possible marriage partners. "My mother and two sisters are on the lookout for me, for which I am grateful." He spoke of his education and belief in Islam "as a moderate and peaceful religion" and that he had "always taught that to my students." He made clear that he was older, wiser, cooperative, and apolitical. He did not address the details of 2001 but conceded that he was naïve and would have done things differently today, that Afghanistan was too dangerous, risky and unstable a place to be in 2001. He put himself at risk and put his family through a nightmare.

Without going into detail (because most of it remains classified), the questions to Fawzi were fairly predictable. Fawzi replied with ease and real charm. Most of the classified questions were directed to me and regarded security arrangements. It was clear that the Board had liked him, and it was hard to know how more detailed assurances of security procedures could be provided. When the guards shackled him and led him out, we hugged again, this time with confidence bordering on joy. Was it enough for a defense and intelligence-dominated tribunal? We had done everything we could. Just over a month later, on July 14, the Board ruled unanimously in Fawzi's favor. A day later, Fayiz Al Kandari, who had stuck with prior counsel who had advised a far more aggressive and confrontational approach, had his petition denied.

Of course, this was Guantanamo, and the ordeal was not over, despite Kuwait being prepared to send an airplane to bring him home. Shortly before Fawzi's hearing, five high-level Al Qaida operatives had been transferred out of Guantanamo to Qatar in exchange for an American soldier, Bowe Bergdahl, who went AWOL in Afghanistan. The Obama administration had not gone through the required process with the exchange, which required thirty days' notice by the Department of Defense to Congress. The Department of Defense had been out of the loop, Congress was enraged, and the administration appeared reluctant to poke the congressional bear with a new repatriation. Weeks went by without a word.

We spent countless hours over nearly three months trying to communicate with the government, but the Department of Defense was not talking. The Department of Defense had its own political and institutional interests, which it would pursue through simple inaction, classic Washington "slow walking." Finally, in October 2014, three months after the PRB decision, the Secretary of Defense gave his approval and notified Congress. Despite some critical comments in Congress and the conservative media generally about releases, Fawzi was sent home on November 14, 2014, the first repatriation since the prisoner exchange in May. One Kuwaiti now remained.

9

And Then There Was One

Fawzi Al Odah's departure from Guantanamo in November 2014 on a Government of Kuwait aircraft was very different from his arrival. He was no longer in a state of sensory deprivation and he was out of shackles. His rehabilitation team had come to pick him up. But he was leaving behind his last countryman with whom he had spent much of the last nearly thirteen years, Fayiz Al Kandari. Saying goodbye was painful for both of them, and there was no way to know when, or if, they would ever meet again.

Why was Fayiz still there? He had lost his CSRT and ARB hearings, then his habeas case, and then his first PRB hearing. Were his actions in Afghanistan so much more heinous or problematic than those of the other detainees? Did he pose a more severe risk? Did the government have real evidence that he was part of Al Qaida, that he had a relationship with Bin Laden, or were they relying on the same jailhouse informants and Fayiz's angry, provocative statements made in response to mistreatment?

Fayiz had taken a confrontational approach to the Board in his first PRB hearing. Barry Wingard, his retired military lawyer, had argued aggressively that Fayiz had been subject to torture, including sleep deprivation, physical abuse, stress positions, extreme temperatures, and attacks by dogs. There was little doubt this was true in Fayiz's case, as in so many others, but a future-oriented PRB hearing was not the forum for airing grievances against the government that was deciding his fate. Indeed, the US government had taken the position that even detainees who were wrongly detained or abused at Guantanamo might become radicalized simply from that experience and pose a future security risk. This was about security, not justice.

Wingard channeled and encouraged Fayiz's outraged approach in his public statements. Responding to a video that the US government had published showing Fayiz at Guantanamo during a visit by a delegation, Wingard said: "My first thought was that there is no way the United States Government sank so low as to show my client to the world, caged like a circus animal."[1] To be sure, there had been many such degrading stunts, in breach of the Geneva Conventions, over many years, but calling attention to it was unlikely to yield remorse by the government.

Wingard had also received questions from a media outlet – *Al Jazeera* – that he put to Fayiz and then transmitted the responses, which were published in November 2012, not long before the first PRB. Fayiz not only commented on his treatment in this mediated interview, which violated the rule that prohibited detainees from making public statements, he dealt as well with sensitive issues of Kuwaiti internal politics. His opinions, not surprisingly, were based effectively on rumor and speculation, the expressions of someone who had been away from his country for over eleven years and effectively subject to a news blackout.

Fayiz's interview answers not only addressed the action or inaction of the Kuwaiti government, a subject upon which he had no personal knowledge, but also inevitably would make the Kuwaiti or US governments less confident that Fawzi was committed to coming home in a peaceful manner:

> I asked my [Kuwaiti] attorney Adel Abdel Hadi to file a lawsuit on my behalf against the Government of Kuwait. He did it last summer. I am planning to pursue this lawsuit until the end. It is a matter of principle. In my opinion, a government that cannot protect its citizens deserves no respect from any individual. The Government of Kuwait has done very little to assist in my case.[2]

The lawsuit accused the Kuwaiti government of conspiring with the United States to torture prisoners and wasting Kuwaiti funds that should have been used to secure Fayiz's release and the release of other Kuwaiti prisoners.

> My brothers in Guantanamo Bay and I speak ill of the Government of Kuwait. We strongly feel it is lame by not protecting and upholding the rights of its citizens. In addition, the United States shows lack of respect to Kuwait officials, although there are thousands of US soldiers deployed in Kuwait. While the drivers of the political tension in Kuwait have much in common with the other Arab uprisings, particularly the impatient and mobilized youth, it is important to keep local conditions well in mind. Most protesters want to see a constitutional monarchy and political reforms, not revolution. But the lessons of other cases suggest that the Kuwaiti regime's current course of action poses a real risk of radicalizing its opposition and setting in motion unpredictable popular forces.[3]

At the risk of stating the obvious, the Core Team would not have allowed, nor would I have ever considered, giving questions to our client for public distribution in violation of the rules for counsel. While other counsel did similar things, in my view it was not helpful to our clients to invite another fight with the US government about conditions regarding access to clients, even if ultimately the rule against republishing statements of detainees through counsel might not have stood up to court challenge. And there were many issues for which a detainee was not in the best position to have the information or the judgment to respond in a way that would contribute to the overall objective of getting him home. No doubt, the PRB panel was aware of the breach of rules and the substance of the *Al Jazeera* interview.

Wingard did more than act as a conduit for Fayiz. His own views in many ways mirrored those of the clients, and he was active in the media, also in ways that did not promote the narrative that Fayiz was at peace with both the US and the Kuwaiti governments and that the Kuwaiti government would be a supportive partner in achieving repatriation and reintegration. Wingard was critical of both governments and did not always give accurate information. He told an interviewer in 2009, for example, that "Fayiz is one of four Kuwaitis still imprisoned in GTMO. Before leaving office, the Bush administration promised the Kuwait government that a rehabilitation center was all that stood between the release of the four detainees. Of interest, the US government is now hedging on releasing at least two of the four Kuwaiti detainees; Fayiz being one."[4]

Neither the Kuwaitis nor I knew of any promise from the US that all four of the detainees would be sent home once there was a rehabilitation center. Indeed, after the early releases of the first two sent home in 2009, it was clear that the United States wanted extensive security guarantees that went beyond the construction of a rehabilitation center. Such comments, effectively accusing the US government of bad faith negotiation or lying, simply made it harder for the remaining detainees, and made the United States dig in more to obtain detailed protocols before any release would be considered. In any event, the Special Envoy at the State Department, Cliff Sloan, made clear from the beginning that, to be sent home, detainees would first need to be cleared for release through the PRB process.

Wingard also decided to give public advice to the Kuwaiti government to be more proactive because of the irrationality and hypocrisy of the US government, which, in his view, could only be solved by Kuwait abandoning diplomacy for invective:

> As a result, I implore the Kuwaiti government not to treat GTMO as just another issue to be resolved through patient diplomacy. The United States' detention policy has become so irrational that polite appeals cannot possibly succeed. Rather, Kuwait must view the United States as one might

view a family member addicted to a powerful substance (in this case fear, paranoia and political pandering). Only immediate and consequential intervention can possibly resolve the problem. As America's strongest ally in the Middle East, Kuwait is the only partner capable of such intervention.[5]

Whatever the validity of these observations, as a potentially viable strategy it was predictably unhelpful. It also fundamentally misread the power dynamics in the bilateral relationship between a superpower and a small Gulf emirate. Kuwait was not going to call out its principal ally as an addict and was not going to force an intervention with the United States. Patient diplomacy was ongoing; it was working; and it was the best tool Kuwait had in its toolkit.

Wingard also made it clear that he did not view the Kuwaiti government as any less brutal than the United States, and so both countries were morally disqualified, again a strategic blunder of real harm to the detainees. He invoked an alleged beating and homicide by Kuwaiti police and tried to analogize it to Fawzi's treatment. He then attacked the Kuwaiti Ministry of Interior for not valuing human life and speculated that this

> ...may help explain why two other Kuwaiti citizens have been confined at Guantanamo Bay for more than nine years without Kuwait ever formally demanding their return. In fact, given the minister of interior's recently leaked opinion that Guantanamo detainees should be returned to Afghanistan to be killed, it is clear neither Kuwait nor the United States retains the moral authority they once held to champion human rights throughout the world.
>
> As Fayiz's attorney, I cannot help but feel the recent death of al-Mutairi [a Kuwaiti prisoner, not a detainee, allegedly beaten to death by Kuwaiti police in 2011] does not bode well for my client. In fact, given President Obama's preference for indefinite detention and the Kuwaiti government's unwillingness to prevent such detention, Kuwait may be responsible for not one, but three, dead bodies.
>
> Like al-Mutairi, al-Kandari was beaten and abused by government officials who believed physical assault was an appropriate means of extracting information, but unlike al-Mutairi, whose fatal abuse was relatively brief, Fayiz was beaten and abused for a much longer period of time. He is arguably fortunate to have survived such an ordeal. But if Fayiz survived only to die in a cage, he has only prolonged the inevitable. His torment will likely continue until he is returned home in a box.[6]

Wingard concluded with a direct appeal to Kuwaitis over the head of their government and a call to direct action in both countries: "[T]he citizens of Kuwait and the United States must ensure their governments take meaningful action and are held accountable for their actions. Otherwise, if such individual human rights abuses are allowed to continue, the clock begins to tick for you, me and those close to us."[7]

Such hostility and contempt toward both governments could not possibly have induced either government to have more sympathy for Fayiz. He would not shame either government into taking action against its own security concerns.

Fayiz had also expressed his frustration and anger to the members of the Kuwaiti members of the Inter-Agency Working Group. He blamed them for his predicament. He had been uncooperative with the medical, spiritual, and security personnel who would be evaluating his state of mind and would be communicating with the United States regularly. It may have given him some satisfaction to claim that his own government was not helping him. In fact, his government was helping him but not in a visibly aggressive way. In any event, he and his lawyer were giving them little to work with in their dialogue with the United States. Would a different approach work? Or was Fayiz regarded as the worst of the worst, a habeas loser without options, and would he be a forever prisoner irrespective of what his government said?

Fayiz's initial PRB file review in March 2014, prior to his first PRB hearing, gave little reason for optimism, as it was far more backward focused on previous conduct than the reviews of other detainees who had come before the PRB:

> Faez Mohammed Ahmed ai-Kandari (KU-552) traveled to Afghanistan for the first time in 1997, returned to the Middle East in 1998, and thereafter served as a recruiter and propagandist for al-Qa'ida. He returned in 2001 to Afghanistan, where he almost certainly received extremist training from al-Qa'ida, provided support to an al-Qa'ida-affiliated charity, and probably fought on the frontlines against Coalition forces. While in Afghanistan, KU-552 probably served as Usama bin Ladin's spiritual advisor and confidant and possibly developed close ties with other al-Qa'ida leaders. He also possibly fought in Bosnia during the 1990s.
>
> During interviews, however, KU-552 consistently has denied involvement with al-Qa'ida or other extremist groups.
>
> Throughout his detention, he has expressed anti-American sentiments, encouraged other detainees to conduct violent jihad after release, and voiced support for his mujahidin "brothers" overseas, indicating he almost certainly retains an extremist mindset.[8]

It appeared that the PRB Secretariat was sticking to the old playbook the government had used in earlier hearings before the CSRTs and ARBs. Accept whatever other detainees may have said, whether or not it was credible or corroborated. Accept that a young, recent Islamic Studies graduate had been accepted into the Bin Laden innermost circle. Take Fayiz's own angry statements at face value as confessions.

Fayiz had just graduated when he went to Afghanistan in 2001. It would be ludicrous to think that Osama Bin Laden, who regarded himself (wrongly) as a sophisticated student of Islam, would have taken spiritual advice from a brand-new graduate from an obscure Islamic college in Ras Al Khaimah. Yet, the PRB file review appeared to accept that Fayiz was a respected senior cleric guiding top Al Qaida officials, as opposed to, at most, one of thousands of pious young men who had come from the Gulf before September 11.

After the March 2014 file review resulting in continued detention, Fayiz was unhappy and pessimistic when he came to his first PRB hearing on June 5, 2014, the day after Fawzi's hearing. The result was consistent with the prior file review – continued detention – but did reference the possibility of some movement in the future:

> The Periodic Review Board, by consensus, determined continued law of war detention of the detainee remains necessary to protect against a continuing significant threat to the security of the United States. In making this determination, the Board considered that the detainee almost certainly retains an extremist mindset and had close ties with high-level Al Qaida leaders in the past. The Board found the detainee credible with respect to his desire to return to his family, which appears willing to help with his reintegration, but also considered the detainee's susceptibility for recruitment due to his connections to extremists and his residual anger at the US. The Board noted a lack of history regarding the efficacy of the rehabilitation program Kuwait will implement for a detainee with his particular mindset but appreciates the efforts of the Kuwaiti government and encourages the officials at the Al Salam Rehabilitation Center to continue to work with the detainee at Guantanamo. *The Board looks forward to reviewing the detainee's file in six months and hopes to see his continued participation in future reviews.*[9]

The decision pointed in contradictory directions. Certainly, Fayiz at his hearing did nothing to convince the Board that he did not hold extremist views or that the rumors of Al Qaida involvement were incorrect. Yes, the Board acknowledged that Fayiz wanted to go home; who wouldn't? But the Board still saw him as someone who had gone from an angry young man to an angry middle-aged man, and his lashing out with extremist statements was viewed not as indicative of frustration with his apparently hopeless situation, but as an admission of his true mental state and predictor of possible future dangerousness.

The Board also acknowledged that the Al Salam Rehabilitation Center was in place and specifically noted its appreciation and encouragement of those efforts, while simultaneously referring to the fact that earlier detainees had been released immediately and that Fawzi had not yet arrived there. Al Salam had no track record. It was a signal that Al Salam's performance when Fawzi got home would be watched and could be an important factor the next time Fayiz's case was considered.

While the decision held out some hope for the next file review in early 2015, it would be difficult to make a case on a paper record without hearing new testimony from Fayiz as well as seeing his family. But a full oral hearing was not required for three years after his first hearing in 2014. He needed another hearing sooner than that, as soon as possible. The year 2017 was a long way away, and who could predict who would be president and what the government's approach to Guantanamo would be then?

Fayiz had spent significant time talking to Fawzi both in the lead-up to their PRB hearings in June 2014, and after Fayiz was cleared. Fayiz knew that Fawzi had taken a very different approach to the hearing, that Fawzi had won, and he had lost. Fayiz now came to realize that short-term bravado would not get him home. He also knew that the Core Team and Lewis Baach had offered to represent both Fawzi and him at the first hearing; that Fawzi had accepted and Fayiz had declined; and now Fawzi was going home. Fayiz spoke to his family, who communicated to the Family Committee that he wanted to change counsel and adopt a new approach.

The Lewis Baach team met with Fayiz for the first time in February 2015. He had been lobbied hard by Wingard, who was representing other detainees with a similarly confrontational approach, not to switch lawyers. Fayiz had appreciated that his previous lawyers were deeply committed to him personally and professionally, and their fighting spirit made him feel a sense of reciprocal commitment and loyalty. Fayiz wanted to show his gratitude for Wingard's efforts, but he knew that the two approaches were diametrically opposed. He would have to choose.

The Lewis Baach team explained that the choice was Fayiz's, but that the Core Team and the firm had formulated a way to fight on his behalf that may have lacked fire but had proven effective. It made no sense to alienate the decision-makers. Fayiz signed the form to change counsel.

Our first goal was to press the US government to drop the requirement that Fayiz wait three years for a new live hearing. Whatever momentum there might have been arising from the PRB report could well be gone by mid-2017. Fayiz's mental state might well not remain optimistic or even stable for that long. And of course, as it turned out, by 2017, Donald Trump was president, and the PRB Boards had become an empty exercise to ratify the policy of an administration committed not to release anyone. Only one detainee was released in those first four years and that was the product of a deal where the detainee would serve the nine years remaining on his sentence after a military commission plea in Saudi Arabia.

The next important goal was to reframe the narrative – to show that Fayiz now understood the PRB process was real and genuinely focused on his future rather than the past. Fawzi's release had given Fayiz something that he had not had for thirteen years. Hope. Hope that he was not wasting his time. Hope that he was not being trapped. Hope that his government was advocating on his behalf. And hope that his own visions for the future would not elicit disbelief and disrespect from his jailers. He could stop being a pointless provocateur and really engage honestly with a new process. But this was a moment in time that might not last. We needed a live hearing.

There was no reason to follow a significantly different game plan in Fayiz's case than in Fawzi's. It was necessary to humanize a man whom the United States had obdurately insisted for more than thirteen years was a hard-core, dangerous terrorist. His family would need to be involved and help present his life story pre-capture with depth and humanity, as well as the care and security they would provide in the future. The Kuwaiti government officials whom Fayiz had treated with hostility in the past would need to be reapproached to meet with Fayiz, observe his optimistic mindset, and provide assurances to the United States that the Kuwaiti government could, in good faith, provide the necessary security guarantees. The success of Fawzi's rehabilitation process was also critical; the United States needed proof that it was working according to the agreed plan, and the same protocol would be followed with Fayiz to the letter. But first Fayiz needed a prompt live hearing outside the normal cycle. We would press the issue as part of the next file review.

After seeing Fayiz at Guantanamo in early February 2015, the Lewis Baach team went to Kuwait the next week and met with his family as well as once again with Dr. Adel, Dr. Al Oteibi, Colonel Al Kandari, and Chief Prosecutor Al Atteqi. Each submitted statements for the PRB File Review, emphasizing the progress that Fayiz had made. Dr. Adel and Dr. Al Oteibi had all seen Fayiz multiple times over a period of years, including twice since Fawzi's clearance, and each spoke candidly about those visits with Fayiz.

Dr. Al Oteibi wrote of his experience with Fayiz:

> In my capacity with the Rehabilitation Center, I have also been a part of the interagency working group of government officials from the United States and Kuwait to develop the conditions under which the remaining Kuwaiti citizens detained in Guantanamo, now only Fayez Al Kandari, will be transferred to the custody of the Government of Kuwait. I have attended five meetings of the working group in Guantanamo, in 2009, 2013, two in 2014, and most recently in January 2015. During those trips, I was part of the Kuwaiti delegation that traveled to Guantanamo Bay and met with Fayez.

Fayez has not expressed any radical or extremist views or intention to commit violent acts at any point. He has always made clear in our discussions, and I believe, that he is a non-violent person. He was open and honest in discussing religion, and his views have always fit within the mainstream of Kuwait, which is a moderate country.

Nevertheless, in previous visits he expressed frustration and a sense of hopelessness as to his future. He was at times frustrated and uncooperative and questioned the efforts of the Kuwaiti government to secure his release.

In the most recent visits in October 2014 and January 2015, however, he had significantly altered his approach in my view. His demeanor was calm; he spoke of going home, getting married, starting a business and living a peaceful, quiet and pious life. He emphasized his desire to look forward. He also emphasized that his love for his religion and its message of peace and good deeds has sustained him and will continue to do so.[10]

Dr. Adel expressed similar views from a psychiatric perspective. He candidly recounted his earlier problematic visits with Fayiz at Guantanamo and the new developments:

In the past, Mr. Al Kandari had not been fully cooperative with me and the delegation. During my last two visits, I was pleased to observe that he was much more fully engaged, calm, cooperative, and forward-looking than he had been during prior visits. Although this recent improvement in Mr. Al Kandari's attitude will significantly aid his rehabilitation, based upon my clinical judgment of his personality issues and my knowledge of the impact on mental health of an experience such as his lengthy imprisonment and separation form his family and society, it is my professional opinion that Mr. Al Kandari will require extended in-patient treatment at the Rehabilitation Center in order to successfully reintegrate with his family and Kuwaiti society. In my view, he is likely to need more intensive rehabilitative services than Mr. Al Odah and we will be prepared to provide them. He will be under the careful and close supervision of the entire team.[11]

Colonel Al Kandari expressed his concern for security but also noted his firm impression that Fayiz had matured over the years of his visits:

I have met Fayez Al Kandari at Guantanamo five times, most recently in January 2015. In the past, he expressed significant feelings of frustration and injustice about his situation. But when I met with him in October 2014 and January 2015, I noted that he had changed his thinking and approach and was much more focused on building a peaceful future in Kuwait, rather than expressing frustration about his past. He expressed appreciation that he was now permitted monthly calls with his family, which I requested, and the US Government kindly implemented. This has significantly strengthened Mr. Al Kandari's family bonds and increased the effectiveness of their communication and positive influence over his thinking and behavior. He plainly feels very close bonds with his parents and other responsible family members. This gives me confidence that he is taking their constructive advice and counsel about his future. He indicated recognition of the value of and need for rehabilitation, which will be extremely useful in continuing that positive adjustment process. As an intelligence official, I cannot speak with 100% certainty concerning whether a former detainee will engage in extremist activities. Nevertheless, I have extensive experience in dealing with extremists. It is my best judgment that upon successful completion of the rehabilitation program, Mr. Al Kandari will present no material risk of engaging in extremist activity, but we will of course remain vigilant to prevent such activity in any event.[12]

He reiterated his commitment to careful monitoring and surveillance and attached documents that Fayiz would need to fill out on a regular basis with respect to his contacts, his social media, his financial transactions, and related matters.

The Lewis Baach team also met in Kuwait with Fayiz's cousin, Dr. Abdullah Al Kandari,[13] who is a prominent ophthalmologist and ophthalmic oncologist in Kuwait. Dr. Abdullah was one of a number of highly educated people in Fayiz's family who had been educated in North America and spoke fluent English. Fayiz had been close to his uncle, who served as a mentor in Fayiz's upbringing and education. Dr. Abdullah offered a nuanced and candid portrait of Fayiz as a young man, perhaps the first such picture offered to a fact finder since Fayiz's capture fourteen years before:

> Before Fayez left Kuwait in the summer of 2001, he was an intelligent and pious young man. He had done very well at school and university. He was a charming and good-humored young man with many friends. As a teenager, he was always skillful at maintaining positive and peaceful relations in his peer group. As the oldest of seven children, he looked after his brothers and sister and served as a warm and loving mentor to them. He was not much interested in politics and his religious beliefs were well within the moderate mainstream here in Kuwait. It was my impression that, upon finishing school, he was, like many young Kuwaiti men, somewhat sheltered and impressionable and unsophisticated for his age by Western standards. He was eager to undertake charitable works and help the poor.
>
> Fayez began as an engineering student at Kuwait University, but did not enjoy engineering and switched to an Islamic Studies college in the United Arab Emirates. When our mutual grandmother and his mother were both diagnosed with cancer, he came home to be with them. Thereafter, he went to Pakistan and Afghanistan to help poor people. Of course, this was before

the terrible events of September 11, 2001. In our religion, it is believed that doing good works for the less fortunate has a beneficial effect in healing the sick. Indeed, the Prophet, peace be upon him, said "Treat your patients with charity." Thus, the family was pleased, and it was viewed as appropriate and beneficial for Fayez to do this charitable work. Indeed, they contributed financially to his doing so.

Fayez has had difficulty over the years coping with indefinite detention at Guantanamo, and most specifically with not knowing when, if ever, he might be released. He has spent his entire young adulthood there and has missed out on many years of professional and personal development. This has caused him at times to be frustrated and unhappy.

The repatriation of Fawzi Al Odah has had a tremendous positive impact on Fayez. First, he is delighted that his friend has gone home. Second, Fawzi's release after so long has clearly restored Fayez's hope that he too can go home in the near future. He believes now that there is a process that is objective and transparent and can lead to his actual repatriation. His whole mindset has changed for the better. In our conversations, he is forward-looking, optimistic, positive and even more happy and joking since Fawzi's repatriation. He is planning a future career in business in Kuwait. He very much enjoys talking with family members on the monthly calls arranged by the Red Cross and is attentive to his parents' feelings and advice. He has talked with the family about getting married and having children. He wants to cooperate fully and get on with his life. In his conversations with me, he expresses no extremist thoughts. He is looking forward to going home.[14]

These statements built a strong case for the PRB to order a full hearing, but it was uncertain, given the Department of Defense bureaucracy and the press of other cases, that it would order another full hearing before July 2017.

On April 14, 2015, however, after receiving our submissions regarding new evidence, the PRB conducted its file review for Fayiz and concluded, "After reviewing relevant new information related to the detainee as well as information considered during the June 12, 2014 full review, the Board, by consensus, determined that a significant question is raised as to whether the detainee's continued detention is warranted and therefore an additional full review should be conducted." We were back on track.

The file review statements from Kuwaiti officials were strong and could be submitted for the hearing in a similar form, updated to account for subsequent meetings with Fayiz. The Core Team and the Lewis Baach lawyers were optimistic after Fawzi's hearing and his first months of effective rehabilitation that the Board would be convinced of Kuwait's continuing commitment to work in good faith to rehabilitate both Fawzi and Fayiz, as well as to make sure that they would be carefully watched. Because Fayiz's family was not English-speaking or experienced in dealing with this kind of sensitive cross-cultural advocacy, it was necessary to spend extensive time with them to be able to show effectively that their commitment was just as great. We would need to submit videos in Arabic with captions and transcripts with respect to his parents. We knew they would not be shown at the hearing, but we had no reason to believe the earlier videos had not been reviewed outside the hearing room.

It was also necessary to decide how to address the allegations of direct interaction with Bin Laden and support of Al Qaida. This issue would need careful handling to be simultaneously both candid and diplomatic. But it would have to be addressed head-on.

From the time Lewis Baach was engaged, the team made four trips to Guantanamo to meet with Fayiz. The new PRB panel was likely to have different agency representatives than the panel that had ruled in favor of Fawzi, as the original panel membership was being replaced. The lead convener of the original PRBs, the much-feared Department of Defense lawyer, J. Allen Liotta, had retired, and other agencies had rotated their official representative. The team needed to check whatever new public material was available and talk to other counsel about the non-classified questions that were being asked at more recent hearings with new personnel.

It was essential to spend time and work in depth with Fayiz. He was extremely sharp and intelligent, quick with a smile or a quip that expressed with dark humor his situation and the nature of his ordeal. He could, however, quickly become emotional and take offense. He knew that he had made strong and pointed statements in the past, which he viewed as rightfully highlighting the unfairness and circular logic of the various interrogations and hearings. But we needed to convince him that pointing out these absurdities would not be good advocacy. Fayiz had a great sense of ironic humor; the United States did not.

After the first meeting with Fayiz, it was clear that he wanted to be cooperative and nonconfrontational. Like Fawzi, he would not admit to anything he did not do, but he was not looking for apologies or regret from the US government. We needed to coordinate his presentation with that of his family members.

As with Fawzi, we made a video of his home and interviewed his father and mother and siblings. Fayiz had a host of nieces and nephews, most of whom he had never met. A few were babies when he left. The children kept everyone cheerful even if the scene was chaotic. Fayiz's parents were anxious, both because they knew how important the next hearing would be and because they had no experience making videos or sharing their feelings about their son in a way that would be viewed by his captors. At one point, a nephew of four or five, fully outfitted in a black ninja costume complete with plastic sword and headband, ran into the sitting room, leapt in the air, and gave a huge ninja shout. Fortunately, he was not captured on video; even tiny ninja residents of the home where Fayiz would reside should probably not debut on Fayiz's family video for the US government.

The United States had expressed concern about one of Fayiz's relatives, and Fayiz's parents and siblings confirmed that he was a distant relative and that he would not be welcome in their house when Fayiz came home. Once again, we did a house tour. The Al Kandari family was warm and humble. Their piety was clear; a digital clock that displayed the daily prayer times hung prominently in their living room. Their love for Fayiz and eagerness to bring him home were just as evident as with the Al Odahs.

The team also met with and made videos of some of Fayiz's other relatives, the Western-trained professionals who spoke fluent English, including Dr. Abdullah Al Kandari, who had also submitted a file review statement, and Dr. Mohamed Al Kandari, who held a doctorate in educational policy and is a Professor at Kuwait University. They both pledged to help mentor Fayiz when he returned home.

The submission contained new statements from the various Kuwaiti authorities reiterating their confidence that the Al Salam Rehabilitation Center would provide necessary services and that these officials had seen changes in Fayiz – changes that were accelerating his positive state of mind, especially now that he would be getting an early full hearing. They also made commitments to convey that their confidence would be backed up with verifiable security requirements. Fayiz would stay for one year at Al Salam under the same parameters as Fawzi, and both Fayiz's father and Fayiz committed that they agreed and would not try to short-circuit his rehabilitation process in court.

The legal team's last trips to Guantanamo took place in June and July 2015. We reviewed with Fayiz the statements and videos that had been obtained in Kuwait. The team also reviewed at length with Fayiz the questions that Fawzi and other detainees had been asked as well as other questions that might be asked only of Fayiz. There were long discussions of the underlying facts as well as the best strategies for approaching what could be difficult, painful, or provocative questions.

The easiest questions had to do with Al Salam Rehabilitation Center. There would be no challenges or surprises. Fayiz himself recognized that after fourteen years, he could not go home and take up where he had left off. He made clear he would be much happier back home in Kuwait where he could see his mother and father in person, even at the Rehabilitation Center. He was concerned that his parents were getting quite old and infirm and feared he might not have much time with them. He recognized that in many ways, he had been a very young and naïve person when he left, having spent most of his time in school or college. He had really not lived as an adult, and now, he was turning forty, with much gray in his hair and beard.

The PRB would know about Fayiz's reputation for being argumentative and a provocateur. How could he account for his current state of mind? How could he convince the Board that this was not just a performance to get home? How could he acknowledge that he had genuinely changed without admitting to alleged terrorist affiliations that he never had? Again, Fayiz had to rely on his process of maturation and the impact of hope after years and years of hopelessness; the impact of the dignity and respect of a fair hearing after years of humiliation. He said he came to Guantanamo when he was twenty-six and now, nearly forty, he had become more patient, more tolerant, and more hopeful. He wanted a private, peaceful life free of disputes.

He also needed to address why there should be a different outcome in 2015 than the one in 2014. He admitted that he had been negative at his 2014 PRB hearing and had feared this was yet another process that would end in failure and disappointment. He could not accept that a board of American security officials would seriously consider what was in his mind and heart. His newfound confidence in the process, after his friend Fawzi had gone home, had made him much more at peace with himself and the world.

Fayiz also had to address some of his hostile, provocative statements about the United States that he conceded he had made. He insisted that, like nearly all Kuwaitis, he had respect and gratitude for the American liberation of Kuwait when he was a teenager. He made clear that Kuwait had always had a large population of Americans in Kuwait City with whom he had interacted amicably throughout his life and that he had close cousins who had trained in America and Canada, including Dr. Abdullah and Dr. Mohammed.

Fayiz was philosophical about his experience. Americans were like anyone else, both good and bad, and he had met both at Guantanamo. He had been treated with kindness and respect and responded accordingly. He also had been treated with scorn and violence and asserted his autonomy by lashing out at those guards or interrogators. Some guards were interested in him and Kuwait's culture and religion. Others were very young and naïve and had neither interest in nor respect for him and his background. He also acknowledged that his detention was a function of government policy decisions, not the guards and interrogators who were essentially doing their jobs, including orders from above to treat detainees harshly.

Because a significant strand of Al Qaida thinking was resentment of non-Muslims in the region and the group sought expulsion of non-Muslims from Muslim lands, it was necessary to discuss at length how Fayiz felt about having Americans, including the American military, in Kuwait and the region.

Fayiz knew Kuwait was in a dangerous neighborhood and that American support, including military support, was vital. He knew there was a close working relationship between the two governments and that the American military was needed to protect vulnerable countries, as the Iraqi invasion and liberation had shown. Fayiz was also unequivocal that he opposes any group that advocates violence or killing – whether Al Qaida or the Al Nusra Front or ISIS or any other group. Fayiz had added to this statement at his first PRB hearing that his opposition to violence extended not just to extreme Islamist groups but also to America's use of Tomahawk missiles in the region. He understood that equating Al Qaida and the American military was deliberately provocative and, in fact, not an equivalence he really accepted. He had been a wise guy, and he knew it.

The team also discussed his views on the caliphate that was advocated by ISIS leadership because he would be asked about ISIS as had other detainees. ISIS did not exist when Fayiz went to Guantanamo but now was perpetrating horrific violence in the region in the name of restoring a Caliph to rule over Muslim lands.

Fayiz was unequivocal that he was strongly opposed, indeed horrified, by the Islamic State and that he was a Kuwaiti who supported the Kuwaiti government, where there is a civilian government and no Caliph. He noted correctly that there had not been a caliphate since the fall of the Ottoman Empire and its Sultan at the end of World War I. He also made clear that he had never made any tapes or recruitment videos for any group. None had ever been produced by anyone in all these years because they did not exist. His only contact with possible extremists, he said, occurred when he met groups of unknown Arabs when he was trying to get to the border and leave Afghanistan; what they shared was fear for their lives, not political views. He never met Bin Laden and found it laughable that he would be accused of being a spiritual mentor to him or anyone else when he was in Afghanistan.

It was also necessary to address some of the statements that he and Wingard had made about the efforts of the Kuwaiti government. Again, those statements were matters of record and could not be denied. Fayiz acknowledged that he owed Kuwait a lot and that it had provided a free quality education to him and his siblings. He was proud to be a Kuwaiti. He did acknowledge that he was often resentful that all the other Kuwaitis had been released for no apparent reason or difference between him and the others. He kept wondering, "Why had Kuwait not gotten him home, when nearly all the others had been sent home?"

Fayiz knew that after 2009, he had been one of only two Kuwaitis, along with Fawzi, who had not been released, and now Fawzi was home. Fayiz had learned that, in fact, his government had helped the detainees and wanted to help him and bring him home, even if he had not been aware of it.

Fayiz was clear that he did not go to Afghanistan to fight; he went to do charitable work because both his mother and grandmother were being treated for cancer. Fayiz knew that his mother feared his going to Afghanistan; she was concerned about his safety and his being apart from her. He told her it would be a short visit and he would find a quiet and safe place to do charitable work in the tradition of Islam. To say the least, that plan had not worked out. His mother, like Fawzi's mother, was right; their boys should have stayed home.

Fayiz also discussed his future plans, including his plans to establish a business and to take classes in accounting, technology, marketing and finance. He wanted to get married. He joked that he wanted his wife to be beautiful, but he said seriously that what he really wanted was a sincere person who would appreciate him for who he is. He would live with his parents, and he would take care of them in their declining years, as they took care of his adjustment. He wanted to cherish his parents in whatever time they had left to them. He made clear that if he could talk to his twenty-six-year-old self as a forty-year-old, he would tell himself to stay close to his parents and remain peaceful and compassionate and that he should have listened to his mother.

Fayiz's hearing took place on July 27, 2015, in the same room at Camp 7 in Guantanamo. Fayiz was also chained to the floor, and again, I was the only member of the counsel team permitted in the room, along with the second military representative as the first had rotated to another assignment. Fayiz was in good spirits and felt comfortable and positive.

We opened the hearing expressing gratitude for the rapid full hearing. The presentation summarized up-front what we viewed as the three principal factors that may have led the Board to render a negative decision the year before – Fayiz's residual anger against the United States; the Board's concern about extremist relatives; and the lack of history regarding the efficacy of the Al Salam Rehabilitation Center. We then explained why those factors no longer applied.

The Al Salam track record was quite straightforward. When Fayiz and Fawzi had their hearings a day apart, there was only expectation, not history. Now there was clear proof that the Kuwaiti government had met its commitments; that the program was in place; services were being provided to Fawzi, and the program was effective.

Fawzi himself played the starring role in the video that was submitted to the PRB, as he conducted the walk-through of the center and showed the Board where he received his services, where he worked out, where he ate, where he saw visitors, and how he conducted his days. Fawzi was the perfect tour guide, upbeat and relaxed. My opening previewed the tour of Al Salam: "You will see Fawzi on video and see what a difference the Al Salam Rehabilitation Center has made in his life. He is optimistic; he is happy; he is ready to resume a full, useful, and peaceful life. He harbors no ill will toward anyone. He just wants to move forward." The 2014 video with Dr. Adel as tour guide had been persuasive. But the new video with Fawzi guiding the Board through the Center where he was living provided powerful proof that it was working.

With respect to being angry at America and wishing harm to the country and its people, we had to concede that Fayiz had been fed up and skeptical in 2014. I tried to put it into context.

> So Fayiz withdrew and tried to preserve his dignity by using this one chance to talk to officials of the United States to express his frustration and sense that his long and seemingly indefinite detention was unfair. To be candid, I do not think he was given much hope in advance that the process would be fair and transparent. So rather than talk about the future, he used the hearing to vent, and this may have come across as hostility.

Now things had changed:

> The defensive cynicism you may have seen last year is gone. Fayiz knows you will listen to him, you will inquire into his mind and spirit and take a fair and honest measure of him. No one can be happy about spending 13½ years here. No one should be. That is human nature. But Fayez bears no ill will toward America or Americans. Fayez is a proud man, but he is a man who engages with others with energy, enthusiasm, and charm. He treats

others with respect; of course, he asks for respect from others. When a man has hope, he is a different man. Fayez has hope. I trust you will get a sense of that today.

But the upbeat words of lawyers would not be decisive; Fayiz would have to convince the Board of his transformation and of his peaceful intentions and lack of resentment. He met that standard easily and exceeded it. He was, in truth, a different man. The Board could perceive this as not an act because it was so heartfelt and real.

The team also dealt with the issue of his exposure to extremists, including family members. Fayiz had not seen any of his family for fourteen years, and he made clear he wanted to be with his parents, and he had no desire to have involvement with possible extremists or involvement in politics in any way. To the extent the US and Kuwaiti governments wanted him to avoid any distant relatives or anyone else, he only needed to be told. Whatever may have been the reality of Fayiz at twenty-six, it was clear that Fayiz at forty wanted to live an apolitical, family-oriented life in Kuwait. At forty, he had no time for anything else. By the end of the hearing, we were cautiously optimistic that the Board agreed.

On September 8, 2015, the Board unanimously recommended his release. On January 8, 2016, he left Guantanamo, more than a year after Fawzi, also on a GoK plane, with his Al Salam caregivers. Finally, his ordeal, his own family's ordeal, the Family Committee's ordeal, and Kuwait's ordeal, was over.

10

Lessons Learned

The original idea for this book was that it would be an analytical review of the steps taken by the Core Team on behalf of the families of Kuwaiti prisoners to gain the release of the Kuwaitis held at Guantanamo. The goal was to provide a legal, historical, and political narrative to elicit strategic and tactical insights for the benefit of governments and lawyers addressing future issues likely to arise in times of global stress.

As the writing progressed, it became clear that an analysis of legal issues and diplomatic initiatives might be of interest to a small group of lawyers and international affairs professionals, but there was a more important narrative to relate. Whenever I talk about Guantanamo prisoners, I am asked whether Guantanamo is still open. It has faded from the public agenda despite the fact that there are, at this writing, fifteen men still there, including those few charged with the most serious crimes related to September 11.

Although the changes to the legal system and the enduring impact of post-9/11 culture are important, it is the stories of the Kuwaiti detainees that are deeply personal yet universal and timeless. Guantanamo not only still exists as a legal and moral challenge but also illustrates a recurring pattern of the weight of fear, panic, and politics coming down on the heads of those whose lives are viewed as not worthy of respect. Politicians knew early on that they had not captured "the worst of the worst," but they suppressed these politically inconvenient facts; many innocent men bore the brunt of this scapegoating and still do. Their lives were collateral damage to a "War on Terror" that was more a political football than an actual, winnable military operation. Their stories illustrate the tragic pattern of dehumanization of the other, those of other religions, colors, or nationalities. There were men at Guantanamo who had done bad things. But there was no honest effort to find out who were and who were not such men. And in any event no one should ever be tortured; yet all were. The rule of law and basic human rights were viewed as dispensable moral luxuries under political pressure. Ultimately, the courts provided some counterweight to a panicked and cruel executive, but it was hesitant, slow, and uneven.

There are some more optimistic lessons as well: that the ruler of a small country can make the difficult choice to commit to getting justice for his nationals abroad and use his diplomatic resources in making their liberty a top priority. There is also the lesson that men who have been tortured and held for years without charge for an indefinite period and the risk of being held forever can maintain a measure of their humanity and perspective through community and faith. Some, however, could not. The "Lessons Learned" discussed here are not so much insights into legal or diplomatic technique; they are lessons about the way people and countries respond, for good and for ill, in difficult times, which are always with us. They are also lessons about how to struggle toward decency and resilience in those times.

Guantanamo Remains an Iconic Part of American Life

"The past is never dead. It is not even past."[1] Faulkner's aphorism applies powerfully to Guantanamo. Not only does Guantanamo continue to operate as a detention center, but the men who were there and those who have fought for their release have not forgotten their experience. Nor have America's enemies.

Many of the remaining detainees have now been there for more than two decades.

The process drags on at *Bleak House* pace. No one has been brought to Guantanamo since 2006 on national security grounds. Fewer than a dozen of the nearly 800 other men were ever charged or will be charged. The high-value detainee process has been marked by incompetence, chaos, endless delays, replacement of personnel, harassment of defense lawyers, and repeated governmental attempts to tweak what minimal due process is given in the hope that a court will accept that the government has finally hurdled the constitutional bar. But the "low-value detainees" suffered from the same bureaucratic incompetence, dishonesty, delay, and attempts to create a legal black hole.

So Guantanamo is not in the past; it is not dead for those men whose lives have been profoundly disrupted, who were tortured, who have blown themselves up, who have become floridly psychotic, who never saw their parents again or missed their children's growing up. It is not past for those who remain there to this day, some of whom may well die there. It is also not past in 2025 for a new cohort of victims, migrants sent to this modern-day Devil's Island or Van Diemen's Land beyond the seas.

Guantanamo is also not past for America's enemies, who take hostages and put them in iconic orange jumpsuits before savagely murdering them. One should not in any way justify or excuse the horrors of Al Qaida or ISIS or their offshoots – and I emphatically do neither – to note that Guantanamo Bay has become a potent symbol manipulated by evil men who try to recruit others to join them or accept their evil deeds.

In the oddly offhand words of President Obama, "We tortured some folks." It was many, many men. It is horrific but should not be shocking that this unspeakable violence against hundreds of Muslim men unleashed sick and unwarranted revenge against not only American military personnel but also innocent civilians. Jimmy Carter invoked the American national conscience. "I think what's going on in Guantanamo Bay and other places is a disgrace to the U.S.A. I wouldn't say it's the cause of terrorism, but it has given impetus and excuses to potential terrorists to lash out at our country and justify their despicable acts."[2]

Guantanamo is also not dead or past as a potent political symbol in American life. The moral panic after 9/11 has been repeatedly rekindled with Guantanamo Bay standing as a shorthand for fighting terrorists, even though, as seen in these chapters, very little fighting or even incapacitation of terrorists was accomplished there. Ginny Thomas, wife of Justice Clarence Thomas, tweeted after the 2020 election that President Biden and the "Biden crime family" "will be living in barges off GITMO to face military tribunals for sedition."[3] And in his first months in office, Donald Trump, who promised to keep it open and put some "bad dudes" there, has cycled more than 700 people through the facility. His Secretary of Homeland Security, Kristi Noem, channeled Donald Rumsfeld, from two decades past, calling these migrants "the worst of the worst," and for good measure, "ratbags." News reports indicate that the vast majority of them have only committed the crime of coming into the United States without permission.[4] It is clear that, yet again for political purposes, an American administration under Trump has conducted a random round-up and has no process in place to sort the guilty from the innocent and no plan to house people under humane conditions.[5] There is a strange recurring attraction to creating lawless enclaves for indefinite arbitrary detention of foreigners far from their families or access to justice.

Guantanamo is also not dead regarding America's relations with other nations, including friends and allies. The widespread use of torture, which the United States tried to hide in black prisons and the "legal black hole" of Guantanamo, has made other nations wary of participating in the dirty work of "enhanced interrogation" as well as in accepting detainees that the United States will not. That is a positive development, to be sure, but American action has greatly diluted American moral authority. Many countries sent interrogators, who assisted in the brutality against their own nationals. Some later provided substantial compensation for this violent treatment; the United States did not.

When President Obama wanted detainees charged with crimes to be taken to the United States to be tried in federal courts, Congress passed a law prohibiting any Guantanamo detainees from being brought to the United States, despite the fact that the United States has been trying serious terrorism cases in federal court without incident for decades.[6] Congress did not trust the US justice system and asked other countries to take steps that it decided were too politically risky to do itself. Alliances require goodwill and reciprocity; the United States offered neither.

Guantanamo is also neither past nor dead as a watershed in American law. The ordeal of the Kuwaiti detainees, which was representative in many ways of the detainees generally, marked a critical breakdown in the rule of law as a powerful and moderating force in American life. The early Supreme Court decisions were generally positive as a matter of principle, declaring that Guantanamo was not a place without law. Detainees were said to have certain due process rights, although it generally left it to the lower courts to decide the parameters of those rights. But the sole reviewing court, as authorized by Congress, was the Court of Appeals for the D.C. Circuit, and it ignored not only the spirit of these decisions but, in certain respects, the letter of Supreme Court rulings. The Supreme Court may have ruled in the poetry of fine abstractions, but the D.C. Circuit administered these rulings in the constricted and contemptuous prose of a court that would do the minimum possible for these men who were presumptively viewed as terrorists. It neutered the rules of evidence. It substituted its own judgment on factual issues for those of the district courts. It stated that it would apply the burden of proof based on its views of terrorism as a new phenomenon to be considered under new rules. It would skew the application of the law to detain the innocent rather than risk acquitting the guilty. It viewed due process as a "charade." And it did so safe in the knowledge that it could thumb its nose at Supreme Court high-minded declarations without any significant likelihood of being called to account or reversed. It became in many ways a rogue inferior court that mocked and defied the higher court whose rulings it was bound to follow. And the Supreme Court simply stopped taking cases, allowing this defiance to become the law. Today's Supreme Court would no doubt do less for detainees.

The legal legacy of Guantanamo is one of hypocrisy and political maneuvering. The Supreme Court virtue-signaled declarations of rights that never resulted in the release of a single man. Lower courts used technical evidentiary doctrines to try to ensure that few men would win their cases and only be released when an all-powerful executive decided that it would do so. The balance of power between the executive and the judiciary has been forever changed: that imbalance continues to accelerate. And Congress fed the flames without caring about any real mechanisms to sort the innocent from the guilty. Indeed, it used its power to eliminate preexisting rights and create obstacles to due process. Terrorism became a special category, a political issue unmoored from fact or justice. And now we see more and more conduct described as terrorism and so subject to its special rules. It is likely to remain so for the foreseeable future.

American Exceptionalism: A City on the Hill without Rules

It is an article of faith in American life that the United States is an exceptional country and Americans an exceptional people. America is the "shining city on the hill," founded to allow freedom of religion, freedom of expression, and other core freedoms not available in Old World autocracies. America is the most enduring democratic republic. It is a melting pot, where people from all nations have come to escape tyranny and to come together based not on blood and soil or national identity but on shared ideals. It is the land of liberty. It is the font of the rule of law.

National ideals can be wonderful things, incentives to enlightened policies and leadership. But American exceptionalism as expressed post-9/11 and its aftermath did much to corrode many of the bedrock ideals of American life. It became a license for lawlessness, an excuse for extraordinary abuses in response to what were viewed as unique, world-historic wrongs committed against this exceptional country.

As Brent Scowcroft, the wise former National Security Advisor to both President Ford and the first President Bush, said after 9/11, "Europeans are familiar with terrorism and violence. We have not experienced a true conflict on our soil in a hundred years, and especially not one that involved 3,000 dead."[7] Americans are fortunate to have spent much of their history between two great oceans protected to some degree from history by geography but that does not convey moral permission for America to ignore the rules of the international order and distort their own Constitutional system. We are no longer insulated from sudden, inexplicable violence but that does not convey a right to abandon the principles laid down by international law and the Constitution that we have espoused through much of our history. To be sure, these principles have not always been followed, but the embrace of torture and indefinite detention without trial as part of a new paradigm in American life represents a new negative American exceptionalism that has taken root in our politics and brutalized our civil society.

September 11 was a terrible event. The United States has had other terrorist events throughout its history, and many other countries have had major attacks over many years. But 9/11 begat Guantanamo Bay, and the Iraq War and the Afghan War and the "Global War on Terror," which entrenched the widespread and largely accepted use of torture and cruel and inhuman treatment of foreigners. It begat a legacy of fear and suspicion of Muslims and a Muslim ban, upheld by the Supreme Court, and more than $2 trillion in spending on national security. It led to a laser focus on the Middle East, including a disastrous war in Iraq, while, as William Galston wrote, it "diverted us from the geopolitical forces that were reshaping the world to our disadvantage."[8] September 11 and Guantanamo are forever linked as hot-button issues in the culture wars that threaten to tear the United States apart. The recent reopening of Guantanamo underlines its symbolic force in accelerating hostility to foreigners and a lack of concern for their safety and dignity. The cruelty is the point; the indifference to the other has become a perverse sign of vitality and strength.

In American culture, there is no real shame about Guantanamo; instead, it expressed in the words of George W. Bush, "The Steel of American Resolve."[9] Just as steel must be tempered, so too should resolve be tempered by justice if not mercy.

There have been significant horrific attacks in London and Paris and Madrid and Riyadh and on the Gaza/Israel border. Terrorism is a major problem throughout the world – not just for the United States – and it requires coordinated, aggressive solutions within the framework of international law and human decency. In that regard, America cannot claim any exception. Nor can it claim the right to create a "new paradigm," where it can portray itself as an entitled victim that is somehow unique in world history. It is not. Retaliation is prohibited by international law. As is torture. American exceptionalism is meant to promote certain positive values and aspects of American life, but it has been used over the last two decades to try to justify breaches of universal principles that it historically has not and should not excuse in others.

After September 11, as Vice President Cheney said, "the gloves came off." Torture was no longer something that happened in medieval dungeons or in the filthy basements of reviled dictators. It became a policy tool within the contemplation of the executive and without effective checks. And, as experience has shown, the "ticking time bomb" scenario, justifying torture to avoid imminent disaster, has become the norm. When torture is justified on instrumental grounds, every arguable source of any information becomes the ticking time bomb, which must be defused with unrestrained brutality. Whether torture works is not a matter of intuition; it does not. But even if it did, its prohibition should be a universal norm of human decency.

Guantanamo lawyers, including our firm, brought suit against the chain of command in the Pentagon for torture, seeking a declaration that torture was always illegal and unconstitutional. We lost.[10] Even today, there is no declaration by the Supreme Court that torture is per se unconstitutional or inherently illegal. And the lower courts held that government officials had "qualified immunity" against suits for torture because they could have reasonably believed they were acting in accordance with the law. And, indeed, they point to the "Torture Memos," the twisted and Orwellian legal advice from the Department of Justice, that enabled them to act as they did.

How could senior government officials reasonably believe that torture was legal? How could the chain of command ignore codes of conduct for military officers that had been codified since the Civil War? How could the Bill of Rights' hallmark protections of the right to due process and to be free from cruel and unusual punishment be construed to permit torture? How could senior officials of the Department of Defense, knowing that Japanese officials were prosecuted and in certain cases executed for authorizing war crimes, including waterboarding, argue that waterboarding did not violate a clearly established norm?[11]

Lawyers can dress up any atrocity in legal language and have done so over history. They are doing so again, and even if a court disagrees, legal cover can be used to cover such actions in qualified immunity. And the Supreme Court has said there is absolute immunity for the President for all official acts, no matter how heinous. The War on Terror, including Guantanamo and Abu Ghraib, knocked down walls and led us to places where, at least officially, we had not and would not go.

During his 2016 campaign, Donald Trump touted the benefits of torture: "Would I approve waterboarding? You bet your ass I would. In a heartbeat. I would approve more than that. It works." Then, he gave up the game – he didn't really care whether it worked as long as it caused pain and terror in those he did not like. "… and if it doesn't work, they deserve it anyway for what they do to us."[12] According to Trump, "The other thing with the terrorists is you have to take out their families, when you get these terrorists, you have to take out their families."[13] But since he also opposes due process to determine who is a terrorist and who is not, he de facto endorses revenge killing of anyone deemed a terrorist and their wives and children, without much interest in how they were caught up in the dragnet. Torture them and see. As the Uruguayan dissident Eduardo Galeano made clear, the purported utilitarian justification for torture masks deeper feelings, "The purpose of torture is not getting information. It is spreading fear."[14] And as history has shown, nothing creates fear more than random killing, including the killing of innocents.

Why does any of this legal history matter? Because the United States had and has again a president who believes in torture, that it is legal and it is justified even if it does not work, because "they" deserve it. Because a head of the CIA was nominated and confirmed despite having run a notorious "black site" in Thailand, where it is admitted that she watched while waterboarding took place.[15] And her own sense of public duty and decency did not prevent her from drafting an order to destroy videotape evidence of that waterboarding.[16] Torture has become established American policy, without inhibition or apology, and the road from 9/11 to Kandahar to Guantanamo played a large role in putting it there. Today, there is nothing other than the hope for idiosyncratic, random decency of particular individuals at particular times that might serve to prevent it from happening again as a matter of executive choice. Justice Scalia put it terribly but succinctly, "The Constitution says nothing whatever about torture."[17] There is little hope that this Supreme Court would rule differently today. The capture and detention of these men at Guantanamo was a trigger for normalizing torture in American life and law.

The Least Dangerous Branch: Law and Its Limits

The Family Committee and the Core Team initially had great faith that the American legal system would provide fair and comprehensive hearings that would adjudicate the guilt or innocence of their sons with respect to the allegations of terrorism. But the Core Team soon realized that Guantanamo Bay was different. The US Government sought for years to deny meaningful access to the American legal system. It argued that the Geneva Conventions did not apply because these detainees were enemy combatants of a non-sovereign, without providing a mechanism to fairly challenge that unilateral conclusion. It purported to discover a lacuna in Common Article 3 that the drafters of the Geneva Conventions did not intend. It argued that under the Law of War, enemy soldiers captured on the battlefield could be held as long as hostilities continued and that it would solely determine the answer to that question. The War on Terror would go on as long as the government thought there was a need for it and a threat of terror.

But terror is a technique, not an enemy. As the Chair Emeritus of the Council on Foreign Relations, Richard Haas, noted, "Terrorists and terrorism cannot be eliminated any more than we can rid the world of disease. There will always be those who will resort to force against innocent men, women, and children in pursuit of political goals."[18] Yet by shoehorning terrorism into a law of war model developed for a very different concept of war, the executive claimed the right to continue to maintain a de facto state of emergency in which it could hold anyone it wished as an enemy combatant forever. Such states of emergency, once validated, have a way of cropping up whenever a regime determines that declaring one gives it a benefit in increasing its power. President Trump has declared a national emergency relating to migrants and, not coincidentally, started sending them to Guantanamo. Guantanamo became and remains a symbol of the employment of fear and special emergency powers to stifle the recognition of meaningful human rights against the state. And now a purported national emergency related to drugs is used to justify skipping the step of detention and simply blowing up alleged drug dealers in small boats on the open seas.

In the government's view, there is no role for federal judges, no need for evidence, and no requirement for neutral determinations of guilt or innocence. Piece by piece, meaningful checks and balances have eroded under perceived emergencies. The decision to hold or release prisoners became an executive decision alone because it controlled Guantanamo, and it controlled the admission or exclusion of noncitizens. Ultimately, these decisions would be political decisions by the executive of the day. Law was an important tool, but only to create some moral and political pressure on the executive to the extent that the executive was susceptible to it. No court would free them; lawyers and judges could send signals, shape public opinion, and attempt to influence executive conduct. As lawyers who take on unpopular cases are accused of "weaponizing the justice system," and brave judges are threatened with impeachment or worse, even that limited leverage on executive power is thrown into doubt.

In the early days of Guantanamo, there seemed to be a significant consensus that the United States was so threatened by terrorism that the Department of Defense could grab whomever it chose, abuse all of them, have no obligation to sort the guilty from the innocent, and could hide, or sometimes literally bury, its mistakes. The law took years to catch up – but major change really required a shift in the political environment with the incoming Obama administration, which did not have political ownership of the post-9/11 fiasco. The Bush administration released a lot of prisoners on a somewhat haphazard basis, but not because the legal system, simple justice, or effective political pressure compelled it to do so. And now there are new dark threats put forward to justify dark measures.

Law was a lever but was only as strong as the political environment in which it was embedded. The fight against terrorism remains a potent wedge issue dividing the United States, and it is likely that there will be numerous periods in the future where it will again decisively overwhelm any moral or due process-based arguments involving foreigners or minorities who have little visibility or claim on the empathy of the American political system or public. It is no accident that the Venezuelan gang – Tren de Aragua – has been classified not as an organized criminal enterprise, which it is, but as a terrorist entity. The "T" word is an all-purpose password for governments looking to augment their power by creating existential fear.

Ignorance and Islamophobia

All of the detainees at Guantanamo were Muslims. To be sure, 9/11 was committed by Muslim men who were part of a Muslim organization. But there are more than a billion Muslims; these acts were committed and supported by a minuscule number of people. Yet, the Guantanamo detainees and the Muslim community generally bore a significant burden in the ensuing moral panic.

Documents found at Bin Laden's compound in Abbottabad, Pakistan, indicated that as of early 2002, shortly after the September attacks, there were perhaps 170 active Al Qaida fighters. There were certainly other groups and other sympathetic people who were supporters of the Taliban and Al Qaida, but most of them were Afghan, and few of them were captured by US forces. The Afghans were largely caught up in their own internal civil war between the Northern Alliance and the Taliban. So, despite a small number of foreign fighters focusing on "the far enemy," the United States, and even fewer members of Al Qaida, nearly 800 men were brought to Guantanamo, more than four times the number of signed-up Al Qaida members. The Department of Defense had no idea who it had taken captive, had abused, or brought to Guantanamo, and the numbers did not add up. It was soon informed that its dragnet had yielded very little. It did not much matter; they were all Muslims found in a dangerous part of the world; they were all presumptive terrorists.

George W. Bush stated his view firmly and with apparent sincerity that this was not a war on Muslims and Muslims should not, as a group, be suspected of terrorist sympathies. But the actions of his administration and the Congress thereafter contradicted those views. And by the time of the first Trump administration, there was no longer much attempt to avoid group libel of Muslims.

A variety of "think tanks" and "terrorism experts" have spent years spreading the narrative that there is something inherent in Islam that was separatist, exclusionary, and potentially violent. Frank Gaffney, a former senior Defense Department official, who runs the Center for Security Policy, claims "most of the Muslim-American groups of any prominence in America are now known to be, as a matter of fact, hostile to the United States and its Constitution."[19] Daniel Pipes, head of the Middle East Forum, makes similar claims and publishes similar perspectives. "In the end ... neither U.S. presidents nor Islamist apologists fool people. Anyone with eyes and ears realizes that the Islamic State, like the Taliban and Al Qaida before it, is 100 percent Islamic."[20] Steven Emerson of The Investigative Project also propagates an intractable Clash of Civilizations, arguing "The level of vitriol against Jews and Christianity within contemporary Islam, unfortunately, is something that we are not totally cognizant of, or that we don't want to accept," says Emerson. "We don't want to accept it because to do so would be to acknowledge that one of the world's great religions, which has more than 1.4 billion adherents, somehow sanctions genocide, planned genocide, as part of its religious doctrine."[21] No serious scholar or journalist would ever say anything like that about any other religious or ethnic group.

Guantanamo Bay is part of a larger narrative of ostracizing Muslims as fundamentally violent, untrustworthy, and irredeemably in conflict with Western, Judeo-Christian norms. Muslims were profiled and surveilled on a massive basis. Women in headscarves were harassed and sometimes physically attacked. A Sikh was murdered because his turban was mistaken for a keffiyeh – bigotry compounded by stupidity.[22] Two brave young men trying to stop the harassment of women wearing headscarves on a Portland tram car were stabbed to death.[23]

Foreign Muslims were questioned for hours at airports before being admitted to the United States (or sent home). FBI informers and provocateurs tried to infiltrate the Muslim community. Public officials tried to prevent mosques from being built and railed against the phantom threat of "sharia law" being brought to their states. And then came the Muslim ban, which the Supreme Court upheld as being legally acceptable because it was limited to citizens of certain predominantly Muslim states where there were, in the views of the executive, valid national security concerns.[24] Again, no attempt was made to sort the real threats from the millions going about their business. A critical lesson from Guantanamo is that the systematic focus on a minority group dehumanizes that group in the eyes of the larger society and numbs much of the public to sympathetic consideration with respect to their treatment or their rights. National security can be used by the executive as a mantra to reify such attitudes into law.

Truth Is the First Casualty of War

Truth, as the old saying goes, is the first casualty of war.[25] Lying is not only central to political propaganda in wartime; it is also a long-used and powerful domestic political tool as well as a tool of bureaucrats to clothe abhorrent actions in morally justifiable raiment. From the false claim of sabotage to start the Spanish–American War, to the fake body counts of North Vietnamese and Viet Cong, to the false claims of weapons of mass destruction in Iraq, all were accepted and cheered on (at least for a time) by a compliant, nationalistic press.

It is impossible to review the treatment of Guantanamo detainees without seeing the widespread acceptance of government lying, by the President and Vice President, the Department of Defense, the CIA, interrogators, and Guantanamo informers. Many of the lies told were incredible on their face. But they served the purpose of creating the perception of omnipresent terrorist threats, the justification of harsh measures, and continued detention. The truth of whatever these defendants may or may not have done was subordinated to the "greater truth" of the threat of terrorism, where justice needed to be sacrificed to an ever-expanding imperative to maximize security of the homeland at any cost. Indefinite detention without trial was collateral damage to which the American public needed to pay little attention.

The various fig leaves to create some appearance of a procedure to get at the truth of who was an enemy combatant or who should be detained were a parody of legal process. Orders were issued; procedures were defined; but ultimately the decision-making process was based on something other than objective fact-finding. The most authoritarian societies all have legal systems and judges and legal codes and written decisions; what they fail to do is subordinate political goals to the truth-finding process.

That is what often happened to the Guantanamo detainees, at least until the habeas cases began more than seven years later and due process remains stillborn in a military commission process that has not advanced in more than twenty years. Judge Jed Rakoff writes, "An application of judicial power that does not rest on facts is worse than mindless, it is inherently dangerous. If its deployment does not rest on facts – cold, hard, solid facts, established either by admissions or by trials – it serves no lawful or moral purpose and is simply an engine of oppression."[26] In a world of "alternative facts," of hearings without evidence or witnesses, of personal representatives who speak for the prosecution not the defense, the truth is subordinated to ever-proliferating claims of national security.

Bureaucracy Responds to Power and Its Own Prerogatives

The driver of any bureaucracy is to increase its own power and resources and to avoid public criticism, budget cuts, and revelation of wrongdoing or error. September 11 and Guantanamo gave rise to enormous and rapid expansion of the national security state. The need to "stay the course" in the war on terrorism not only hollowed out core aspects of our legal system; it justified endless blank checks for the bureaucracy and vast payments to the emerging defense–national security complex. Counterterrorism has driven the agendas of big government and big business. The Department of Homeland Security was created in 2002. Its first budget for FY 2002 was $19 billion. The next year, it was $32 billion. Then, $52 billion. For Fiscal Year 2025, Congress appropriated $64.81 billion, $4.27 billion more than was requested.[27] These amounts do not include funding for national security within numerous other departments, including the Departments of Defense and State and the intelligence agencies. Bureaucracies that make requests in the name of security are rarely if ever told that there is already enough security. You can never be criticized for too much security, only when there is too little. DOGE is unlikely to send its minions into the national security space.

Proceedings in Guantanamo have been cloaked in secrecy with liberal use of classification and the state secrets doctrine. Often, when district judges have reviewed classification designations in habeas proceedings, they have found that information had been classified to hide from public scrutiny, not important secrets, but instead governmental failures or senseless cruelties. From Abu Ghraib to Bagram to black prisons to Guantanamo, the Department of Defense and intelligence agencies have much to hide, and they have used their rarely challenged classification power to limit revelation of their most egregious and indefensible actions. Even those who do not agree with the actions or methods of Julian Assange would be inclined to agree with his statement, "Intelligence agencies keep things secret because they often violate the rule of law or of good behavior."[28]

Navigating a New Paradigm for Foreigners

The first part of this chapter addressed the lessons of Guantanamo from a US legal and political perspective. But having seen the limited power of law, the dulling of moral impulses with respect to torture, and the political and bureaucratic mendacity and incompetence, what can be done to try to remedy the failings of a political and legal culture that has seemingly lost its bearings? What are the lessons for Kuwait or other countries faced with a problem like that posed by Guantanamo – unjust detention and mistreatment of its nationals by a powerful government that has the momentum of public support for such actions in the face of a panic stoked by fear and political opportunism?

Don't Be in a Hurry and Never Give Up

American culture is often accused of suffering from Mass Attention Deficit Disorder. With the twenty-four-hour news cycle, issues do not remain in the front of the national cortex for very long. What was the first impeachment about? Is Yemen still in civil war? WMD? Travelgate? Koreagate? Deflategate? Emails? Laptops? After a while, no one remembers or cares.

But terrorism and 9/11 are different. People may forget that Guantanamo is still open, but politicians continue to play the terrorism card effectively with the American people. Terrorism remains a potent issue more than two decades later. The American public makes a distinction between "real terrorism," coded as committed by Muslims, and "domestic terrorism," mass shootings or bombings committed by white supremacists or anti-Semites or other Americans who do not have any apparent foreign ties.

So, any lawyer or diplomat or country taking on a project similar to the Family Committee project must understand that results, when allegations of terrorism are involved, are unlikely to happen quickly if they happen at all. Fear of violence from outsiders, especially Muslim outsiders, on American territory will slowly dissipate, if ever.

There will be political diatribes to justify further restrictions of liberty and human rights violations in the name of containing terrorism. A new strategy that responds to the new paradigm must be adopted. To take on a project like the Guantanamo detainees or its future iterations, one must be ready for a long haul, constant analysis, and adjustment of strategy, persistence, patience, and a stubborn refusal to give up. Aggressive and illegal detention and invocation of emergencies will be a first blow that will take time and resources to undo through political or legal responses, and will be attacked as unpatriotic, naïve, or worse. The Core Team had the stamina to do so and was willing to commit resources for the duration, but that is not often the case. Courts are often essential to changing public opinion, as brave judicial decisions can sometimes puncture the convenient lies that governments tell. But courts are increasingly deferential to executive prerogatives. The legal profession can organize, as it eventually did in litigating Guantanamo cases. It is no accident that the Trump administration is trying to intimidate judges that do not uphold its actions and lawyers and law firms that take on unpopular causes. Brave lawyers and judges need to be prepared to fight long and hard against an overreaching state. They will make few friends.

Know the Rules: Keep Calm and Carry On

Guantanamo was a multidimensional puzzle, involving the executive, the Congress, the judiciary, the media, and other sovereigns. Each had its own agenda, which changed over time. President Bush initially wanted to be seen as reasonable and not motivated by Islamophobic animus. He had severe constraints within his administration – his Vice President and Defense Secretary – as well as Congress and the media, which fed on the narrative of existential panic. Bush could not be seen as soft on terrorism. His 2004 campaign was run on the basis that he had kept America safe from terrorism, despite the fact that 9/11 had occurred on his watch and in the face of escalating warnings that were ignored. And he could not be seen as releasing someone who would possibly go out and commit violent acts. Whatever his better angels may have told him, his political calculus skewed toward taking the hardest conceivable line.

Bush released some detainees from the United Kingdom because Prime Minister Tony Blair was providing cooperation to the United States on Iraq, despite getting extreme flak from the left wing of the Labor Party.

The British detainees were sent home without a real examination of their cases on the facts. It was political backscratching between allies.

The Emir did not have the same bargaining power as Blair and the United Kingdom. But Bush was an oilman and had an affection for the Emir and valued their relationship. Nevertheless, Bush was unwilling to take much political risk for the benefit of the bilateral relationship. Ongoing dialogue was essential over a long period of time. The first Kuwaiti was released in 2005. Others at the beginning of the Obama administration. But when one Kuwaiti detainee became a suicide bomber, the relationship dynamic took second place to the political dynamic. Any politician can envision the commercial in the next election cycle with grainy footage of anonymous Middle Eastern men: "He released terrorists who went on to kill again." Predicting future dangerousness is perilous at best; better to make a mistake through wrongful incapacitation than wrongful release.

No administration would want to accept responsibility for releasing someone who was obviously disturbed and at risk. But the United States could or would not bear the financial or logistical burden of keeping 800 men at Guantanamo or take on the daunting and complex task of setting up some rational basis for deciding how to deal with overcapacity. So, the process became haphazard, and one Kuwaiti, to the surprise of no one, committed a tragic suicide bombing in Iraq. The United States was not going to take the blame. Instead, Kuwait paid the price for the United States' failure of administrative competence. All dialogue ceased, but the team could not let this become an entrenched situation; it could not lash back and announce that it was the United States' own fault. This leads to another lesson.

Try to Keep Talking

The Obama State Department made clear that it would not talk to Kuwait about Guantanamo detainees. It was angry about the political blowback of quick releases in Kuwait. It was sick of the complaints of lawyers. The United States was also suspicious about Kuwait's commitment to fight terrorism, without expressing any concrete concerns or making specific requests. And the Obama administration did not have any preexisting relationships or particular affinities in the region.

The Core Team would not accept that such a state of affairs was permanent. Everyone talks in Washington eventually, and the team made careful, polite efforts to restart dialogue. Without dialogue, the process stagnated, and the prospect of two Kuwaiti "forever prisoners" became more likely. With communication, even not very friendly communication, the situation could potentially move forward. Secretary Clinton made clear her anger toward Kuwait and initially gave Marcia Newell a strongly negative view about the detainees. But when asked whether there could be a reopening of dialogue, the message was: "Call Dan Fried." Things change.

Fried was initially cautious; he would still not meet with lawyers and would only meet on an unofficial basis in a noisy coffee shop. But he was the right person with the right responsibilities. It took some time to go from coffee shop whispering to the Inter-Agency Working Group, but patient dialogue was a critical key to the repatriation of all the Kuwaitis. Fried was crucial to getting buy-in through the bureaucracy. His replacement, Cliff Sloan, came to the job with access at the highest levels and without the baggage and history of seven years of the War on Terror; he viewed his mission as clearing out Guantanamo as much as possible consistent with national security requirements. What started slowly with Fried could accelerate with Sloan.

Trust building through ongoing communication is a slow and nonlinear process, but a necessary one. Even bad news provides clues to future solutions. The Core Team showed that it would never put down its tools, never show frustration publicly and never conclude that there was nothing more to be done.

What Does Your Counterparty Need? What Can You Do?

Constructive dialogue with Ambassador Fried, his interim successor Mike Williams, and Special Envoy Sloan allowed an informal exchange for the team to understand the developing PRB process and learn what the US government expected and required to release the last two detainees. It also allowed the Core Team to avoid minefields and so determine in advance what would be nonstarters to either government. It is counterproductive and wasteful of goodwill to fight about issues where there will be no agreement. Although the US government made clear that this was a new forward-looking process, smiling faces and upbeat future plans were not by themselves going to undo a long and tortuous history or lead to radical rethinking of positions. The Core Team understood that it had a secret weapon – Marcia Newell was not only an adept Washington networker; she was not a lawyer. She could break through the wall of silence. She also understood how governments negotiate and how to give each side what it needs to make an agreement.

Whether justified or not, there was continued concern within the government about the commitment of Kuwait to oversee a rehabilitation and surveillance process and to ensure that there would be no moral or financial support for terrorism. The US government demanded that Kuwait show its work – produce detailed plans and punch lists for the rehabilitation center; produce statements from security figures, law enforcement, and senior leaders of the country; and provide specifics on what they would do to ensure security and fight extremism and terror finance. Marcia Newell, and then she and I working together, were able to figure out what the Americans would just about accept, and ARH and William Brown worked to make sure that it could just about be delivered.

The process was iterative. Kuwait did not want to just create a rehabilitation center in the dark and then be told it was not good enough or had deficiencies that could not be fixed within its existing parameters. The dialogue allowed the United States to indicate what it wanted, what compromises it might accept and the Kuwaitis to say what it could and would do consistent with Kuwaiti law and where it might be able to stretch. It allowed negotiation to find solutions where the American and Kuwaiti needs and capabilities were not entirely congruent but bridgeable. The communication through nongovernment intermediaries prevented the parties from taking and then digging in on official positions that would lead to a stalemate. Dialogue creates possibilities.

Know the Rules of Decision and the Mindset of the Decision-Makers

Ultimately, whether the detainees were released was going to be decided by the US defense, intelligence, diplomatic, and intelligence apparatuses. If the security people were not convinced that the risks were manageable, there would be no releases. The Obama administration no doubt created openings that were not present during the Bush administration, but its willingness and interest in confronting the security apparatus were limited. The decisions would largely be made by career people who had been laser-focused on terror issues for more than a decade. They wanted to release detainees where it seemed feasible, but the idea that there would be "forever prisoners" did not make them uncomfortable. Indefinite detention without trial, perhaps for life, would be a policy of the executive until a court ruled otherwise, and to this day, no court has done so. Our goal was not to convince the executive decision-makers that it was untenable and fundamentally inconsistent with American justice to detain indefinitely; it was to convince them that our clients did not fit within that category.

There was on the part of the detainees and certain of their lawyers a tremendous temptation to turn the hearings into a Festivus-style "airing of grievances."[29] They had true stories to tell about torture, about medical mistreatment, about sexual and religious humiliation, and about findings in earlier proceedings that were ridiculous and showed real ignorance about basic cultural and historic facts. There was much to attack and criticize. But the decision-making process was not going to be positively affected by hearing such criticisms. The PRB officers would not be intimidated or shamed into releasing anybody. The decision-makers needed to be made comfortable that they were not facing detainees who were hostile or would present danger. Ultimately, this was not a trial of past facts by a neutral judge or jury. It was an impressionistic evaluation of the characters of two men and their country by six agencies that had counterterrorism in their DNA.

To the extent that criticisms could be effectively leveled against the conduct of the US government, there were countless others who would and could make those criticisms. Academics and journalists could write articles and books. Federal judges could render harsh evaluations of government conduct in habeas opinions. The bureaucracy could also be nudged to use the PRB process pragmatically as a safety valve to avoid a confrontation between branches regarding the power and predicates to order release. The US government might, on the margin, prefer to approve a quiet release than be embarrassed in court or make bad law on the rights of detainees.

But criticizing the honesty, capability, or decency of the decision-makers directly could lead to only one result. It was critical for both detainee and counsel to be the most reasonable people in the room, even if the room was in Guantanamo and one person was shackled to the floor. The Core Team not only had good ideas; they had good manners, and the Lewis Baach legal team knew how important they would be in the PRB process.

Be Prepared in Tone and Substance

It is often the case that decision-makers decide whom to trust based on the level of preparation and the tone of presentation. Litigators too often are ego-driven; they shout and rail and fail to read the room. They push versions of the facts that overreach and make them untrustworthy to the tribunal. Or because they are proceeding on limited budgets or with limited time, they do not treat hearings with the thoroughness that they require. Videos, for example, took a great deal of time and effort to prepare, shoot, and edit. The Core Team believed that videos were essential to show the rehabilitation center so that it was no longer an abstraction but a concrete place. Videos were also important to show family members as real people with real emotions in real homes who were longing for their sons and were committed to their supervision. In addition, the videos helped show the commitment of senior Kuwaiti officials to taking the US government's requirements and the PRB process seriously.

"Facts are stubborn things."[30] At too many junctures, facts were ignored in favor of emotions, conjecture, politics, and stereotypes. But for the Kuwaiti detainees at their long-awaited hearings, both the detainees and the legal team calmly presented a cascade of facts that could not be ignored. Facts not about what happened in the fog of war, but the facts of their previous lives, the reality of their family ties and support, and the infrastructure of security and monitoring that could provide confidence that Kuwait was a serious and reliable partner. The methodical presentation of facts was the final chapter in this odyssey for the Kuwaiti detainees and, perhaps, provides some hope someday for a return to the quotidian operation of the rule of law and ordinary human decency in the treatment of those who continue to be detained or those who may be detained in future times of stress or panic.

Inshallah.

NOTES

1 The Long Journey beyond the Rule of Law

1. US Navy, Southeast Command, Naval Station Guantanamo Bay, History.
2. Fayiz Al-Kandari was charged by a military commission in 2008; the charges were dropped without explanation in 2012. Fouad Al Rabiah was briefly charged in 2008, but the charges dropped without explanation in 2009.
3. For a detailed description of the rushed decision and rapid repurposing of Camp X-Ray to house the detainees, see Karen Greenberg's excellent *The Least Worst Place: Guantanamo's First 100 Days* (Oxford University Press, 2009).
4. K. Greenberg, *The Least Worst Place*, at 42–44.
5. Ibid., at 18, 19.
6. V. Larson (September 23, 2008), "Sailor Volunteers to Help Base Environment." Joint Task Force Guantanamo Public Affairs: www.businessinsider.com/inside-guantanamo-bays-camp-x-ray.
7. journals.ku.edu/reptiles and amphibians.
8. www.pbs.org/wnet/nature/cuba-wild-island-of-the-caribbean-cuban-crab-invasion/1247.
9. K. Greenberg, *The Least Worst Place*, at 80, 81.
10. K. Greenberg, Ibid., at 91.
11. J. Hafetz, *Habeas Corpus after 9/11* (NYU Press, 2012), at 31.
12. Ibid.
13. See K. Greenberg, *The Least Worst Place*, at 211–12.
14. J. Hafetz, *Habeas Corpus after 9/11*, at 32.
15. See Standard Operating Procedures Camp Delta, University of Minnesota Human Rights Library, at section 6.3.
16. www.obama.org/stories/obl-ten/.
17. www.nbcnews.com, "Guantanamo Inmates Say They Were Sold," May 31, 2005; www.theguardian.com/us-news/2015/aug/25/guantanamo-detainees-captured-pakistan-afghanistan.
18. J. Hafetz, *Habeas Corpus after 9/11*, at 35.
19. K. Greenberg, *The Least Worst Place*, at 160.
20. Center for the Study of Human Rights, UC Davis, Declaration of Col. Lawrence Wilkerson, *Hamad v. United States,* Paragraph 9.
21. J. Hafetz, *Habeas Corpus* after 9/11, at 36, 37.
22. Ibid.
23. https://academic.oup.com/cid/article-abstract/34/Supplement.
24. https://merip.org/2011/08/afghan-arabs-real-and-imagined/.

25. https://islamic-relief.org/where_we_work/afghanistan/.
26. https://merip.org/2011/08/afghan-arabs-real-and-imagined/.
27. www.aljazeera.com/program/fault-lines/2016/9/14/the-dark-prison-legacy-of-the-cia-torture-programme. See, generally, Richard Abel's excellent two-volume series, R. Abel, *Law's Trials* (Cambridge University Press, 2018); R. Abel, *Law's Wars* (Cambridge University Press, 2018). See, especially, R. Abel, *Law's Wars* at 208–60.
28. https://papers.ssrn.com/sol3/papers.cfm?abstract_id=2003598.
29. casebook.icrc.org/case-study/united-states-status-and-treatment-detainees-held-guantanamo-naval-base.
30. www.americanprogress.org/article/alberto-gonzales-a-record-of-injustice/.
31. https://humanrightsfirst.org/library/two-retired-generals-denounce-former-vice-president-cheney/.

2 Why Should Kuwait Be Different?

1. See Steve Coll's brilliant, Pulitzer Prize-winning history of this period, S. Coll, *Ghost Wars* (Penguin Press, 2004).
2. https://humanrights.ucdavis.edu/reports/guantanamos-children-the-wikileaked-testimonies/guantanamos-children-the-wikileaked-testimonies.
3. www.ohchr.org/en/instruments-mechanisms/instruments/united-nations-rules-protection-juveniles-deprived-their-liberty.
4. https://bridge.georgetown.edu/research/guantanamo-bay-data-project.
5. https://freedomhouse.org/country/kuwait/freedom-world/2022.
6. https://freedomhouse.org/countries/freedom-world/scores.
7. https://atlanticcouncil.org/blogs/menasource/parliament-kuwait-sabah-democracy.
8. www.state.gov/reports/2021-report-on-international-religious-freedom/kuwait.
9. https://pomeps.org/the-rise-of-the-islamic-constitutional-movement-in-kuwait.
10. www.eslah.com/; www.icmkw.org/portal/pages/aboutus.php#.ZGO1DXbMJD8.
11. https://carnegieendowment.org/2013/11/20/kuwait-s-muslim-brotherhood-under-pressure.
12. Ibid.
13. file:///26ModernizationandFamilyStructureinKuwait.pdf.
14. Traditionally, Kuwaiti daughters who marry move in with their husband's family, although that is not always the case, and nearly all children who live in Kuwait regularly visit both sides of the family. As time goes on, more Western nuclear family-style arrangements are becoming common.
15. www.nbcnews.com/science/environment/kuwait-worlds-hottest-places-lags-climate-action-rcna20830.
16. https://2009-2017.state.gov/documents/organization/160074.pdf.
17. https://bti-project.org/en/reports/country-report/KWT.
18. https://digitalcommons.butler.edu/cgi.
19. www.jstor.org/stable/163796.
20. R. Simon, P. Mattar, R. Bulliet, *Encyclopedia of the Modern Middle East – Volume 1* (Macmillan, 1996), at 119.
21. www.britannica.com/place/Kuwait/Resources-and-power.

22. www.kockw.com/sites/EN/Pages/Profile/whoAreWe/KOC-History.
23. Later reorganized and renamed the Kuwait Investment Authority.
24. www.bibalex.org/he_funding/donors/Details.
25. https://2001-2009.state.gov/r/pa/ei/bgn/35876.htm.
26. www.weforum.org/docs/WEF_TheGlobalCompetitivenessReport2019.pdf.
27. www.nationsencyclopedia.com/Asia-and-Oceania/Kuwait-JUDICIAL-SYSTEM.html.
28. www.kuwaittimes.com/freedom-of-press-narrows-in-kuwait/#:~:.
29. S. Coll, *The Achilles Trap* (Penguin Press, 2024), at 158.
30. Ibid. at 156.
31. https://adst.org/2016/09/sparking-iraqs-invasion-kuwait-loans-land-oil-access.
32. S. Coll, *The Achilles Trap*, at 167.
33. www.nytimes.com/1990/09/23/world/confrontation-in-the-gulf-excerpts-from-iraqi-document-on-meeting-with-us-envoy.
34. www.nybooks.com/articles/1990/09/27/the-thief-of-baghdad/=.
35. See S. Coll, *The Achilles Trap*, at Chapter 11, for a detailed discussion of the Iraqi invasion of Kuwait.
36. See R. Hermann, "Coercive Diplomacy and the Crisis over Kuwait, 1990–1991," in A. George and W. E. Simons, eds., *The Limits of Coercive Diplomacy*, 2nd ed. (Boulder: Westview, 1994); Baram; "The Iraqi Invasion of Kuwait," A. Baram and B. Rubin, eds., *Iraq's Road to War* (St. Martin's Press, 1993), at Chapter 1.
37. www.middleeastmonitor.com/20220225-remembering-the-iraqi-withdrawal-from-kuwait-and-the-highway-of-death.
38. W. Kälin, Special Rapporteur of the *Commission on Human Rights*, prepared in accordance with Commission resolution 1991/1967.
39. www.latimes.com/archives/-2003-feb-23-fg-martyrs23-story.html.
40. www.nasa.gov/mission_pages/landsat/news/40th-top10-kuwait.html.
41. Badil Center, "Palestinian Forced Displacement from Kuwait: The Overdue Accounting." This monograph argues that the Palestinian community in Kuwait was not monolithic, and the subsequent deportation of Palestinians was unwarranted.

3 Strategizing in a New World: Navigating the New Paradigm

1. www.researchgate.net/figure/guantanamo-bay-population-and-releases-transfers-of-guantanamo-detainees-by-month_fig2_333632050; 780 was the total number sent to Guantanamo, but the maximum at any one time was just under 700.
2. www.gao.gov/assets/gao-13-31.pdf.
3. Author interviews with ARH and William Brown, 2020–2021.
4. P. Musharraf, *In the Line of Fire* (Free Press, 2006), at 237.
5. https://papers.ssrn.com/sol3/papers.cfm?.
6. J. Steyn, "Guantanamo: The Legal Black Hole," *International and Comparative Law Quarterly*, January 2004. International Committee of Jurists, June 28, 2004.
7. *Terminiello v. City of Chicago*, 337 U.S. 1 (Jackson, J. dissenting). See Khawaja, "Not a Suicide Pact: The Constitution in Time of Emergency," Book Review, *Dissent*, Spring 2007, at 1–18.

8. In dissent, Justice Sotomayor found the repudiation of *Korematsu* to be so much window dressing to disguise a similarly racist ruling. She wrote that the decision "redeploys the same dangerous logic underlying *Korematsu* and merely replaces one gravely wrong decision with another." *United States v. Hawaii*, 138 S.Ct. 2392, 2448 (2018) (Sotomayor, dissenting).
9. *Korematsu v. United States*, 323 U.S. 214 (1944); www.cnn.com/2016/12/03/politics/trump-guantanamo-bay. John Walker Lindh, a US citizen who had joined Al Qaida and was captured in Afghanistan, was not brought to Guantanamo but taken directly to the United States and indicted in a US federal court with all constitutional protections provided to a citizen in a US criminal trial. casebook.icrc.org/case-study/united-states-trial-john-phillip-walker-lindh.
10. Author interview with Marcia Newell, 2022.
11. Author interviews with Marcia Newell, 2021–2022.
12. Columbia University Oral History Project, The Reminiscences of Thomas B. Wilner (Columbia University, 2010).
13. 339 U.S., 763 (1950).
14. Ibid., at 778.
15. Ibid., at 779.
16. 02CV00299, 00828, 00130 (D.D.C. 2003).
17. 321 F. 3d 1134 (D.C. Cir. 2003).
18. Ibid., at 1143.
19. Ibid., at 1140.
20. Ibid., at 1145.
21. Ibid., at 1141.
22. *Rasul v. Bush*, 542 U.S. 466 (2004).
23. Ibid., at 476.
24. Ibid., at 480.
25. Plutarch, *The Parallel Lives*, "The Life of Pyrrhus," (Loeb Classical Library, 1920) Vol IX.
26. With regard to Abu Zubaydah, our client, who remains at Guantanamo, the Senate Select Committee on Intelligence documented his complete isolation, including being confined for eleven days in a coffin-sized box, and twenty-nine hours in an even smaller confinement box, just 21 inches wide, 2.5 feet deep, and 2.5 feet high.
27. "The goal of the facial slap is not to inflict physical pain" but "to induce shock, surprise, and/or humiliation," Assistant Attorney General Jay Bybee wrote. Bybee was subsequently promoted to be a federal Court of Appeals judge on the Ninth Circuit.
28. With regard to Abu Zubaydah, "You have orally informed us that you would not deprive Zubaydah of sleep for more than 11 days at a time and that you have previously kept him awake for 72 hours," Mr. Bybee wrote.
29. Three detainees were waterboarded, including Abu Zubaydah 83 times and Khalid Sheikh Muhammed 200 times. Videos were made by the CIA, which were subsequently destroyed, in anticipation that they were likely to be subpoenaed.
30. *New York Times*, "A Guide to the Memos on Torture," with memos attached.
31. www.theatlantic.com/daily-dish/archive/2008/06/yoo-testifies/214822/.
32. www.ohchr.org/en/statements/2014/12/feinstein-report-un-expert-calls-prosecution-cia-officers-and-other-us.
33. *Rasul v. Myers*, 563 F.3d 527 (D.C. Cir. 2009).
34. Department of Defense, Order Establishing Combatant Status Review Tribunals, signed by Deputy Secretary Paul Wolfowitz, July 2004.

35. J. Margulies, "Guantanamo and the Abuse of Presidential Power," *Political and Legal Anthropology Review* (2007), at 170.
36. https://supreme.findlaw.com/legal-commentary/the-supreme-court-faces-the-kangaroo-courts.html.
37. See Chapter 1, at 16–22.
38. P.L. 109–148, 10 U.S.C. §§ 100–86.
39. 548 U.S. 557 (2006).
40. P.L. 109–366, 10 U.S.C. §§ 948–49.
41. For an excellent discussion of the litigation over habeas corpus rights, see R. Abel, *Law's Trials* at Chapter 8.
42. The Suspension Clause states that the right to habeas corpus may not be suspended other than during wartime or civil unrest. US Constitution Section IX.
43. R. Abel, *Law's Trials*, at 358 and n. 90.
44. www.scotusblog.com/2007/11/abraham-takes-on-top-security-echelon/.
45. *Boumediene v. Bush*, 553 U.S. 723 (2008).
46. Ibid., at 765.
47. Ibid., at 794–95.
48. R. Abel, *Law's Trials*, at 361.
49. Ibid., at 364.
50. R. Epstein, "How to Complicate Habeas Corpus," *New York Times*, June 21, 2008.
51. *Boumediene v. Bush*, 553 U.S., at 827.
52. R. Abel, *Law's Trials*, at 365.

4 The Rules of the Road: The Lower Courts Define a Narrow Path

1. *Boumediene v. Bush*, 553 U.S. at 776.
2. Ibid.
3. Ibid., at 798.
4. Editorial "President Kennedy," *Wall Street Journal*, June 13, 2002.
5. W. Blackstone, *Commentaries*, at 358 (1853).
6. *Jackson v. Virginia*, 443 U.S. 307 (1979).
7. In *Addington v. Texas*, 441 U.S. 418 (1979), the Supreme Court held that the clear and convincing standard is required in civil commitment hearings. Similarly, in *United States v. Salerno*, 481 U.S. 739 (1987), the Supreme Court upheld pretrial detention under the Bail Reform Act, noting the Act's requirement of "clear and convincing evidence that no conditions of release can reasonably assure the safety of the community or any person" struck an appropriate balance between individual liberty and community security.
8. *U.S. v. Salerno*, 481 U.S. 739 (1987).
9. See Government's Brief Regarding Preliminary and Procedural Framework Issues at 15, *In re Guantanamo Bay Detainee Litig.*, No. 08-0442, 2008 WL 4858241 (D.D.C. November 6, 2008).
10. 590 F.3d 866 (D.C. Cir. 2010).
11. Ibid., at 878.
12. Ibid.
13. *Al-Bihani v. Obama*, 590 F.3d 866, 871 (D.C. Cir. 2010).

14. 613 F.3d 1102 (D.C. Cir. 2011).
15. 639 F.3d 1075 (D.C. Circ. 2011).
16. Ibid., at 1078.
17. Ibid.
18. *Al-Adahi v. Obama*, 613 F.3d 1102, 1110–11 (D.C. Cir. 2010), cert denied, 562 U.S. 1194 (2011).
19. See *Almeferdi v. Obama*, 654 F. 3d 1 (D.C. Cir. 2011), cert. denied, 132 S. Ct. 2739 (2012).
20. 677 F.3d 1175 (D.C. Cir. 2012).
21. In *Al Mutairi v. Obama*, 644 F. Supp2d 48 (D.D.C. 2009), the district court even pointed to evidence that "for over three years," the government had, "based on a typographical error in an interrogation report," erroneously insisted "that Al Mutairi manned an anti-aircraft weapon in Afghanistan." See also *Al Rabiah v. United States*, 658 F. Supp. 2d 11, 18 (D.D.C. 2009) (noting "discrepan[cies]" between two reports summarizing the same interrogation that the government had made no attempt to reconcile); *Al Odah v. United States*, 648 F. Supp. 2d 1, 6 (D.D.C. 2009) ("interrogators and/or interpreters included incorrect dates in three separate reports that were submitted into evidence based on misunderstandings between the Gregorian and the Hijri calendars.")
22. 677 F.3d at 1208, 1212 (Tatel, J., dissenting) (internal citations omitted).
23. www.aclu.org/press-releases/fbi-inquiry-details-abuses-reported-agents-guantanamo; www.oversight.gov/sites/default/files/documents/reports/2018-03/s0910.pdf.
24. U.S. Department of Justice, *Review of the FBI's Involvement in and Observations of Detainee Interrogations in Guantanamo Bay, Afghanistan and Iraq* (2009); FOIA Document 5053.
25. www.propublica.org/article/a-guantanamo-detainees-case-has-been-languishing-without-action-since-2008-the-supreme-court-wants-to-know-why.
26. www.nbcnews.com/id/wbna9956644.
27. J. Gerstein, "We Tortured Some Folks," *Politico* (August 1, 2024).
28. www.npr.org/trump-has-vowed-to-fill-guantanamo-with-some-bad-dudes-but-who.
29. See, e.g., S. O'Mara, *Why Torture Doesn't Work* (Harvard University Press, 2015); "Torture does not work," *Nat Hum Behav* 1, 0077 (2017), www.brennancenter.org/our-work/research-reports/review-why-torture-doesnt-work-neuroscience-interrogation.
30. https://propublica/assets/detention/gitmo/khalifh_trial_court_opinion.pdf.
31. *Al Rabiah v. Obama*, 658 F. Supp. 2d 11,36 (D.D.C. 2009).
32. *Al Adahi v. Obama*, 613 F.3d 1102 (D.C. Cir. 2010) cert. denied, 131 S.Ct. 1001 (2011).
33. *Ali Ahmed v. Obama*, 613 F. Supp.2d 51, 62 (D.D.C. 2010).
34. Ibid.
35. 696 F. Supp. 2d 1 (D.D.C. 2010).
36. Ibid., at 7 (citations omitted).
37. Ibid., at 9, 10.
38. "Judge to the White House: Gitmo Gets Top Priority," NBC News, July 8, 2008.
39. www.wsws.org/en/articles/2008/07/guan-j12.html.
40. *Boumediene v. Bush*, C.A. No. 04-1166 (D.D.C., November 20, 2008).
41. See discussion in R. Abel, *Law's Trials* at 366–67.

42. www.washingtonpost.com/archive/national/2008/10/31/motives-of-justice-lawyers-questioned-in-detainees-case/.
43. J. Sutton, "U.S. Drops Charges against 5 Guantánamo Captives." Reuters; www.theguardian.com/uk/2009/feb/23/binyam-mohamed-guantanamo-plane-lands.
44. https://foreignpolicy.com/2018/11/01/for-them-afghanistan-is-safer-than-china/.
45. www.washingtonpost.com/wp-dyn/content/article/2006/12/04/AR2006120401191.html.
46. www.nytimes.com/2008/07/15/us/15gitmo.html; https://doj-inspector-general-report-review-fbi-involvement-and-observations-detainee-interrogations.
47. *In Re Guantanamo Bay Detainee Litigation*, 581 F. Supp. 2d (D.D.C. 2008). For a detailed discussion of the Uighur experience and litigation, see R. Abel, *Law's Trials*, at 368–74.
48. *Al Gharani v. Bush*, C.A. No. 05–429 (D.D.C.) (RJL).
49. C. Stafford Smith, "Why 17 years on our job isn't over at Guantanamo," Reprieve, January 11, 2019; Mem. Order, January 14, 2009.
50. www.washingtonpost.com/wp-dyn/content/article/2006/09/28/.l.
51. 639 F.3d 1075 (D.C. Circ. 2011).
52. www.andyworthington.co.uk/2009/06/11/guantanamos-youngest-prisoner-released-to-chad/.
53. www.nytimes.com/2009/10/04/world/middleeast/.
54. "Judge: U.S. hiding evidence in detainee case," NBC News, January 6, 2009.
55. aclu.org/sites/default/files/pdfs/safefree/alhalmandyvobama_jawadresponse.pdf. See R. Abel, *Law's Trials*, at 389–91.
56. Hearing before Judge Huvelle, July 16, 2009.
57. J. Hafetz, *Habeas Corpus after 9/11*, at 3.
58. www.reuters.com/article/world/top-court-rejects-appeals-by-guantanamo-prisoners-/.

5 Twelve Men

1. J. Hafetz, *Habeas Corpus after* 9/11, at 34–36.
2. Secretary Powell's Chief of Staff, Colonel Lawrence Wilkerson, submitted a declaration years later stating: "Secretary Powell received frequent phone calls from British Foreign Minister Jack Straw, who had consulted with Secretary Powell frequently about repatriating the British Guantánamo detainees. I also know that several other foreign ministers spoke with Secretary Powell urging him to repatriate their countries' citizens. During [daily] morning briefings, Secretary Powell would express frustration that more progress had not been made with detainee releases." Center for the Study of Human Rights, UC Davis, Declaration of Col. Lawrence Wilkerson, *Hamad v. United States*, Paragraph 8.
3. www.theguardian.com/world/2002/jan/28/september11.afghanistan.
4. BBC Five Live, Interview with Shafiq Rasul and Asif Iqbal, January 2010, quoted in "Tipton Three," Wikipedia.
5. www.nytimes.com/2023/01/11/us/politics/guantanamo-bay-landmark-cases.html.
6. Interviews with the author in London. August–September 2004.
7. theguardian.com/world/2017/feb/22/how-jamal-al-harith-became-isis-suicide-bomber-manchester-iraq-guantanamo.

8. www.theguardian.com/world/2017/feb/23/british-suicide-bomber-jamal-al-harith-radicalised-decade-after-guantanamo-release.
9. Ibid.
10. Interview with author, November 2021.
11. Ibid.
12. Ibid.
13. Ibid.
14. Ibid.
15. wikileaks.org/gitmo/prisoner/65lwikimedia.org/wikipedia/commons/0/0b/Publicly_filed_CSRT_records_-_Omar_Rajab_Amin.pdf.
16. Interview with author, November 2021.
17. Ibid.
18. CSRT Summary of Findings, Omer Rajab Amin.
19. Ibid.
20. Author interviews, November 2021 and September 2022.
21. See *New York Times*, "Guantanamo Docket," Khalid Abdullah Mishal Al Mutairi, ISN 213.
22. See discussion of Khalid's habeas hearing in Chapter 6 at 208–16.
23. *New York Times*, "Guantanamo Docket," Khalid Abdullah Mishal Al Mutairi, ISN 213.
24. See discussion of habeas proceeding in Chapter 6, at 208–16.
25. *New York Times*, "Guantanamo Docket," Fouad Mahmoud Al Rabiah, ISN 551.
26. Author interview with Fouad Mahmoud Al Rabiah, November 2021.
27. www.hrw.org/report/2004/03/08/enduring-freedom/abuses-us-forces-afghanistan.
28. Interview with author, November 2021.
29. Ibid.
30. Ibid.
31. *New York Times*, "Guantanamo Docket," Fouad Mahmoud Al Rabiah, ISN 551.
32. Ibid.
33. www.miamiherald.com/news/nation-world/world/americas/guantanamo/article11141825.html; www.seattletimes.com/nation-world/obese-prisoner-at-guantanamo-appeals-for-release/ Ironically, when Al Sawah was cleared for release, medical personnel indicated his health was so poor that there was a risk that he would quickly die, and his release was delayed while he lost weight.
34. Author interview with Fouad Al Rabiah, November 2021.
35. https://edition.cnn.com/2011/10/28/world/meast/guantanamo-former-detainees/.
36. *New York Times*, "Guantanamo Docket," Abdulaziz Al Shammeri, ISN 217.
37. Ibid.
38. Ibid.
39. Ibid.
40. Ibid.
41. Ibid.
42. Ibid.
43. Ibid.
44. Ibid.
45. www.pewresearch.org/religion/2010/09/15/muslim-networks-and-movements-in-western-europe-tablighi-jamaat.
46. *New York Times*, "Guantanamo Docket," Abdullah Kamal Al Kandari, ISN 228.
47. Ibid.

48. https://int.nyt.com/data/documenttools/76370-isn-228-abdullah-kamel-abudallah-kamel/full.pdf.
49. Interview with author, November 2021.
50. *New York Times*, "Guantanamo Docket," Abdullah Kamal Al Kandari, ISN 228.
51. Interview with author, November 2021.
52. Democracy Now, "Meet the Muslim Army Chaplain who Condemned Torture at Guantanamo," January 11, 2022.
53. Interview with author, November 2021.
54. Ibid.
55. Ibid.
56. *New York Times*, "Guantanamo Docket," Abdullah Kamal Al Kandari, ISN 228.
57. www.aljazeera.com/features/2012/3/22/life-after-guantanamo-bay.
58. Interview with author, November 2021.
59. Ibid.
60. humanrights.ucdavis.edu/projects/the-guantanamo-testimonials-project/testimonies/testimonies-of-the-defense-department/csrts/csrt_ap_isn_045.pdf.
61. *New York Times*, "The Guantanamo Docket," Adel Zamel Al Zamel, ISN 568.
62. T. Lassseter, *McClatchy News Service*, "Day 2: U.S. abuse of detainees was routine at Afghanistan bases," June 15, 2015; A. Worthington, "Guantanamo Prisoners Released after the Tribunal," T. Lasseter, *McClatchy News Service*, "Guantanamo Inmate Database: Adel Al Zamel," June 16, 2008.
63. https://archive.org/details/mysticaldimensio00schi/page/232/mode/1up.
64. *New York Times*, "Guantanamo Docket," Nasser Najiri Al Amutairi ISN 205.
65. Ibid.
66. Ibid.
67. Ibid.
68. *New York* Times, "Guantanamo Docket," https://int.nyt.com/data/documenttools/76299-isn-205-nasser-najiri-amtiri-combatant-status/1c8c0fb7d9b0e5ac/full.pdf.
69. https://arabist.net/blog/2012/1/9/kuwaitis-denied-justice-in-guantanamo-bay.html.
70. www.dia.mil/FOIA/FOIA-Electronic-Reading-Room/FileId/161790/; https://wikileaks.org/plusd/cables/05KUWAIT1501_a.html.
71. *New York* Times, "Guantanamo Docket," Abdullah Saleh Al Ajmi, ISN 220.
72. JTF-GTMO Detainee Assessment (2004–2008)Administrative Review Board Round 1 Transcript Administrative Review Board Round 1 Summary Combatant Status Review Tribunal Summary.
73. www.nytimes.com/2008/05/09/world/middleeast/09mosul.html.
74. *New York* Times, "Guantanamo Docket," Abdullah Saleh Al Ajmi, ISN 220; https://web.archive.org/web/20080802031333/http://law.shu.edu/news/final_no_hearing_hearings_report.pdf.
75. www.nytimes.com/2008/05/09/world/middleeast/09mosul.html.
76. Author interviews with Fawzi Al Odah, Fayiz Al Kandari, Omar Rajab Al Amin, Abdulaziz Al Shammeri, Abdullah Kamal Al Kandari, November 2021.
77. R. Chandrase Karan, "From Captive to Suicide Bomber, "*Washington Post*, February 21, 2009.
78. www.columbia.edu/cu/libraries/inside/ccoh_assets/transcript.pdf.
79. www.nbcnews.com/id/wbna29341889.
80. Ibid.

81. www.defenselink.mil/news/d20080613Returntothefightfactsheet.pdf.
82. Author interview with Khaled Al Odah, February 2025.
83. www.cnn.com/2011/10/28/world/meast/guantanamo-former-detainees.
84. Author interviews with Fawzi Al Odah, Fayiz Al Kandari, Omar Rajab Al Amin, Abdulaziz Al Shammeri, Abdullah Kamal Al Kandari, November 2021.
85. Author interview with Khaled Al Odah, February 2025.
86. www.cnn.com/2011/10/28/world/meast/guantanamo-former-detainees.
87. www.washingtonpost.com/wp-dyn/content/article/2009/02/21/topnews.
88. *New York Times*, "Guantanamo Docket," Abdullah Saleh Al Ajmi, ISN 220.
89. Ibid.
90. Ibid.
91. https://int.nyt.com/data/documenttools/76338-isn-220-abdallah-saleh-ali-al-ajmi/f34f98dbfd1811ee/full.pdf.
92. https://int.nyt.com/data/documenttools/76338-isn-220-abdallah-saleh-ali-al-ajmi//full.pdf.
93. www.columbia.edu/cu/libraries/inside/ccoh_assets/transcript.pdf.
94. Ibid.
95. Ibid.
96. Ibid.
97. Ibid.
98. www.andyworthington.co.uk/2008/05/11/identification-of-ex-guantanamo-suicide-bomber-unleashes-pentagon-propaganda/.
99. www.columbia.edu/cu/libraries/inside/ccoh_assets/transcript.pdf.
100. Ibid.
101. Ibid.
102. www.washingtonpost.com/wp-dyn/content/article/2009/02/21/AR2009022101234.html?hpid=topnews.
103. www.columbia.edu/cu/libraries/inside/ccoh_assets/transcript.pdf.
104. Author interviews with Abdullah Kamal Al Kandari and Abdulaziz Al Shammeri, November 2021.
105. www.columbia.edu/cu/libraries/inside/ccoh_assets/transcript.pdf.
106. Author interview, November 2021.
107. NPR, "Guantanamo Detainees Attempted Mass Suicide in 2003," January 24, 2005. Associated Press, "Detainees Attempted Suicide in Protest at Base, Military Says," January 25, 2005.
108. *Reuters*, "Afghan Prisoner at Guantanamo dies in in apparent suicide," May 18, 2011.
109. www.columbia.edu/cu/libraries/inside/ccoh_assets/transcript.pdf.
110. *New York Times*, "Guantanamo Docket," Abdullah Saleh Al Ajmi, ISN 220.
111. www.dod.mil/pubs/foi/detainees/csrt_arb/000201-000299.pdf.
112. Ibid.
113. *New York Times*, "Guantanamo Docket," Mohammed Al Daihani, ISN 229.
114. Ibid.
115. Ibid.
116. Ibid.
117. https://2009-2017.state.gov/j/ct/rls/other/des/123085.htm.
118. www.nytimes.com/2006/09/17/magazine/17guantanamo.html.
119. https://int.nyt.com/data/documenttools/77062-isn-571-saad-madi-saad-al-azmi-combatant-status/26022d181cc0d705/full.pdf.

120. Ibid.
121. *New York Times*, "Guantanamo Docket," Saad Al Azmi, ISN 571.
122. Ibid.
123. Ibid.
124. Ibid.
125. web.archive.org/web/20080920042929/http://detainees.mcclatchydc.com/detainees/61.
126. Ibid.
127. Ibid.
128. Ibid.
129. Author interviews, November 2021 and February 2022.
130. *New York Times*, "Guantanamo Docket," Fawzi Al Odah, ISN 232.
131. *New York Times*, "Guantanamo Docket," Fawzi Al Odah, ISN 232.
132. Author interview with Khalid Al Odah, February 2025.
133. *New York Times*, "Guantanamo Docket," Fawzi Al Odah, ISN 232.
134. Ibid.
135. www.mc.mil/Portals/0/pdfs/alKandari/Al%20Kandari%20(Government%20Sworn%20Charges).pdf.
136. *New York Times*, "Guantanamo Docket," Fayiz Al Kandari, ISN 552.
137. www.mc.mil/Portals/0/pdfs/alKandari/Al%20Kandari%20(Government%20Sworn%20Charges).pdf.
138. Ibid.
139. www.nytimes.com/2002/10/09/world/threats-responses-skirmish-us-marine-killed-kuwait-gunmen-strike-training-site.html.
140. Ibid.
141. Ibid. Author interview with Fayiz Al Kandari, November 2021.
142. Author interview with Fayiz Al Kandari, November 2021.
143. Ibid.
144. Ibid.
145. www.nytimes.com/2002/10/09/world/threats-responses-skirmish-us-marine-killed-kuwait-gunmen-strike-training-site.htm.
146. www.nytimes.com/interactive/2021/us/guantanamo-bay-detainees.html#detainee-213.
147. T. Lasseter and C. Rosenberg, "Wikileaks: Just 8 at GTMO Gave Evidence against 255 others," *Miami Herald*, March 3, 2015.
148. Ibid.
149. Author interview with Fayiz Al Kandari, November 2021.
150. www.nytimes.com/2002/10/09/world/threats-responses-skirmish-us-marine-killed-kuwait-gunmen-strike-training-site.htm.
151. Author interview, November 2021.
152. www.theguardian.com/us-news/2016/jan/21/two-guantanamo-bay-detainees-transferred.
153. See discussion of Judge Kollar-Kotelly's ruling on informer credibility, at 257–59.
154. *New York Times*, "Guantanamo Docket," Fayiz Al Kandari, ISN 552.
155. Author interview with Fayiz Al Kandari, November 2021.
156. Ibid.
157. Ibid.

158. https://abcnews.go.com/International/guantanamo-detainees-historic-interrogation-torture-cia-psychologists-denia; www.nbcnews.com/storyline/cia-torture-report/cia-paid-torture-teachers-more-80-million.
159. Author interview with Fayiz Al Kandari, November 2021.
160. Ibid.
161. Ibid.
162. Ibid.
163. Ibid.
164. Ibid.
165. Ibid.
166. Ibid.
167. YouTube, Fayiz Al Kandari, "Surviving Jinns and Black Magic in Guantanamo Bay" and subsequent episodes.
168. Author interview, November 2021.

6 The Final Four: Habeas Hearings for the Last Four Kuwaiti Detainees

1. See discussion regarding standards of proof in Chapter 4.
2. The language used in the "Authorization for the Use of Military Force ("AUMF")," the resolution passed by Congress shortly after September 11, 2001.
3. 644 F. Supp. 2d, at 85.
4. Ibid.
5. Ibid., at 86, 87.
6. Ibid., at 89, 90.
7. Ibid., at 84.
8. Ibid., at 86.
9. Ibid., at 87–89.
10. Ibid.
11. Ibid., at 89–91.
12. Ibid., at 89.
13. Ibid., at 96.
14. Ibid., at 91–94.
15. Ibid., at 90, 91.
16. Ibid., at 91.
17. Ibid., at 94.
18. Ibid., at 95.
19. Ibid., at 95, 96.
20. See discussion in Chapter 5 of Al Rabiah's background.
21. The discussion and quotations are taken from *Al Rabiah v. United States*, 658 F. Supp. 3d 11 (D.D.C. 2009).
22. Ibid., at 20, 21.
23. Ibid., at 22.
24. Ibid., at 25.
25. Ibid., at 24–26.
26. Ibid., at 27.
27. Ibid., at 27, 28.
28. Ibid., at 29–31.

29. Ibid., at 32, 33.
30. Ibid., at 39, 40.
31. Ibid., at 33.
32. Ibid., at 34.
33. Ibid., at 42.
34. Author interview with Fouad Al Rabiah, November 2021.
35. Ibid.
36. Ibid.
37. *Al Odah v. United States*, 648 F. Supp. 1, 5–8 (D.D.C. 2009).
38. Ibid., at 8, 9.
39. Ibid., at 9, n. 9.
40. Ibid., at 9.
41. www.kayak.com/flight-routes/Dubai-Intl-DXB/Karachi-Quaid-E-Azam-Intl.
42. 648 F. Supp. 2d at 9, 10.
43. Ibid., at 12–15.
44. Ibid., at 15, 16.
45. Ibid., at 11.
46. Ibid., at 16.
47. Ibid., at 15.
48. See Chapter 4 at 52–60.
49. *Al-Adahi v. Obama*, 613 F.3d 1102, at 1104–06.
50. https://papers.ssrn.com/sol3/papers.cfm?abstract_id=1540601; www.brookings.edu/wp-content/uploads/2016/06/0122_guantanamo_wittes_chesney.pdf.
51. 744 F. Supp. 2d 11 (D.D.C. 2010).
52. Ibid., at 25.
53. Ibid., at 27, 28.
54. Ibid., at 28–35.
55. Ibid., at 33, 34.
56. Ibid., at 30, 31.
57. Ibid., at 33, 34.
58. Ibid., at 34, 35.
59. Ibid., at 35.
60. "[The] explanation provided is consistent with Al Qaida counter-interrogation tactics, and therefore supports a reasonable inference that Al Kandari was not in Afghanistan solely to assist with, and did not engage solely in, charitable work, as claimed. While this inference standing alone is insufficient to find that Al Kandari became 'part of the forces of the Taliban or Al Qaida,' the court finds that this evidence is probative and shall be considered in the context of the other record evidence." 744 F. Supp. 2d at 35.
61. 744 F. Supp. 2d, at 46, 47.
62. Ibid., at 23, 48.

7 The US Government Re-engages

1. Author interview with Marcia Newell, February 2022.
2. Ibid.
3. Ibid.
4. Ibid.

5. Ibid.
6. See Executive Order (CEO) 13567, March 7, 2011, prs.mil.
7. Ibid., at Section 2.
8. Federal News Radio Interview with Cully Stimson, January 11, 2007.
9. "Guantanamo remarks cost policy chief his job," cnn.com, February 2, 2007. www.cnn.com/2007/US/02/02/gitmo.resignation/.
10. J. Rood, "Lawmakers Blast Obama 'No Visit' Gitmo Policy," July 17, 2009, https://abcnews.go.com.
11. See Chapter 6 for a discussion of habeas proceedings of Al Rabiah and Al Mutairi at 246–64.
12. D. Roberts, "Senate Passes Legislation Barring Transfer of Prisoners to Guantanamo," *Guardian*, November 10, 2015.

8 The First Periodic Review Board

1. Of course, what we did not know was that there would still be troops in Afghanistan for another seven years, until a new Democratic President, Obama's Vice President Joseph Biden, finally and chaotically withdrew all forces in the summer of 2021.
2. Geneva Conventions, Article 3, Section 118, Commentary of 1960.
3. *Hamdi v. Rumsfeld*, 547 U.S. 507 (2004).
4. *Rasul v. Bush*, 542 U.S. 466 (2004).
5. www.nytimes.com/2021/11/26/us/politics/guantanamo-bay.html.
6. Author interview with Khalid Al Odah, September 2022.
7. Ibid.
8. Ibid.
9. Ibid.
10. Author interview with Khalid Al Odah, May 2014.
11. Ibid.
12. Transcript of Khalid Al Odah video, May 2014.
13. Transcript of Dr. Adel Al Zayed video, May 2014.
14. Ibid.
15. Statement of Dr. Al Oteibi to PRB, May 2014.
16. Statement of Colonel Abdullah Al Kandari to PRB, May 2014.
17. Letter of Sheikh Mohammed Khaled Sabah Al Sabah to PRB, May 2014.
18. Ibid.
19. Statement of Abdul Rahman Al Haroun to PRB, May 2014.
20. See discussion of Zamel Al Zamel in Chapter 5 at pp. 134–39.

9 And Then There Was One

1. J. Leopold, "Outrage over Pentagon's Guantanamo Propaganda Video," *Truthout*, November 19, 2011.
2. J. Fenton, "A Voice from Guantanamo," *Al Jazeera*, November 23, 2012.
3. Ibid.
4. www.cage.ngo/articles/interview-with-lt-col-barry-wingard-counsel-for-fayiz-al-kandari.
5. truthout.org/articles/guantanamo-a-cold-sore-on-the-face-of-america/.
6. truthout.org/articles/three-dead-bodies-2-2/.

7. Ibid.
8. www.prs.mil/portals/60/documents/ISN552/140611_U_ISN552_Government_Summary_PUBLIC.pdf.
9. www.prs.mil/Portals/60/Documents/ISN552/141016_U_ISN552_Detainee_Summary_Approved_For_Public_Release.pdf.
10. Statement of Dr. Al Oteibi for File Review, January 2015.
11. Statement of Dr. Al Zayed for File Review, January 2015.
12. Statement of Colonel Al Kandari for File Review, January 2015.
13. No relation to the head of counterintelligence with the same name.
14. Statement of Dr. Al Kandari for File Review, January 2015.

10 Lessons Learned

1. W. Faulkner, *Requiem for a Nun* (Chatto & Windus, 1953).
2. CBS, "Guantanamo a 'disgrace,' says Carter," July 31, 2005.
3. www.businessinsider.com/ginni-thomas-thought-biden-crime-family-would-be-sent-to-barges-off-gitmo-2022-3.
4. www.dissentmagazine.org/online_articles/the-worst-of-the-worst/; abcnews.go.com/Politics/1st-migrant-flight-heads-guantanamo-bay-carrying-worst/story?id=118456073; abcnews.go.com/US/confinement-unbearable-migrants describe-held-guantanamo/story?id=119270282.
5. E. Lewis, "Trump is using Guantanamo to rob migrants of their humanity" *The Independent*, March 13, 2025.
6. newhouse.house.gov/media-center/weekly-column-and-op-ed/column-president-cannot-legally-transfer-guantanamo-.
7. www.azquotes.com/quote/545676?ref=years.
8. wp-content/uploads/2021/09/21-Sept-Nash-911-Legacy-Reading-List.pdf.
9. www.georgewbushlibrary.gov/explore/exhibits/911-steel-american-resolve.
10. *Rasul v. Myers*, 563 F. 3d 527 (D.C. Cir. 2009).
11. www.motherjones.com/criminal-justice/2009/04/yes-we-did-execute-japanese-soldiers-waterboarding-american-pows/; www.cbsnews.com/news/mccain-japanese-hanged-for-waterboarding/.
12. www.theguardian.com/us-news/2015/nov/24/donald-trump-on-waterboarding-even-if-it-doesnt-work-they-deserve-it.
13. www.cnn.com/2015/12/02/politics/donald-trump-terrorists-families/index.html; www.washingtonpost.com/news/worldviews/wp/2017/05/27/trump-said-he-would-take-out-the-families-of-isis-fighters-did-an-airstrike-in-syria-do-just-that/.
14. quote.org/quote/the-purpose-of-torture-is-not-getting-263627.
15. www.nytimes.com/2022/06/03/us/politics/cia-gina-haspel-black-site.html.
16. www.pbs.org/newshour/nation/probe-cleared-gina-haspel-in-destruction-of-waterboarding-tapes-cia-memo-says.
17. apnews.com/article/6bfd8d97e865451c95fc266e1c29be82.
18. www.project-syndicate.org/commentary/9-11-in-perspective.
19. islamophobianetwork.com/misinformation-expert/frank-gaffney/.
20. islamophobianetwork.com/misinformation-expert/daniel-pipes/.
21. islamophobianetwork.com/misinformation-expert/steven-emerson/.
22. www.nbcnews.com/id/wbna41962756.

23. www.nbcnews.com/news/us-news/oregon-man-gets-life-without-parole-killing-2-portland-train-n1232067.
24. *Trump v. Hawaii*, 585 U.S. 667 (2018).
25. Attributed variously to Aeschylus, Samuel Johnson, and Senator Hiram Johnson.
26. www.washingtonpost.com/business/economy/judge-rakoff-on-free-love-the-death-penalty-defendcrooks-and-wall-street-justice/2012/01/05/gIQAIGKrDQ_story.html.
27. appropriations.house.gov/news/press-releases/committee-releases-fy25-homeland-security-appropriations-bill#:~:text=.
28. allauthor.com/quotes/5649/.
29. Seinfeld, "The Strike" Episode, NBC, December 18, 1977.
30. Credited to John Adams.

INDEX

Abdah (Esmail) v. Obama, 56
Abraham, Stephen, Lt. Colonel, 48–49
Administrative Review Board, 96, 104, 106, 108, 111, 112, 116, 249
affidavit, 48
Al Adahi v. Obama, 56–57, 246
Al Ajmi, Abdullah Saleh, 104
Al Amutairi, Nasser Najiri, 103
Al Azmi, Saad, 114, 251
Al Bihani v. Obama, 55
Al Daihani, Mohammed, 111, 250
Al Farouq Training Camp, 115
Al Harith, Jamal, 74–75
Al Haroun, Abdul Rahman (ARH), 1–2, 31–33, 35, 76, 157, 160–61, 163, 173, 196, 238
Al Kandari, Abdullah, Dr., 212, 215
Al Kandari, Abdullah Kamal, 76, 95, 249–50
Al Kandari, Fayiz, 2, 4, 7, 8, 65, 76, 77, 100
Al Mutairi, Khalid Abdullah Mishal, 84
Al Odah, Dalal, 180, 182, 184, 188
Al Odah, Fawzi, 1–2, 4, 8, 48, 50, 65, 76, 84, 118–20, 122, 143, 147, 166, 171–72, 174, 194, 203, 213, 249, 251
Al Odah, Khalid, 1, 4, 31, 39, 76, 105, 174, 184, 201, 251, 254
Al Oteibi, Khaled, Dr., 190
Al Qaida, 11, 13, 15, 31, 34, 54, 57–58, 63, 66, 68, 77, 79–80, 82, 83, 86–87, 90–94, 96–97, 99, 102, 104–5, 107, 110, 112, 115, 117–18, 120–25, 127–28, 133–38, 143, 147, 150–53, 180, 197–98, 200, 203, 217, 230, 244, 253
Al Rabiah, Fouad, 87, 90–91, 118, 123, 142, 146–47, 150–51, 241, 248, 253

Al Rabiah v. Obama, 63, 246
Al Sabah, Sheikh Mohammed, 4, 195, 254
Al Sabah, Sheikh Sabah al-Ahmad al-Jaber, 22
Al Salam Rehabilitation Center, 131
Al Shammeri, Abdulaziz, 76, 92, 248–50
Al Wafa, 83, 85, 87, 96, 98–101, 115, 117–18, 124, 133, 136, 146, 150–51
Al Zamel, Adel Zamel Abd Al-Mahsen, 98
Al Zayed, Adel, Dr., 164
Amin, Omar Rajab, 76–77, 248

bayat, 121–22, 134
Bin Laden, Osama, 9, 86, 137, 139–40
Boumediene v. Bush, 57, 245, 247
bounties, 10, 34, 39
Brown, William, 1, 31, 35, 163, 238, 243
burden of proof in the habeas hearings, 52
Bush, George W., 61, 178, 226, 231

Camp Delta, 8–9, 84, 89, 241
Camp X-Ray, 8–9, 78, 84, 107, 120, 241
Combatant Status Review Tribunals, 45, 112, 244
Core Group, 154
Court of Appeals (D.C. Circuit), 40, 42, 45, 52, 65, 224, 244
Cynamon, David, 132

Department of Homeland Security, 157, 159, 233
Detainee Treatment Act, 46
District Court (District of Columbia), 43, 53, 55, 57–59, 62, 64, 70, 84, 246

INDEX

Emir of Kuwait, 7, 33
enhanced interrogation, 44, 47, 61, 71, 129, 140, 223

Family Committee, 1–2, 4, 7, 13, 30–33, 35–37, 39, 71, 76, 119, 157, 166, 209, 220, 228, 234
First Gulf War, 16, 34, 88, 185
Fried, Daniel, Ambassador, 154, 237

Geneva Conventions, 12, 63–64, 71, 158–59, 172, 204, 228, 254
Global War on Terror, 170
Government of Kuwait, 13, 33, 37, 98, 157, 161, 174, 203–4, 210, 219
Greenberg, Karen, 241
Guantanamo Bay Bar Association, 162, 166

habeas corpus proceedings, 51
Hafetz, Jonathan, 70, 247
Hamdan v. Rumsfeld, 48
hearsay, 59–60, 132, 134
high value detainees, 4, 12
Hood, Jay, Major General, 11
hunger strikes, 77, 119, 143, 162, 179, 183
Hussein, Saddam, 13, 16, 18, 23–24, 34, 88, 94, 184–85, 201
Huvelle, Ellen, Judge, 69, 247

Johnson v. Eisentrager, 40

Kennedy, Anthony, Justice, 49, 51, 171
Kessler, Gladys, Judge, 64, 68, 127
Kollar-Kotelly, Colleen, Judge, 63, 134, 138, 140, 143–44, 149, 151–52, 251
Kuwait Chief Prosecutor, 195, 210
Kuwait Foreign Minister, 33, 195–96

Latif v Obama, 58
Leon, Richard, Judge, 65
Lewis Baach, 162, 166, 172, 181, 189, 209–10, 212–14, 239
Lucenti, Marin, Brigadier General, 11

Military Commissions Act, 48

Newell, Marcia, 1, 32, 35–37, 123, 154, 162, 173, 189, 237–38, 244, 253
Northern Alliance, 3, 15, 34, 81, 89, 102–4, 106–8, 135, 144–45, 147, 230

Periodic Review Board hearings, 118, 164
Pillsbury, 132

Randolph, A. Raymond, Senior Judge, 56
Rasul, Shafiq, 41, 73, 247
Rosenberg, Carol, 73–74, 175
Rumsfeld, Donald, 12, 223

Scalia, Antonin, Justice, 50, 228
September 11th, 3, 85, 90, 113, 137
Shearman & Sterling, 37, 104
Silberman, Laurence, Judge, 56–57
Sloan, Cliff, 163, 205, 237
Stafford Smith, Clive, 67, 166, 179
Stevens, John Paul, Justice, 42, 163
Suad Al Odah, 181–85
suicide bombing, 104–5, 110, 160, 236
Sullivan, Emmet, Judge, 66
Supreme Court, 29, 35, 39–42, 44–53, 56–57, 61, 65, 67, 71, 80, 84, 91, 119, 132, 134, 143, 163, 171, 186, 224, 226–29, 231, 245

Tatel, David, Circuit Judge, 59
Tipton Lads, 72–74
Tora Bora, 87, 90–91, 104, 107, 121, 125–26, 135, 137, 139–41, 143, 145–47, 150, 152–53
torture, 2, 10, 13, 26, 30, 44–45, 47, 54, 60–65, 68–69, 71–72, 76–77, 89, 91, 98, 102, 108–11, 129–30, 140, 142, 148, 150, 158–59, 162, 166, 173, 178, 203–4, 223, 226–28, 234, 239, 242, 246, 251, 255

Vice President Cheney, 13, 226

Wilkerson, Lawrence, Colonel, 10, 247
Wilner, Thomas, 37–38, 42, 104–5, 107–8, 110, 132
Wingard, Barry, 203
working group, 131, 156, 210

For EU product safety concerns, contact us at Calle de José Abascal, 56–1°,
28003 Madrid, Spain or eugpsr@cambridge.org.

www.ingramcontent.com/pod-product-compliance
Lightning Source LLC
LaVergne TN
LVHW011810060526
838200LV00053B/3726